WITHDRAWN

UN~

KW-255-321

This book is to be returned on or before
the last date

WITHDRAWN
FROM
UNIVERSITY OF PLYM...
LIBR...

DEPARTMENT OF INDUSTRY

The economics of
the profits crisis

Edited by W E Martin

Papers and Proceedings of the Seminar on
Profits held in London on 1 April 1980.

PLYMOUTH POLYTECHNIC
LIBRARY

Accn.
No.   1285?8
Class.
No.
Contl.
No.

LONDON

HER MAJESTY'S STATIONERY OFFICE

© *Crown copyright 1981*
First published 1981

Design by HMSO Graphic Design

HER MAJESTY'S STATIONERY OFFICE

Government Bookshops

49 High Holborn, London WC1V 6HB
13a Castle Street, Edinburgh EH2 3AR
41 The Hayes, Cardiff CF1 1JW
Brazennose Street, Manchester M60 8AS
Southey House, Wine Street, Bristol BS1 2BQ
258 Broad Street, Birmingham B1 2HE
80 Chichester Street, Belfast BT1 4JY

*Government publications are also available
through booksellers*

PLYMOUTH POLYTECHNIC
LIBRARY

Accn. No.	128519-1
Class. No.	© 339.2 ECO
Contd. No.	011 512 9774

Printed in England for Her Majesty's Stationery Office
by Hobbs the Printers of Southampton
(2063) Dd0698006 K24 4/81 G327

ISBN 0 11 512977 4 ✓

Contents

Foreword

The papers in this volume were presented at a seminar on profitability held on 1st April 1980 by the Department of Industry in London. The seminar was attended by academics, representatives of industry, the TUC, CBI, the Bank of England and civil servants (a list of participants is given on pages ix and x). An opening address was given by the Secretary of State for Industry, the Rt Hon Sir Keith Joseph.

The main aims of the seminar were to review current thinking on the causes and consequences of falling profitability in the UK, to extend our understanding of certain key elements in the problem and to discuss the appropriate policy responses. A fuller description of the background to the seminar and what it achieved is provided in the introduction.

I would like to thank the contributors to the seminar—the authors of the papers, the discussants, and the participants in the debates—as well as those involved in organising it. I would like to pay a special tribute to Mr W E Martin; he took a leading part in arranging the seminar, he wrote the introduction as well as a large part of the substantial background paper, and he edited the volume.

H H LIESNER
Chief Economic Adviser

List of seminar participants

Dr G Anderson   University of Southampton
Dr M Beenstock   London Business School
Mr L Berman   Department of Industry
Mr K Blackburn   Trades Union Congress
Dr C Bowe   Department of Industry
Mr E Butler   Inland Revenue
Mr S Charik   Department of Industry
Mr K Coutts   Cambridge Economic Policy Group
Mr L Dicks-Mireaux   Bank of England
Mr W Eltis   Exeter College, Oxford
Mr J Evans   Courtaulds
Mr J Flemming   Bank of England
Mr J Fowler   Department of Industry
Mr A Glyn   Corpus Christi College, Oxford
Mr P Goate   Department of Industry
Mr P Gordon-Potts   Imperial Group
Dr R Goss   Department of Industry
Mr J Graham   Department of Industry
Mrs F Heaton   HM Treasury
Mr J Hibberd   HM Treasury
Professor T Hill   University of East Anglia
Mr S James   Department of Industry
Professor M King   University of Birmingham
Mr A Lane   Department of Trade
Mr D Lewis   Department of Industry
Mr H Liesner   Department of Industry
Mr I Lightman   Department of Industry
Mr D McWilliams   Confederation of British Industry
Mr W Martin   Department of Industry
Professor R Matthews   Clare College, Cambridge
Professor G Maynard   Chase Manhattan Bank
Dr G Meeks   University of Cambridge
Mr R Mountfield   Department of Industry
Mr M Neifield   Department of Industry
Miss M O'Connor   Department of Industry
Mr E Price   Department of Energy
Mr J Schneider   Inland Revenue
Mr J Shepherd   Department of Industry

Mr D Stout   National Economic Development Office
Mr A Threadgold   Bank of England
Mrs G Wenban-Smith   National Institute of Economic and Social
  Research

Notes on contributors

DR G J ANDERSON
Gordon Anderson lectures at Southampton University. He has published several papers on applied econometric methods and is the author of a series of discussion papers on the determinants and financing of investment.

MR J S FLEMMING
John Flemming, previously a Fellow of Nuffield College, Oxford, has recently been appointed a chief adviser at the Bank of England. His publications include articles on company profitability, the cost of capital and investment and a book on inflation (1976). He was a member of the Meade Committee on Tax Reform.

MR J HIBBERD
Jim Hibberd is an economic adviser at HM Treasury responsible for forecasts of the UK company sector, including investment and employment. He published a study of UK imports of manufactures (with Simon Wren-Lewis) in 1978.

PROFESSOR M A KING
Mervyn King is Esmée Fairbairn Professor of Investment at the University of Birmingham. Previously he was a Fellow of St John's College, Cambridge and a member of the Meade Committee on Tax Reform. His publications include Public Policy and the Corporation (1977) and, with John Kay, The British Tax System (1978).

MR W E MARTIN
Bill Martin is an economic adviser at the Department of Industry responsible for advice on macro-economic policy matters and the econometric interpretation of the Department's investment intentions survey, on which he has published an article (with P Lund and A Bennett).

PROFESSOR R C O MATTHEWS
Robin Matthews is Professor of Political Economy at Cambridge and Master of Clare College. He was a member of the OECD expert group on Non-Inflationary Growth (1975–1977) and now chairs the Bank of England Panel of Academic Consultants which recently investigated the profitability question. His many publications include A Study in Trade Cycle History (1954) and The Trade Cycle (1958).

PROFESSOR G W MAYNARD

Geoffrey Maynard is Visiting Professor of Economics at Reading
University, a Vice-President of the Chase Manhattan Bank and the
Director of Economics for the Bank's operations in Europe and the
Middle East. He was previously an Under-Secretary (Economics) at
HM Treasury (1972–1974) and Deputy Chief Economic Adviser at
HM Treasury (1976–1977). His publications include Economic
Development and the Price Level (1962), International Monetary
Reform and Latin America (1966), A World of Inflation (1976).

DR G MEEKS

Geoffrey Meeks is Assistant Director of Research at the Faculty of
Economics and Politics, University of Cambridge. His publications
include: The Financing of Quoted Companies in the United Kingdom
(1976), Disappointing Marriage: A Study of Gains from Merger (1977)
and Public Money in Private Industry (1979).

MISS M O'CONNOR

Moira O'Connor is a statistician at the Department of Industry
responsible for domestic financial statistics. Previously she has worked
and published articles on the measurement of stocks, capital
expenditure and investment intentions of manufacturing industry.

MRS G WENBAN-SMITH

Gay Wenban-Smith is a research officer at the National Institute of
Economic and Social Research responsible for forecasts of the North
American economies and of investment and stockbuilding in the UK
and for analysis of productivity trends. She has published articles on
investment and consumption.

The profits crisis: introduction

by W E Martin

In 1960, the real pre-tax rate of return of private manufacturing
companies in the UK was, in aggregate, about 13 per cent. By
1973—like 1960, a year of peak economic activity—manufacturers'
profitability had fallen to 8 per cent. There followed a collapse of
profitability in 1974–75, a partial recovery up to 1978 and then a
further fall, partly because of recession. In 1980, profitability may
prove to be only a quarter of the level achieved 20 years earlier. That,
in a nutshell, is the "profits crisis".

The Seminar

Concern about these trends has, not surprisingly, varied with the
intensity of the decline in profitability. However, our worries today
arise not only from the low recorded levels of profitability but also
from a continuing inability to tackle the problem. With regard to the
underlying causes, it is immodest but, nevertheless, relevant to quote
my own thoughts expressed in the background paper in this volume
which notes 'there has been a low rate of return to the dismal science
of explaining secular movements in income distribution'. Equally, we
appear little further forward in our efforts to understand the consequences of low profitability and what, if anything, should be done
about it[1]. That all this is of concern to the Department of Industry
goes without saying.

In designing the seminar, we were conscious that much of the
ground had been gone over several times by academics and others. In
particular, the Bank of England's Panel of Academic Consultants had
considered the profits question as recently as October 1978. (The
paper by Ball (1978) is a slightly abridged version of the main paper
presented to the Panel.) Wishing to build upon, rather than duplicate,
the Bank's efforts, we decided to survey the ground ourselves, with a
view to identifying particular gaps in our understanding which could
then usefully be explored by specialists. This survey resulted in the
paper by my colleague Miss Moira O'Connor and myself which
provides the background for the four specialist papers taken at the
seminar.

Another guiding principle in designing the seminar arose from a
desire to make the debate more accessible to non-academics. Clearly,
low profitability is of special concern to those who work in industry as

[1] In view of the recent large revisions to the profits figures (see *Economic Trends*,
April, 1980, p76; "Blue Book", 1980), one might well add that even the basic facts
are highly uncertain. In the time available before going to print, it was not possible to
reflect all these upward revisions in the papers in this volume.

well as to those who study it, and it is possible that some of the theories and policies put forward by academics have not been sufficiently well aired in public. The authors of all the papers were asked to write in a style accessible to the layman; in addition they have each provided a short, non-technical summary. The papers are published subject to some revision made in the light of discussant's formal comments, also published here[1], and the lively debate during the seminar sessions. My record of the general discussion is appended to the relevant papers. By agreement, remarks have not been attributed.

Our approach to the subject has meant that the specialist papers do not fall neatly into the categories of 'causes, consequences and cures', which is perhaps the most natural way to slice the topic. The relevance of each paper should be largely apparent from the background paper—which therefore takes the first position in the volume—but a few words of introduction may be in order. One theory of the secular decline in profitability is that governments have been over-generous with the provision of investment incentives so that it has been possible for businessmen to secure a particular post-tax return whilst scoring progressively lower pre-tax rates of return. More generally, it is alleged that the tax/subsidy system is a major source of distortion in the capital market and has thereby led to a misallocation of resources. Professor King's paper is a step towards answering these questions. The papers by Dr Meeks and Dr Anderson on investment and cash flow need little in the way of introduction. Given the fragility of the company sector's financial position, it seemed worthwhile re-examining the profits-investment link and these two papers represent quite distinctive approaches to the topic.

The specialist paper which came closest to an analysis of 'causes, consequences and cures' was the one by Professor Maynard. He develops two central themes concerning the pressure in the labour market for increased real wages and the acquiescence of governments in this respect, given an increasingly politicised trade union movement. The result, according to Professor Maynard, was low profitability and industrial inefficiency; difficulties which were compounded by the oil crisis in 1973–74. An increase in the rate of return is seen as a precondition for economic survival in the UK. As may be imagined, this paper stimulated a good deal of debate both in its own session at the seminar and at the more general final session devoted to policy, for which a specialist paper was not invited.

---

[1] To prevent endless iteration, discussant's comments have not been substantially revised in the light of revisions to the main papers.

Future Work

A one-day seminar could not hope to do full justice to the wide range of issues that have a bearing on the profitability question. Quite apart from the enormous scope of the subject, it is also a very difficult one, and one which attracts a considerable amount of controversy. Readers of this volume should not therefore expect a new conventional wisdom to emerge. The extent to which the seminar succeeded in answering the particular questions it set itself may be judged in detail from the reports of the discussions. It suffices to note here that many of these issues still remain to be resolved. In particular, the seminar was unable to reach firm conclusions on the magnitude of any fiscal contribution to the fall in the rate of return, nor on the empirical significance of the investment-cash flow link, though few doubted that the link did exist. Stimulated by Professor Maynard's paper, hypotheses of causes and cures bloomed like flowers in the Spring, quite in keeping with the date on which the seminar was held.

The main value of the seminar was to suggest areas for future work and two particular ideas stand out. First, there is the international point. Academics who retain their faith in standard international trade theory (and, in particular, in the Lerner-Samuelson 'factor price equalisation theorem') will perhaps not have been surprised by Hill's (1979) discovery that the decline in the rate of return was widely experienced in industrialised countries. Both trade and movements in factors of production between these economies would tend, according to this theorem, to equalise the movement, at least, of rates of return, (strictly, post-tax rates of return). Of course, it would be little help to say that the decline in UK rates of return was simply a reflection of developed world trends. For one thing, this is not so−the UK has fared worse than others and this may be a reflection of peculiar British difficulties and the very long run erosion of profitable investment opportunities to which Professor Matthews draws attention in this volume. However even if there were not special British factors, we would still need to explain the trends in the developed world.

What is implied here is a need to start the analysis at a higher level of aggregation−treating the industrialised countries as a bloc rather than in isolation. This would have important implications for a number of the prevailing hypotheses regarding declining rates of return. For example the idea that declining profitability was due to the inter-play between trade unions pushing up money wages and inter-national competition between industrialised countries pushing down prices could not be sustained. The simple point is that the implied movements in competitiveness within the industrialised bloc would cancel out: we might explain, by these means, the pattern of profitability between industrialised countries but not the behaviour of profitability in the industrialised world as a whole! In this respect, one is naturally drawn towards a more complete analysis of trade between developed and developing countries and associated international movements of factors of production.

The second interesting idea that deserves further consideration is Matthews' contention that the decline in profitability has been a very long run phenomenon in the UK. It is quite possible that important perspectives on the problem are lost by considering only the period for which data are most readily available—that is, the post war period. Combining this idea with the international point leads one to suggest an ambitious piece of research—perhaps in the tradition of Schumpeter—which would look at the very long run evolution of capitalist economies and the interactions between them. This approach to the study of profitability would not be easy but it would at least be one response to the present unsatisfactory state of the art.

These are then areas for future work which appear especially interesting. But there is no shortage of suggestions for research on, for example, the effects of the tax system and the nature of the investment-profits link; these suggestions may be found in the reports of the various discussions. It is to be hoped that the papers and proceedings recorded here will stimulate wider debate of, and further research into, this contentious subject. At the very least, we might establish whether low levels of profitability constitute a crisis and so justify the title to the volume.

References

See reference list appended to the background paper.

---

[1]A similar point is raised by Duesenberry in his comment on Sachs (1979).

Profitability: a background paper

by W E Martin and M O'Connor

Section B is by Miss M O'Connor; the remainder is by
Mr W Martin. We would like to thank our colleagues at the
Department of Industry and the Bank of England for helpful
advice. We are responsible for remaining errors and omissions.
The views expressed in the paper do not necessarily represent
those held by the Department of Industry.

Section A   Introduction and summary

The decline in the profitability of UK industry over the long term and its relative stagnation in recent years has been the cause of increasing concern. Yet despite a considerable amount of analysis and discussion there exists little consensus about the causes of the decline or its implications. This paper draws together various strands of the debate concentrating, in particular, on the analysis of 'causes'. There are four sections—Factual background, Causes, Consequences and Policy—which are summarised below.

Factual background

All the measures of real profit shares and rates of return for the UK set out in this paper show a downward trend from at least 1960, with a sharp decline in 1974—75, a partial recovery up to 1978 and a further sharp drop in 1979. The international comparisons, based mainly on the work of Professor Hill for OECD, suggest that UK profit shares and rates of return are generally among the lowest encountered but that most other countries have also shown a declining trend. Germany is the only one where the steepness of the decline approaches that of the UK.

Causes

Under this head, possible causes of low profitability—particularly in UK manufacturing industry—over the last few years are considered as well as those explaining the secular decline. The dramatic fall and relative stagnation of profitability since 1973 seems largely symptomatic of the macro-economic problem of 'stagflation'. Chronic excess capacity, pricing policies misguided by a reverence for historic cost accounting principles and unexpected increases in costs as inflation accelerated have probably been major influences depressing profitability. These difficulties have been compounded by the rise in real energy prices which directly squeezed profits, especially in manufacturing industry, and also added to inflationary pressures.

   While the influences on recent profit performance seem fairly clear cut, the causes of the secular decline since at least the mid 1950s are much less well understood. Concentrating on theories which have received some empirical support, the paper considers four possibilities:

   (a) a fall in the marginal productivity of physical capital;
   (b) a fall in the corporate tax burden;
   (c) a shift in market power from 'capitalists' to 'labour';
   (d) crowding-out by the public sector.

The first proposition is that post-war optimism and an increasingly generous tax treatment of company profits has encouraged the adoption of less profitable investment projects at the margin and a substitution of capital for labour in productive processes. There is however little reliable evidence pointing to a secular fall in risk premiums in the UK and, despite a number of different studies, the actual evolution of the corporate tax burden is unclear. Furthermore, the mechanism by which the substitution of capital for labour is secured does not receive fully convincing support from econometric studies of investment in the UK.

The second theory considered holds that a fall in the effective tax burden on manufacturing industry profits has been passed on in prices leading to a fall in the pre-tax profit share. Apart from the conflicting evidence on tax burden it is unclear whether the direction of causation is as suggested: it is quite possible that a fall in pre-tax profitability (for whatever reason) would cause a fall in the average tax rate.

Trade unions are thought to have squeezed profits largely by exercising their market power to secure higher money wages which are not fully passed on in prices because of international competition. The theory is taken to imply that real product wages in manufacturing industry (money wages deflated by the price of output produced by the labour employed) have grown in excess of labour productivity and that the UK has lost unit labour cost competitiveness in international trade. However during the 1960s and between 1972 and 1978, average rates of growth of real product wages and labour productivity in manufacturing industry have been roughly equal. Furthermore, until very recently, the UK experienced a trend gain in competitiveness. While it is true that real product wages have, at times, grown faster than labour productivity over the full business cycle (late 1950s, late 1960s/early 1970s), it is not clear that these instances were due to any shift in market power from capitalists to the workers.

Given the assumption that there exist constraints on domestic prices due to international competition and/or price controls, the growth of public expenditure may have crowded out industrial profits by reducing labour resources available to industry, by pre-empting funds for investment, by causing inflation, by raising the corporate tax burden or by increasing the tax burden on wage-earners, the latter leading to increased money wage claims—the 'tax-push hypothesis.' The evidence, for the 1950s and 1960s at least, is against these explanations. Growth of public sector employment largely benefitted females whereas the decline in industrial employment since 1966 was concentrated on males. Given conditions of relatively stable prices, akin to the world of the 1950s and 1960s, evidence from studies of investment behaviour in the UK and the simulation properties of macro-economic models is against any significant fiscal crowding out, though the issue is less clear cut in the inflationary conditions of the 1970s. As mentioned previously, the evidence on the evolution of the corporate tax burden is mixed and the tax-push hypothesis is subject to the same objections raised regarding the market power theory of the secular decline.

The broad conclusion is that the reasons for the secular decline in profitability remain something of a mystery though, because the decline is concentrated in the manufacturing sector, the possibility of some market process encouraging a shift of resources out of manufacturing cannot be dismissed. The complexities of the economy may however preclude any clear identification of the major causes.

Consequences

These are divided into short- and long-run effects. The short-run effects are concerned with the question of whether the economy has become supply constrained—due to low profitability—rather than demand constrained. If the former is true, the implication is that conventional macro-economic policies of demand stimulus would fail to work. There is little firm evidence on this point—the impression is that supply conditions have worsened over time but the role played by lower profitability is unclear.

The long run effects of low profitability mainly relate to investment. Profitability may influence the volume and kind of investment by affecting incentives and the ability to finance expenditure but econometric evidence has generally failed to reveal a significant effect. However, because of the difficulties of, for example, econometric specification, it is felt that the case is an open one. Surveys indicate that prospective profitability is an important influence on investment decisions and it may be that the financial role played by realised profitability will be a more important influence in the future.

Policy

The uncertainty surrounding the causes of the secular decline in profitability does not admit of any positive policy conclusions—indeed the possibility that declining profitability over the longer term is not a doomsday machine and thus does not call for special cures cannot be ruled out. For the immediate future, the problem of stagflation at home and abroad and the rise in real energy prices augur a further fall in profitability. The broad question for policy is whether a monetarist prescription of disinflation and 'supply management' will suffice to put the economy and profitability back on track or whether more far reaching institutional reforms will be required, reconciling the perceived self-interests of nation states and indigenous social groups.

Section B   Factual background

This part of the paper first of all considers some of the conceptual and measurement problems in deciding what 'facts' are relevant; it then summarises the available data for the UK, mainly for the period since 1960, in terms both of the share of profits in total domestic income and in value added and of rate of return on capital; finally, it discusses how the levels and trends in the UK compare with those in other countries.

B1   Conceptual and measurement problems

B1.1   CONCEPTUAL PROBLEMS

There are numerous ways of defining profits and profitability depending on the purpose of the exercise (see for example Walker 1974). In most of the discussion which follows, profits are defined as gross trading profit, before deduction of any interest payments, plus rent received, less stock appreciation and less capital consumption at current replacement cost. The calculations of rates of return are designed to measure the profitability of production or trading operations in the UK and therefore relate to the rate of return on physical assets regardless of how they are financed; for this purpose 'real' rates of return are the most relevant, ie profits as defined above as a percentage of the capital stock of fixed assets (excluding land because of lack of data) at current replacement cost plus the book value of stocks[1]. It could be argued that net current assets should be included in the denominator as they are part of trading assets but statistics on the national accounts basis used are inadequate. If this could be done it would also be appropriate to make a monetary working capital adjustment (MWCA) as required by SSAP16[2]. It seems likely however that the effect of the MWCA at the aggregate levels of all industrial and commercial companies or even manufacturing as a whole, which are used here, would be very small.

Of other definitions of profit discussed, one suggestion which applies to entity profits is adding to (or subtracting from) profits calculated as described above the notional capital gains (losses) made because prices of the fixed assets and stocks used in the business have

---

[1] Strictly this should be replacement value of stocks but the methods used to value stocks in the UK are such that overall the book value is likely to be a reasonable approximation.

[2] *Current Cost Accounting* Statement of standard accounting practice No 16, March 1980.

risen by more (less) than prices in general[1]. Such revaluation surpluses, however, bear no relation to the operating efficiency of the business or industry concerned and their inclusion could give a misleading impression of the long-term viability of an industry. In any case they are not necessarily a measure of real capital gains or losses because the net present value (ie the discounted value of future earnings) of the assets may not be the same as their replacement cost. (For discussion of the valuation ratio or Tobin's q, which measures the ratio of the financial valuations of companies' physical assets, based on market prices, to the tax-adjusted replacement cost of those assets, see Flemming 1976 (b) and *Bank of England Quarterly Bulletin* June 1979 and June 1980; also pages 51, 53 below).

In any attempt to relate these rates of return to trends in investment the several ways in which they will differ from internal rates of return as observed (or forecast) by companies have to be remembered. Firstly they are averages over all existing projects rather than marginal returns on a particular project. In addition, national accounts estimates of capital consumption are based on straight line depreciation and, although this may often be a reasonable approximation to economic depreciation, Professor Hill (1979) shows that net rates of return based on this assumption can in some cases be much greater than internal rates of return. An average of the gross (ie before depreciation) and net rates of return, both measured after deduction of stock appreciation, can sometimes be a better approximation to an internal rate. Further, in assessing investment projects, companies will take account of taxes, grants etc; some reference is therefore made below to post-tax rates of return on physical assets (as calculated by the Bank of England) but they differ from the calculations likely to be made by companies in that the Bank of England deduct taxes on dividends and interest in the hands of recipients (in order to compare returns with those earned by savers on holdings of financial assets)[2] and ignore certain government grants such as Regional Development Grants and the various sectoral assistance schemes and selective assistance granted under the Industry Act 1972.

For some purposes it is useful to consider the return on equity only. This cannot readily be done from national accounts data but estimates

---

[1] Over short periods these capital gains or losses could alter the movements of profits considerably although they are unlikely to have an appreciable effect on long-term trends. The deflator for gross domestic fixed capital formation in the whole economy for example rose by 2 per cent more than the retail price index between 1960 and 1978 although between 1971 and 1974 it rose by 14 per cent more.

[2] Which also has the incidental advantage that continuity is not affected by the change to the imputation system of taxation in 1973.

have been made using the Department of Industry's analysis of the accounts of large listed companies mainly operating in the UK. It involves adjusting current cost profit as defined above by deducting interest payments and adding an allowance for the capital gains accruing to equity owners on that part of the physical assets financed by debt; net monetary liabilities have to be deducted from capital employed (which in calculations based on company accounts data is usually defined as net trading assets rather than physical assets alone).

The main point of contention is the allowance which should be made for capital gains to equity holders. SSAP16 provides for a gearing adjustment which would add back into equity profits the proportion of the adjustments from historic cost to current cost profit (the additional depreciation, cost of sales adjustment and MWCA) represented by net borrowing to net borrowing plus shareholders interest. It has been argued that the gearing proportion should be applied to the whole of the increase in value during the year of physical assets or that the gain to equity holders should be taken as the fall in the real value of the company's net monetary liabilities. The latter can be measured either by an index appropriate to the physical assets of the company (which should give approximately the same result as applying the gearing proportion to the increased value of physical assets, apart from any complications due to non-trading assets etc) or by a general price index[1]. The main argument against this wider gearing adjustment is that it is inappropriate to include in earnings unrealised holding gains which could not be made available for distribution without eroding the operating capability of the business. The counter-argument is that additional borrowing could be undertaken to bring the 'real' gearing ratio back to its original level.

The Bank of England have calculated (Clark and Williams 1978, supplementary note in *Bank of England Quarterly Bulletin,* June 1979 and article by N P Williams in the December 1979 issue) the rates of return on equity for companies in the DoI analysis in manufacturing, distribution and service industries on three bases. The first is equivalent to SSAP16 (then exposure draft 24, in the June and December 1979 *Bulletins*), the second uses what is described as a 'natural' gearing adjustment, which is the method mentioned above of crediting to equity holders the fall in the real value of net monetary liabilities as measured by the retail price index, and the third adjusts equity profits on the latter basis by the capital gains or losses

---

[1] Estimating the gain by applying a general price index to the net monetary liabilities is equivalent to converting the deduction of interest payments into a deduction of *real* interest payments only.

discussed above–attributing the whole of them to equity holders. If they really represented capital gains (but see the reservations above) there might be more case for the latter adjustment in considering returns to equity in general than returns to entity trading operations but they are still rather inappropriate in the context of a continuing business. The relationship between these returns to equity and the returns to entity on trading assets depend partly on how the rate of interest compares with the overall rate of return. From 1960 to date the Bank's calculations show that all three measures give higher rates of return than returns to entity trading assets but they show a similar falling trend. The decline in the third measure of return to equity[1] is less marked than in the other series.

B1.2 MEASUREMENT PROBLEMS

A problem in any analysis of rates of return which involves using estimates of net capital stock of fixed assets is the uncertainty attached to the estimates mainly because of the assumptions which have to be made about lives of assets. It has been argued that the lives assumed for the UK in the national accounts estimates are too long and it is true that they are in general longer than those assumed by other countries in their calculations. However, although they are still based mainly on Inland Revenue depreciation allowances in the 1950s and Barna's work on fire insurance valuations in 1955 (Barna 1957), a range of evidence from surveys of particular industries which became available in 1975–76 indicated that they were reasonable (Griffin 1976). A sensitivity analysis showed that reducing all asset lives by 20 per cent would have reduced net capital stock at end 1975 by 13½ per cent and an earlier analysis (Hibbert *et al* 1977), covering only plant and machinery in the chemical industry, showed that reducing lives gradually from 37 years in 1947 to 30 or 22 years by 1972 would have reduced capital stock at end 1973 by 9 per cent or 19 per cent respectively.

However it cannot be assumed that such reductions would necessarily increase rates of return. The increase in capital consumption in the above three instances was 11 per cent, 19½ per cent and 44 per cent respectively. The last two figures of course relate only to one sector of manufacturing industry and the precise effect will vary

---

[1]In addition to its doubtful conceptual basis, the adjustment involved in going from the second to the third measure of return is to some extent a question of introducing timing effects which present statistical difficulties when dealing with data based on a mixture of accounting years; the Bank therefore emphasise the uncertainty of this measure.

considerably depending on the pattern over the years of capital formation. The effect on the rate of return also depends on the relative
importance of capital consumption to gross trading profits, which
varies considerably. In some recent years when profits have been low,
capital consumption has been greater than net profit after deduction
of capital consumption and stock appreciation, and calculations with
the sort of adjustments set out above would almost certainly have led
to lower rates of return. It is however impossible to generalise about
the effects.

In rates of return based on the DoI company accounts analysis,
lengths of lives are those used in the company accounts. To the extent
that they have been artificially shortened as an indirect method of
making some allowance for increased replacement cost, the use of the
same assumptions when making calculations of 'real' rates of return is
not strictly correct.

There are, of course, numerous measurement problems in the other
elements entering into rates of return calculations, especially in gross
trading profits and figures on stocks. These are discussed in Maurice
(1968) and the notes in each edition of the National Income and
Expenditure 'Blue Book'.

B2   The UK position

B2.1   SHARE OF PROFITS IN TOTAL DOMESTIC INCOMES AND IN VALUE ADDED IN THE UK

Table B1 gives data from 1960 for the share of profits, after deducting
stock appreciation and capital consumption at replacement cost, of
industrial and commercial companies (ICC), before and after
deducting profit from North Sea oil and gas exploration and
extraction (NSO), and of private manufacturing companies[1] in total
domestic income (TDI). Chart B1a shows the same series plus one
slightly longer series for all ICC before deduction of stock
appreciation and capital consumption, ie at historic cost. Chart B1b
indicates trends in the share of profits in value added[2] (ie profits plus
employment income) for all ICC.

All series show declining trends although the historic cost series
decline much more slowly than the current cost series and the shares
in value added more slowly than in TDI. The shares of current cost
profits in TDI for all three groups of companies dropped particularly
sharply between 1973 and 1975, and, despite improvements in

[1] more accurately described as companies whose main activity is manufacturing.
[2] for which only approximate estimates can be made.

1976–78, were still below 1973 levels in 1978. Shares fell sharply in 1979, reaching the lowest levels yet recorded for ICC excluding NSO and for manufacturing companies. The recovery in ICC profit shares in 1976–78 is much more pronounced if North Sea activities are included and the fall in 1979 less marked (profits from these activities are estimated to have accounted for nearly 30 per cent of the current cost profits of all industrial and commercial companies in 1979).

A longer term analysis for ICC (Clark and Williams 1978) indicates that the share of current cost profits in the late 1960s was about the same as in the 1920s and higher than in the depression of the early 1930s. It is only in the 1970s that the share of profits has fallen below the shares recorded over any of this period from 1920.

The share of ICC value added in TDI has fallen from about 58 per cent in the early 1960s to 51–53 per cent in recent years; if the earlier share had been maintained, the share of ICC current cost profits in TDI would have been about 1½–2 percentage points higher in each year since 1971 than it has actually been. The share of current cost profits in value added has fallen from 26 per cent in 1960 to about 20 per cent in 1970 and to a low point of 12 per cent in 1975 from which it has recovered to about 18 per cent in both 1977 and 1978 (the 1979 figure is not available at the time of writing but is likely to show a fall).

B2.2   RATES OF RETURN IN THE UK

Table B2 and Charts B2a and B2b give data on real rates of return for the years 1960 to 1979 based on national accounts data. Chart B2a, on pre-tax rates, shows that, between 1960 and 1972, there were three cycles in a steady downward trend but since then a much more severe recession than in the past has been experienced and it is possible that the trend is now more steeply downward. The pattern has been very similar to that described above for shares of TDI; sharp falls between 1973 and 1975, a partial recovery in 1976–78 and a fall to new low points (except for all ICC) in 1979. In that year, the 'real' rate of return for ICC excluding NSO is estimated at 4 per cent and for manufacturing companies 3 per cent.

Rates of return in manufacturing (which are less reliable) have been consistently below those for all ICC and have shown even sharper movements since 1973. An alternative set of estimates for real rates of return in manufacturing industry is provided by the DoI analysis of large listed company accounts. This shows a similar downward trend to the national accounts series but the cyclical variations are more pronounced and figures for particular years can differ considerably. There are differences in definition and coverage between the two series[1], each having advantages and disadvantages, and it is useful to have them both as a cross check on the general level and pattern of returns in manufacturing companies.

Post-tax rates of return as calculated by the Bank of England (see Chart B2b) show a less marked downward trend than pre-tax rates but a similar pattern since 1973.

In summary, all measures of real profit shares and rates of return considered above show a downward trend from at least 1960, with a sharp decline in 1974−75, a partial recovery up to 1978 and a further steep drop in 1979[2].

B3   International comparisons

This section is based mainly on the work of Professor T P Hill for the OECD (originally published in Hill, 1979, but use is made here of updated figures produced by Professor Hill for the OECD earlier this year). To try to ensure comparability between countries, the figures are derived from national accounts statistics as returned to OECD and the UN on the SNA system. UK figures in this section are on the same basis as those of other countries and differ in various respects from those quoted above.

The SNA uses the term 'operating surplus' rather than 'profit' but, when the reference is to companies, the meaning is practically the same. Even if all countries conform exactly to SNA definitions for the operating surplus, it is difficult to be sure of consistency because of the two completely different methods used to derive data−the production account (input-output) method, used by most European continental countries and, starting recently, Japan, and the income approach method, based on company accounts or tax returns, used by UK, USA and Canada. Some countries attempt to reconcile results from the two approaches while some use one method to estimate totals and the other to subdivide by sector or industry. This basic difference has to be borne in mind in examining the comparisons below.

[1] For details, and the data from the company accounts analysis, see article 'Companies' rate of return on capital employed 1960 to 1978', *Trade and Industry* 28 September 1979.

[2] The only detailed published series of which we are aware that does not show a long-term downward trend is that on post-tax profit shares produced by King (1975), discussed on p 54 below and in annex 2.

The most interesting international comparison would be that relating to private industrial and commercial companies or to all non-financial corporations (including publicly owned). Nothing is available on the former basis and figures for only three countries on the latter. Most of the comparisons therefore relate to industries.[1]. The operating surplus of an industry corresponds to the gross trading profits of companies, the trading surplus of public corporations and the self-employment income of the owners of unincorporated businesses, all net of stock appreciation and (except when stated to be 'gross') of capital consumption at current replacement cost. Comparisons will therefore be affected by differences between countries and over time in the relative importance of public corporations and unincorporated businesses within the industry or industries concerned. To approximate as closely as possible to the non-financial corporate sector, industries in which unincorporated businesses predominate (agriculture, distribution and miscellaneous services) have been omitted.

Comparisons are made for 'industry plus transport' (manufacturing, mining, construction, public utilities, transport and communications) and for manufacturing on its own, in each case for the share of the operating surplus in value added in the industries concerned and for rate of return on capital (fixed assets only). Figures have been calculated both gross and net of capital consumption and some comparisons of gross rates of return are shown on the charts although the tables and most of the discussion in the text relate to the net figures.

Tables B3a, B3b, B4a and B4b summarise the data for the major countries for which long runs are available, tables B3a and B3b covering 'industry plus transport' and non-financial corporations and B4a and B4b manufacturing industry. In tables B3b and B4b net rates of return are given for all the countries for which reasonably reliable data can be obtained. The charts show shares and rates of return for individual years from 1955 or 1960 to 1978 and those on profit shares include one or two countries additional to those in the corresponding tables. For most countries, data for 1970 onwards are more soundly based than for earlier years.

Operating surplus and value added should be consistently defined as

---

[1] The production account method of estimating the operating surplus probably gives a better industry split as the data are normally on an establishment basis or at least relate to a more homogenous unit than the whole company, which has to be the basis of the income approach. The USA attempts to translate its company-based profits data to an establishment-based series (used here) but neither UK nor Canada do so.

between countries (apart from the effect of different methods, as discussed above) and comparable with each other. For measurement of capital stock and hence for rates of return, it is inherently more difficult to be sure of comparability between countries or even of the profit figures with the capital stock figures for any one country. The latter point is more likely to be a problem with disaggregated data and, because of this and the fact that some estimation was often required to obtain the necessary industry breakdown of net capital stock, estimates for manufacturing are probably more suspect than for the broader industry group. Particular caution should therefore be used in drawing conclusions from table B4b.

In all *industry and transport* (table B3a and chart B3a) the UK has the lowest *profit share* through the whole period, except for 1971/2 and 1976/8 when Sweden and Norway are both lower. All five countries for which a long run of data is available show a declining trend although it is only marked in the case of Germany. No net figures are available for Japan but gross operating surplus has been a declining proportion of gross value added. For net *rates of return* in the same group of industries, Norway has generally had the lowest rate, followed by UK, then Canada with Germany the highest. Although the rate in Germany has declined more steeply than elsewhere, it was still nearly twice as much as UK even in 1973 (before the UK's steep decline). A comparison of gross rates of return shows Sweden only just above UK (and below it in 1976/7) and Japan way above any other country.

Tables B3a and B3b also give comparisons of profit shares and rates of return for *non-financial corporations* (illustrated in chart B3c). In the early 1960s profit shares were similar in UK, USA and France but from about 1968 to 1973, France remained at a high level while shares in UK and USA fell, with the USA being the lowest of the three. Since 1974, UK has been the lowest and USA rose above France in 1975 and 1976 (the latest available for France). In 1977–78 UK was only a little below USA. In rates of return, by contrast, USA[1] has been the highest throughout the whole period with France rising to be very close in the early 1970s. UK and French rates of return were similar in the early 1960s but then diverged, the UK becoming considerably lower by the 1970s.

In *manufacturing* (table and chart B4a), the lowest net *profit shares*

[1] The USA's low profit share and high rate of return are consistent because capital productivity appears to be very much higher than elsewhere.

have been experienced by USA, Sweden and UK and the highest
mostly by Germany in the 1960s and (of the countries in the chart) by
Canada in the 1970s. New Zealand and Finland, for which estimates
are available only from 1971 and 1970 respectively, have had shares as
high or higher than Canada. The share in Australia is also fairly high.
Again Japanese figures are not available net but on a gross basis are
far above those of other countries. The fluctuations in shares are more
marked than for the broader group of industries, making trends
difficult to discern. There is a fairly steeply declining trend in
Germany and UK and, in recent years, Australia and some downward
trend in Canada and USA. The picture for Sweden is less clear and
for other countries there is too short a run of figures to judge.

In *manufacturing* net *rates of return* (table and chart B4b), UK has
the lowest rates of the four countries for which estimates can be
made, over the whole period from 1955. USA[1] has the highest from
1962 onwards but for 1960−61 Germany is higher (for 1955−59 no
figures for Germany are available; during this period the USA is the
highest of the other three countries). There are again steeply declining
trends in Germany and UK and a less marked decline in Canada.
There is some evidence of a declining trend in USA but the marked
upswing in the mid 1960s makes conclusions difficult. In gross rates of
return, Sweden was as low as UK in the mid 1960s, there is less difference between Germany and USA, and Japan shows rates of return
far higher than elsewhere.

France is not covered in the OECD industry comparisons because of
lack of data but another study (King and Mairesse 1978), comparing
UK and French rates of return in manufacturing industry excluding
food, drink and tobacco and metal manufacture in the period
1956−75, suggests that the trend in France was, if anything, slightly
upwards.

Additional qualifications can be made to these comparisons, particularly the element of self employment income included in the
operating surplus which, for example, would inflate rates of return
and shares in Japan compared with the UK, but the general picture of
a declining trend in many countries in rates of return and profit shares
is fairly clear. In manufacturing industry, Germany has suffered as
much decline as the UK although from higher levels and in all
industry and transport it shows a much sharper decline than UK. The
UK is at or near the bottom of the range on all comparisons except

[1] See footnote p 20.

for profit shares in manufacturing industry, in terms of which the UK occupied a medium position until recent years.

Table B1   Share of profits in total domestic incomes*   per cent
(after deducting stock appreciation and capital consumption)

| | Industrial and Commercial Companies | | Private Manufacturing Companies |
	Including North Sea activities	Excluding	
1960		15.5	10.1
1961		13.7	8.6
1962		12.7	7.9
1963		13.8	8.3
1964		14.3	8.8
1965		14.6	8.3
1966		12.3	7.4
1967	12.2	12.3	7.2
1968	12.0	12.1	7.0
1969	12.1	12.2	6.9
1970	10.9	10.9	5.8
1971	11.2	11.3	6.0
1972	11.6	11.6	6.2
1973	11.2	11.3	6.1
1974	7.4	7.6	2.9
1975	6.2	6.6	2.7
1976	7.2	7.1	2.7
1977	9.2	8.2	4.0
1978	9.5	8.4	4.3
1979	8.5	6.0	2.5

*Gross trading profit plus rent received (rent taken as nil for manufacturing) less stock appreciation, less capital consumption at replacement cost, as percentage of total domestic income less stock appreciation (ie income-based estimate of gross domestic product), less capital consumption at replacement cost.

Source: Profits, stock appreciation and total domestic incomes 1974 onwards *Economic Trends* April 1980 (HMSO); data for 1970−73 on consistent basis from Central Statistical Office. Earlier data and other data for 1970−78 mainly from *National Income and Expenditure* 1979 Edition (HMSO 'Blue Book')

Table B2   Real rates of return* (pre-tax)   per cent

| | Industrial and Commercial Companies | | Private Manufacturing Companies |
	Including North Sea activities	Excluding	
1960		13.2	12.9
1961		11.4	10.7
1962		10.4	9.7
1963		11.5	10.4
1964		12.0	11.1
1965		11.3	10.4
1966	10.0	10.0	9.0
1967	10.0	10.1	9.0
1968	10.1	10.2	9.1
1969	9.9	10.0	8.9
1970	8.7	8.7	7.3
1971	8.9	9.0	7.5
1972	9.2	9.2	7.8
1973	8.5	8.6	7.6
1974	5.1	5.3	3.3
1975	4.4	4.7	3.1
1976	5.0	5.1	3.2
1977	6.3	5.8	4.7
1978	6.4	5.9	5.0
1979	5.4	4.1	2.9

*Gross trading profit plus rent received (rent taken as nil for manufacturing) less stock appreciation, less capital consumption at replacement cost, as percentage of net capital stock (fixed assets other than land) at replacement cost plus book value of stocks.

Source: see table B1. Net capital stock fixed assets consistent with data in 1979 National Income Blue Book, 1979 estimated; book value of stocks takes account of data revisions in April 1980.

INTERNATIONAL COMPARISONS OF PROFITABILITY 1955–78

Table B3a Profit shares[a]: industry plus transport, non-financial corporations

per cent

	Industry plus transport[b]					Non-financial corporations[c]		
	Canada	West Germany	Sweden	Norway	United Kingdom	United Kingdom	United States	France
Averages for years[d]								
1955–59	30	32	26		22	23		
1960–62	28	29	24		23	22	20	21
1963–67	29	28	22		22	22	23	21
1968–71	27	23[e]	22	22	21	20	19	23
1972–75	28		7	21	18	15	17	20
1976–78	26			14	17	15	18	
Years								
1975	26	21	17	19	13	10	17	16
1976	26	23	9	16	15	13	18	17
1977	26	23	3	11	19	16	18	
1978	27		8	16	18	16	18	

Notes

a defined as net operating surplus as percentage net value added.

b ie manufacturing, mining, construction, public utilities and transport and communications industries.

c non-financial corporate and quasi-corporate enterprises (including public corporations)

d Apart from the first two and the last, which are governed by availability of data, the groupings of the years are related to the cycles in UK rates of return for industry plus transport, each starting in the year after a trough and ending in a trough year. Figures for other countries for the same years may cover more or less than a complete cycle and in this sense can only provide a broad comparison with UK.

e 1976–77

Source: T P Hill, OECD. UK figures 1970 onwards revised by Department of Industry.

INTERNATIONAL COMPARISONS OF PROFITABILITY 1955–78

Table B3b Net rate of return[a]: industry plus transport, non-financial corporations

per cent

	Industry plus transport[b]				Non-financial corporations[c]		
	Canada	West Germany	Norway	United Kingdom	United Kingdom	United States	France
Averages for years [d]							
1955–59	14			11	13	18	
1960–62	11	22		10	12	17	11
1963–67	12	18	5	10	11	22	12
1968–71	10	17	6	9	8	17	15
1972–75	11	14	6	7	5	15	13
1976–78	9		3[e]	6	5	15	
Years							
1975	9	12	5	4	3	13	9
1976	9	13	4	5	4	14	9
1977	9		2	6	5	15	
1978	9			6	5	15	

Notes

a defined as net operating surplus as percentage net capital stock of fixed assets (excluding land)

b ie manufacturing, mining, construction, public utilities and transport and communication.

c non-financial corporate and quasi-corporate enterprises (including public corporations)

d Apart from the first two and the last which are governed by availability of data, the groupings of the years are related to the cycles in UK rates of return for industry plus transport, each starting in the year after a trough and ending in a trough year. Figures for other countries for the same years may cover more or less than a complete cycle and in this sense can only provide a broad comparison with UK.

e 1976–77

Source: T P Hill, OECD. UK figures 1970 onwards revised by Department of Industry.

INTERNATIONAL COMPARISONS OF PROFITABILITY 1955–78

Table B4a   Profit shares[a]: manufacturing industry   per cent

	Canada	United States	West Germany	Sweden	United Kingdom
Averages for years [b]					
1955–59	30	21			28
1960–62	28	20	32	24	26
1963–67	28	23	29	20	24
1968–71	25	19	28	21	21
1972–75	27	17	21	25	16
1976–78	23	19	21[c]	12	13
Years					
1975	25	17	19	23	10
1976	23	19	21	16	10
1977	22	19	21	10	14
1978	24	19		11	15

Notes
a defined as net operating surplus as percentage net value added.
b apart from the first two and the last, which are governed by availability of data, the
   groupings of the years are related to the cycles in UK rates of return in industry plus
   transport, each starting in the year after a trough and ending in a trough year.
   Figures for other countries for the same years may cover more or less than a complete
   cycle and in this sense can only provide a broad comparison with UK.
c 1976–77

Source: T P Hill, OECD. UK figures 1970 onwards revised by Department of Industry.

INTERNATIONAL COMPARISONS OF PROFITABILITY 1955–78

Table B4b   Net rate of return[a]: manufacturing industry   per cent

	Canada	United States	West Germany	United Kingdom
Average for years[b]				
1955–59	22	29		17
1960–62	19	27	29	15
1963–67	18	36	21	14
1968–71	16	26	22	11
1972–75	17	22	16	7
1976–78	13	24		5
Years				
1975	15	19	14	4
1976	13	23	16	4
1977	12	24		6
1978	13	24		6

Notes

a defined as net operating surplus as percentage net capital stock of fixed assets (excluding land)

b apart from the first two and the last, which are governed by availability of data, the groupings of the years are related to the cycles in UK rates of return for industry plus transport, each starting in the year after a trough and ending in a trough year.
Figures for other countries for the same years may cover more or less than a complete cycle and in this sense can only provide a broad comparison with UK.

Source: T P Hill, OECD. UK figures, 1970 onwards, revised by Department of Industry.

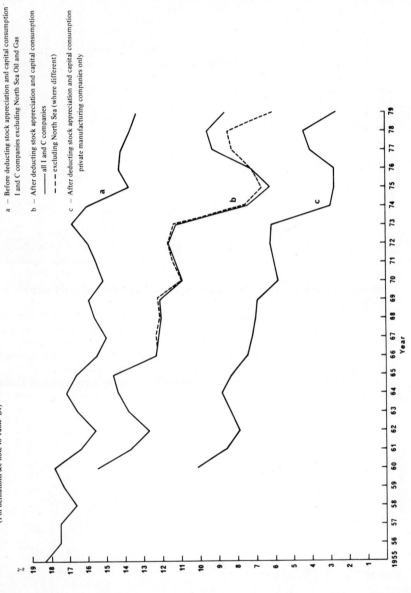

CHART B1a SHARE OF PROFITS IN TOTAL DOMESTIC INCOMES
(For definitions see note to Table B1)

a – Before deducting stock appreciation and capital consumption
    I and C companies excluding North Sea Oil and Gas
b – After deducting stock appreciation and capital consumption
    —— all I and C companies
    – – – excluding North Sea (where different)
c – After deducting stock appreciation and capital consumption
    private manufacturing companies only

CHART B1b   SHARE OF PROFITS* IN ALL INDUSTRIAL AND COMMERCIAL COMPANIES
VALUE ADDED†

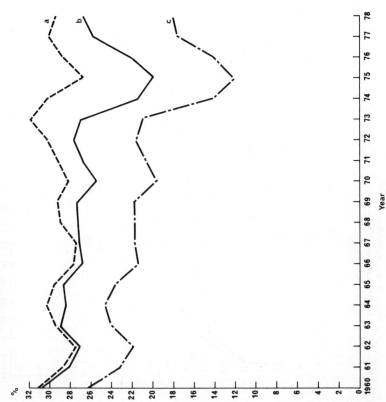

a   before deducting stock appreciation or
     capital consumption

b   After deducting stock appreciation but
     before deducting capital consumption

c   After deducting stock appreciation and
     capital consumption at replacement cost

*   gross trading profit plus rent, including
     profits from North Sea activities

†   numerator plus estimated income from
     employment

CHART B2a   PRE–TAX REAL RATES OF RETURN 1960–79
(For definitions see notes to Table B2)

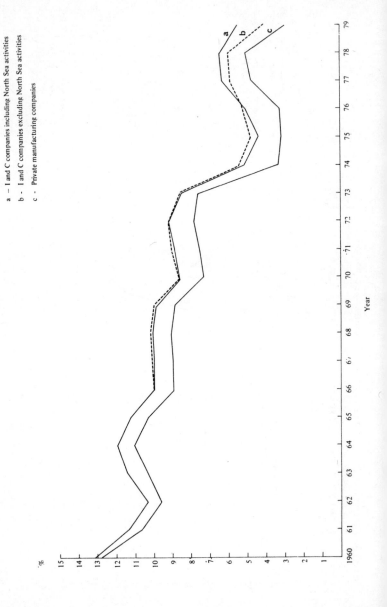

a – I and C companies including North Sea activities
b - I and C companies excluding North Sea activities
c - Private manufacturing companies

CHART B2b   REAL RATES OF RETURN: INDUSTRIAL AND COMMERCIAL COMPANIES
EXCLUDING NORTH SEA ACTIVITIES PRE– AND POST– TAX
(For definitions see notes to Table B2)

a – Pre-tax

b – Post tax (backward looking)

Source of post-tax rates

Bank of England Quarterly Bulletin June 1980

The basis of the post-tax rates of return is set out in detail in the BEQB March 1976. Taxes, including those on dividends and interest in the hands of recipients, are deducted from earnings and the capital base is reduced to allow for the proportion financed by tax allowances etc on investment. The backward looking measure computes tax allowances by reference to those in force when the capital was installed.

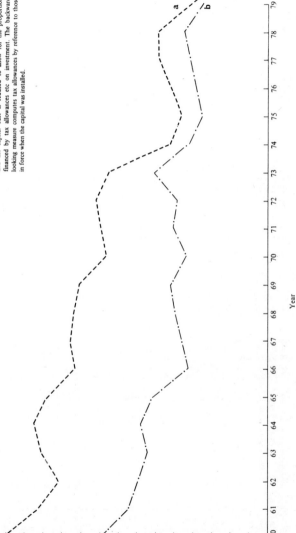

International Comparisons of Profitability 1955-78

Chart B3a Profit Shares: Industry plus Transport

(net operating surplus as % of net value added)

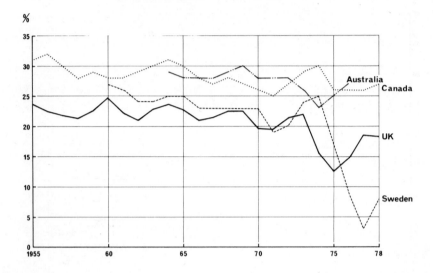

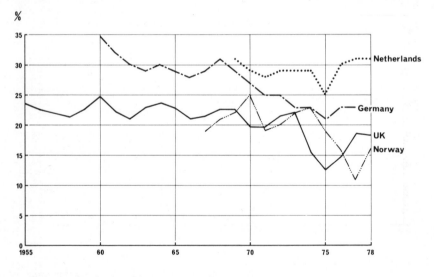

International Comparisons of Profitability 1955-78

Chart B3b Rates of Return: Industry plus Transport

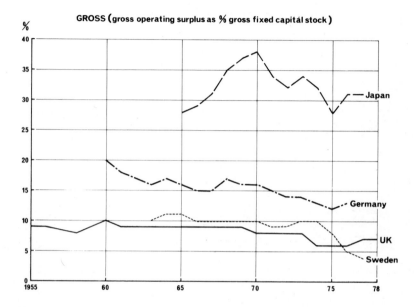

GROSS (gross operating surplus as % gross fixed capital stock)

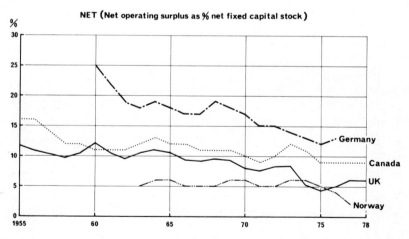

NET (Net operating surplus as % net fixed capital stock)

International Comparisons of Profitability 1955–78

Chart B3c Non–Financial Corporate and Quasi–Corporate Enterprises

Net Rate of Return (net operating surplus as % net fixed capital stock)

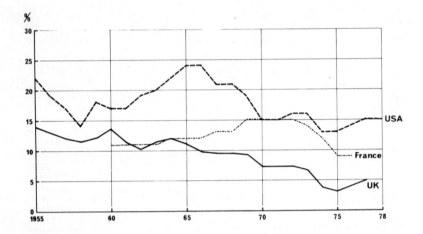

Profit Shares (net operating surplus as % net value added)

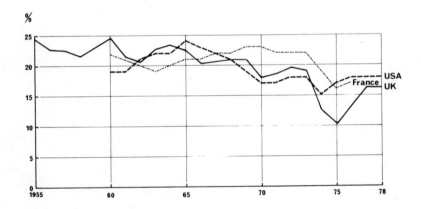

International Comparisons of Profitability 1955-78
Chart B4a Profit Shares: Manufacturing
(net operating surplus as % net value added)

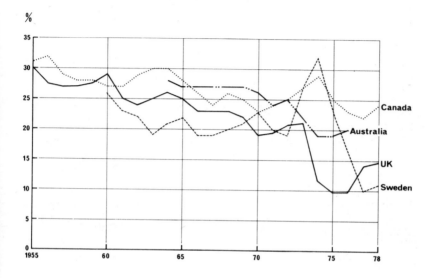

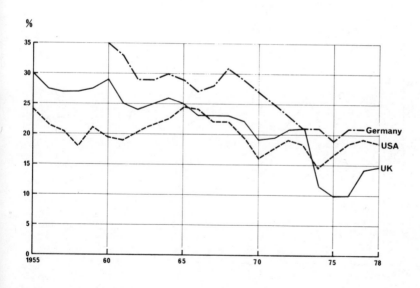

International Comparisons of Profitability 1955-1978

Chart B4b Rates of Return : Manufacturing

GROSS (Gross operating surplus as % gross fixed capital stock)

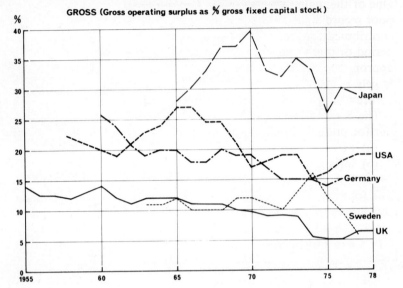

NET (Net operating surplus as % net fixed capital stock)

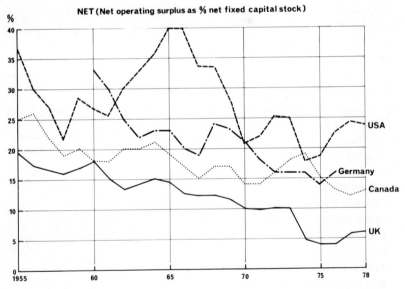

Section C   Causes of declining profitability

One of the main features of profitability in the UK is the especially poor record since 1973. This suggests either that those factors which contributed towards the secular decline became more intense in this period or that there emerged new adverse influences. It seems appropriate to consider therefore the main factors thought to be largely responsible for the performance of profits since the early 1970s before looking at theories explaining secular movements.

The explanations of the recent debacle are inevitably inter-related but for presentational reasons it is useful to distinguish between:

    (a) excess capacity;

    (b) inflation;

    (c) increase in real material/energy prices.

The following paragraphs consider these factors in general terms; a concluding section attempts some modest empirical analysis.

C1   Causes of the recent fall

C1.1   EXCESS CAPACITY

One explanation of the sharp fall in profitability is that the decline in output in relation to capacity was more marked in the recession of 1974–75 and, perhaps, subsequently than at any other time in the post-war period. The Bank of England, for example, noted in September 1978 that 'most indicators suggest that capacity utilisation has fallen since the last peak in 1973; and that the margin of unutilised capacity is now considerable'.

Cyclical changes in capacity utilisation are thought to affect profitability because of the associated effects on labour productivity and the spreading of non-labour overheads and because of the particular pricing policies adopted by firms. Labour productivity tends to be pro-cyclical, at least in manufacturing industry, because of lags in adjusting any variable labour input to variations in demand and because some proportion of the employed labour force is, in any case, more akin to a fixed factor of production. Whether or not such movements in productivity lead to contra-cyclical movements in unit costs – rising in recession – depends, of course, on the response of nominal factor costs (eg average earnings) to demand pressures. This is a complex issue which cannot be considered here in detail; it suffices to say that most empirical models of the inflationary process do not suggest that the effect on unit costs of pro-cyclical movements in productivity are offset, in the short term at least, by movements in nominal factor costs.

For one reason or another, contra-cyclical movements in unit costs are not fully reflected in prices charged – hence profit margins vary pro-cyclically. One hypothesis is that firms use a measure of 'normal' unit costs – unit costs incurred when operating at a satisfactory level of capacity utilisation – to which is added a *non-cyclical* margin[1]. As a result, 'the customer is not asked to pay for the higher overhead per unit and the lower productivity of recession' (Okun, 1975), so observed profit margins fall. The alternative hypothesis is that the profit margin is affected by competitive pressures which vary with the degree of excess capacity[2]. All these considerations are relevant to cyclical movements of profit share in value added as well as profitability. The latter is affected additionally of course by pro-cyclical movements in the ratio of output to the capital stock[3].

Whatever the merits of the alternative pricing hypotheses, it is clear that profits move with the business cycle (see, eg, Ball, 1978; Brown, 1978; Coutts, 1978; Jenkinson, 1978). Of particular note is Jenkinson's observation that 'most of the decline in the real share [of profits] between the second half of 1973 and the second half of 1975 can be attributed to the impact of the recession'. Also Ball states '. . . . over 60 per cent of the fall in the rate of return since 1973 [until 1976] can be accounted for by the recession' though he regards this as a top estimate.

The hypotheses regarding *short run* pricing behaviour and the movements in unit costs are helpful in explaining cyclical movements in profit share and profitability. However it is less clear that they can be applied confidently to an economy which, as the Bank of England noted, suffers from chronic excess capacity (as conventionally measured). Added to this difficulty, it is possible that the persistence of excess capacity is due, not to demand deficiency, but to structural inefficiencies and market distortions, ie 'supply constraints'. Since conventional theory provides little guidance in these circumstances, it is worth anticipating the results of the later empirical enquiry. Perhaps not surprisingly, these suggest that the clearest direct impact of chronic excess capacity (there may be other effects) has been to reduce, almost by definition, the ratio of output both to the capital stock at constant prices and to the volume of capital consumption. The increased importance of capital consumption in net incomes and the decline in

---

[1] Some advocates, eg Godley and Nordhaus, 1972, 'normalise' earnings as well as labour productivity when testing this proposition.

[2] For a survey of the evidence see Laidler and Parkin, 1975.

[3] Note that the rate of return (profitability) is identically equal to profit share multiplied by the output to capital ratio.

the output-capital ratio help account – ex post – for the persistent low levels of real profit share and real profitability.

C1.2 INFLATION

In a textbook economy in which (a) there were no adjustment lags, (b) where prices and costs were rising at the same rate and (c) where this rate was fully anticipated by all economic agents, real profitability would not be affected by inflation. However, these conditions are unlikely to be met in practice, the most obvious (inter-related) reasons being:

    (a) adverse activity effects arising as a result of inflation;
    (b) lags between increases in costs and subsequent movements in prices;
    (c) unexpected increases in costs.

(a) *Inflation: adverse activity effects*

Inflation, in a general sense, may adversely affect profits because it can exert contractionary influences on the economy and acts as a constraint on demand management policy. In so far as capacity utilisation is thus reduced, profits will be squeezed for reasons already described. On the question of policy, there has been a shift of government priorities, in the UK and elsewhere, from the pursuit of full-employment towards the control and reduction of inflation which has led at times to a more restrictive budgetary stance, both here and abroad. Inflation at the high and volatile rates experienced in the 1970s seems also to have been a direct cause of recession. Examples of contractionary effects include the rise in the propensity to save – the result probably of greater uncertainty and the erosion of the real value of accumulated savings as inflation rapidly increased[1] – and, possibly, a fall in investment demand by companies facing liquidity problems[2], partly as a consequence of lags in price-setting/unexpected cost inflation (see below). Inflation may also have contributed towards supply constraints by obfuscating market signals.

All this serves to amplify the somewhat obvious point that the especially poor performance of profitability in the UK in the 1970s is not due simply to excess capacity but to its combination with inflation. The fact that the UK has fared worse than other countries in terms of

[1] Taylor (1978) shows the increased saving propensity to be a major proximate cause of UK recession, 1975–77.
[2] The liquidity problem was compounded by the effects of inflation working through the tax system – ie the problem created by taxing 'paper stock profits' prior to the introduction of stock relief (a relevant analysis is in Godley and Wood, 1975).

profitability over this period also bears a superficially appealing correlation with the UK's worse record on inflation and growth.

(b)   *Inflation: price-cost lags*
The relevance of price/cost lags can be illustrated by a simple numerical example. It is assumed in Table C1 that the price of output is a constant mark-up (of 25 per cent) on (unit) wage costs in the previous period. (Profits are implicitly defined net of stock appreciation.) With stable prices, this mark-up is achieved in the first two periods. In period 3, there is a sudden change in the environment, with wage inflation proceeding at a constant rate, until period 6, of 10 per cent. Because of the price-cost lag, prices do not alter until period 4. Consequently, the effective profit margin falls in period 3 and remains at a new lower level while inflation of both prices and wages stay at 10 per cent. Consistently, the real product wage – the average wage divided by the price of (gross) output[1] – rises to a new level. Rising inflation, beginning in period 6, leads to a falling effective profit margin and a rising real product wage. Price inflation lags behind wage inflation. (A more elaborate discussion can be found in Flemming 1976(a).)

The essential result, which holds qualitatively whatever the structure of the price-cost lag, is that a move to a higher rate of inflation will cause a once-and-for-all fall in the level of profit share (net of stock appreciation); accelerating inflation will cause a continuing fall. However, as a general proposition, this result depends on the view that industrial prices are essentially cost-determined – ie price inflation is always initiated by inflation of costs, for whatever reason. If price adjustment always preceded wage adjustment, converse conclusions apply. The 1970s in fact provide examples of both possibilities. In 1972–73, the inflationary process was characterised in part by the increase in prices ahead of costs – as evidenced by the rapid rise in manufactured export prices above domestic prices, both in the UK and in the OECD area generally (McCracken Report, 1977, p 62). At the same time, there were very strong cost pressures, to which industrial prices responded, arising from world supply and demand conditions: the upsurge in food prices and, subsequently, commodity prices generally and later still, the oil price hike in October 1973/January 1974. In turn, these external cost pressures may have sparked off a rise in domestic labour costs – a contentious issue which is briefly

---

[1] Real product wages are variously defined in the literature. The present definition is consonant with Maynard's (1978) concept of the 'own product real wage' but differs from definitions to be found in, for example, Sachs (1979) and *Midland Bank Review*, Summer, 1979.

considered later. Thus it is no easy matter to distinguish price-led from cost-led inflation; nor therefore to assess the impact of observed inflation on profit margins, given lags in adjustment.

Table C1   Hypothetical example of the effect of inflation on the profit margin, assuming a price-cost lag

	Price (i)	Wage (ii)	Effective Mark-Up (%) (iii)	Real Product Wage (iv)	Price Inflation (%) (v)	Wage Inflation (%) (iv)	
Period							
1	10	8	25	0.8	0	0	Stable
2	10	8	25	0.8	0	0	Prices
3	10	8.8	13.6	0.9	0	10	
4	11	9.7	13.6	0.9	10	10	Constant Inflation
5	12.1	10.6	13.6	0.9	10	10	
6	13.3	12.2	8.7	0.9	10	15	
7	15.3	14.7	4.2	1.0	15	20	Rising Inflation
8	18.4	18.4	0	1.0	20	25	

Notes:
  (i) Assumed that price = 1.25 × average wage in previous period and that the level of labour productivity is equal to unity
  (ii) Column (iii) = ((column (i) ÷ column (ii)) − 1) × 100
  (iii) Alternatively, column (iii) = $(\dfrac{1.25}{1 + \text{rate of wage inflation}} - 1) \times 100$
  (iv) Real product wage = average wage ÷ price of output

One reason for the existence of a price-cost lag may be institutional, reflecting the cost valuation practices of firms. In addition, the apparent lag between prices and actual costs will be greater if firms follow a normal cost-plus pricing policy – since self-reversing cyclical movements in unit costs are not, ex hypothesi, passed into prices. There will also be administrative lags. The institutional factor has been cited as particularly relevant to recent experience. Analogously to the problem of stock valuation, prices may be based on historic or replacement costs, or some average of the two. The assumption of historic cost pricing is 'extreme because, under it, firms do not adjust final prices in a period of rising prices until stocks of inputs bought at lower prices are completely exhausted. At the other extreme is the assumption that firms practice replacement cost pricing, adjusting their selling prices instantaneously to changes in cost' (Coutts, Godley and Nordhaus, 1978, p 36)[1].

It appears therefore that the more cost-plus pricing approximates to an historic rather than replacement cost rule, the greater the susceptibility of profits to an increase in cost inflation. If this is to explain why profits actually fell, the question arises why firms should adhere, apparently irrationally, to a pricing policy which is against their own interests.

The main reason adduced for the possibility of such behaviour is the prevalence of historic cost accounting (see, eg Brown, 1979). It may be noted, for example, that the fall in profit share net of stock appreciation which, as illustrated above, will accompany a rise in cost inflation, given a price-cost lag, will be matched – and under certain limiting conditions, exactly matched (Coutts, 1978) – by the associated increase in stock appreciation. Profit share including stock appreciation may therefore not fall at all; it will certainly not fall as fast as profit share excluding stock appreciation if cost inflation increases. Thus, it may be alleged, by adopting profit margins inclusive rather than exclusive of stock appreciation as a signal, those taking pricing (and output) decisions were misled.

The general objection to this explanation is that there is no logical necessity for a firm practising historic cost accounting also to practise historic cost pricing. More specifically, to the extent that the rapid increase in the importance of stock appreciation after 1972 was due directly to historic cost pricing policies, it may be argued that the sheer problem of financing that stock appreciation would have prompted management to switch to a more rational pricing rule, irrespective of managers' comprehension and acceptance of current cost accounting principles. This argument has some force but it may be that firms were prevented from making such a switch between 1973 and 1975 by the operation of a price code which attempted to control domestic selling prices on the basis of historic costs.

(c)   *Unexpected cost inflation*
The importance of these issues has not been resolved empirically. However, even those who question the simple mechanics of price-cost

---

[1] For manufacturing industry, there is evidence that there exists a price-cost lag, though shorter than that implied by strict historic cost pricing (Coutts, Godley and Nordhaus, 1978, Chapters 3, 4).

lags as an explanation of profit's decline would not dismiss cost inflation – more particularly, unexpected cost inflation – as a possible causative factor. In principle, the potential difficulty posed for profits by the existence of a price-cost lag could be overcome simply by removing the lag. While there may be good practical reasons (such as information and implementation lags) why this would not be feasible, a broadly equivalent procedure would be (in effect) to index-link the profit margin to the expected rate of cost inflation. For example, if the desired margin (net of stock appreciation) and the expected rate of cost inflation from the current period to the date of implementing a future price change are both 10 per cent, the future price may be reckoned at a margin of $(1.1^2 - 1) = 21$ per cent above present day costs. This is equivalent to applying a 10 per cent margin to the expected future level of costs.

What matters for profits in this case is the extent to which cost inflation is accurately predicted: if expectations are met, profit margins will be as desired (other things equal); if cost inflation continually exceeds expectations, profit margins will fall. In this context, it may well have been the case that the commodity/oil price shocks and the subsequent rapid acceleration of labour costs were associated with considerable underprediction of cost inflation. It seems unlikely however that such a state of affairs would have persisted in any serious degree after inflation peaked in 1975[1], though the very recent rise in labour/material costs in 1978–79 may have led to some re-enactment of the same set of adverse processes.

Overall, it is difficult to judge the importance of price-cost lags/ unexpected cost inflation. The problem of deciding which came first – the price rise or the rise in costs – the unknown extent to which firms attempt to incorporate future cost increases in their pricing decisions and their success in so doing make empirical analysis extremely difficult. The one piece of traceable evidence is due to Jenkinson (1978) who contends, on the basis of some 'rather unsatisfactory' equations, which make no formal distinction between actual and expected cost inflation, that 'The influence of accelerating costs in reducing profitability over this period [1973H2 to 1975H2] was .... a good deal less important than declining capacity utilisation'.

---

[1] Some evidence from the Department of Industry's investment intentions enquiry – admittedly in relation to the rate of inflation of prices of capital goods rather than wages or material costs – suggests that manufacturers and those engaged in distributive and service industries underpredicted the rate of inflation a year ahead up to 1975 but fairly accurately predicted its deceleration after 1975. See Lund, Martin and Bennett (1980).

C1.3   RISE IN REAL MATERIAL/ENERGY COSTS

In 1972–74, the prices of materials and fuel purchased by the UK manufacturing sector rose by 95 per cent compared with a 32 per cent increase in output prices of goods sold at home. By definition, such a rise in real material prices would have squeezed manufacturers' profit margins. This rise reflected the sharp depreciation of sterling (a 12 per cent fall in the effective exchange rate, 1972–74) and the rise in real commodity and oil prices on world markets. After 1974, some real commodity prices fell back; real oil and energy prices on the other hand remained permanently at a much higher level than pre-1973 (though varying from year to year). Some estimates reflecting the impact of these commodity and oil price shocks are presented in the next section.

To the extent that these shifts in relative prices contributed towards the inflation of 1974–75, the full impact of them on profits – through the kind of routes discussed above – may have borne little resemblance to, and may have been of greater significance than, the direct impact. Whether shifts in relative prices will cause inflation is a contentious issue which can be dealt with but briefly here. A number of monetarists (eg Laidler, 1976) dismissed the possibility that the oil crisis could have fuelled inflation: given that nominal monetary growth fell back in the UK in 1974–75, there would have been an offsetting fall in the price of those goods which did not use oil intensively, matching the rise in the price of oil and oil-intensive goods.

The most important counter-argument, due especially to Hicks (1975), is the contention that wage bargaining is subject to 'real wage resistance',[1] and the attempt to restore real wages by the workforce in the face of the rise in prices of imported commodities and oil led to a general rise in wages and prices. Whatever the merits of the idea of 'real wage resistance' as a general description of wage bargaining processes, it would seem a very accurate approximation to UK conditions in 1973–74. The reason is simply that, between November 1973 and October 1974, 'real wage resistance' was institutionalised by the threshold agreements, operating under Stage 3 of incomes policy, linking money wages to the retail price index (see Miller, 1976). It seems clear therefore that the inflationary outburst of 1974–75 and the problems it created for profitability can be traced to the commodity/oil crises as well as the synchronised excessive monetary expansions in OECD countries in 1972–73.

[1] There is of course no universally accepted view of the nature of the wage bargaining process (see Blackaby, 1978(a), p 389 on this point) but evidence supporting the real wage resistance or target real wage theory is to be found in, eg, Coutts, Tarling, Wilkinson, 1976; Henry, Sawyer, Smith, 1976.

C1.4   AN ACCOUNTING EXERCISE

This section attempts to draw some of the threads of argument together by conducting a simple investigation into the pattern of real factor costs and productivities which bear upon the evolution of profit share and profitability. For profit share (net of stock appreciation and capital consumption) the relevant considerations are[1]: real product wages/earnings and labour productivity, real material costs and material productivity, the real implicit price of capital consumption and the volume of output in relation to the volume of capital consumption. In each case, 'real' implies deflation by the wholesale price of output. It hardly needs emphasizing that a simple accounting exercise of this kind can provide at best only rough guidance as to the importance for profits of the various causative factors cited at the beginning – excess capacity, inflation, increased real material/energy costs – since no account is taken of the various inter-relationships emphasized in the preceding sections.

The following concentrates on the UK manufacturing sector, partly for reasons of data availability and partly because it is here, rather than in non-manufacturing, that the profitability record is so poor. This contrast is illustrated in table C2, showing profit shares before and after deducting capital consumption at replacement cost, for the manufacturing sector[2], and a miscellaneous group corresponding to Hill's (1979) definition of industry and transport less manufacturing industry less mining and quarrying. (The latter exclusion is adopted to abstract from the direct impact of North Sea oil.) The share of profits in manufacturing industry plunges in 1974 (and remains flat in 1973 despite the output peak in that year). Thereafter, profit share recovers (quite sharply in 1977), but the recovery, in relation to the 1972 level, is more marked for gross profit share than that net of capital consumption (ie real profit share). Profit share in the miscellaneous group on the other hand falters only in the depths of the 1975 recession: gross profit share is back to, and slightly above, its 1972 level by 1978, real profit share is only slightly down on the 1972 level by 1978.[3]

---

[1] This list can be inferred from the identity for pre-tax net profits (ignoring indirect and employment taxes): net profits ≡ the value of gross output less the wage and salary bill less the cost of purchased materials and fuel less capital consumption at current prices. These components can be broken down into their respective price and volume terms – eg the value of gross output is the output price multiplied by the volume of gross output.

[2] Including firms in the public sector cf Section B.2.

[3] Within the miscellaneous group, there is some diversity of experience: over the period 1973–78, real profit share rose in the public utilities (reflecting the rise in real energy prices), fell slightly in construction and more markedly in transport and communication.

Table C3 shows the pattern of real capital prices and 'productivities' which bear upon the evolution of real profit share and profitability in manufacturing industry. The relevance of the output-capital ratio in terms of the identity for profitability is obvious; the ratio also reflects, in a crude way, the degree of excess capacity. The recession of 1974–75 and the subdued rate of output growth, apparently[1] below potential, in subsequent years is thus reflected in a maintained fall in the output-capital ratio and, partly as a result of the arbitrary method of calculating depreciation, in the ratio of output to the volume of capital consumption. It is these volume movements rather than the pattern of real prices of capital goods (rows C and D) which account for the more adverse movement in profitability compared to profit share after 1973 and the increased divergence between the gross and real profit shares in table C2.

Table C4 turns to the impact of labour costs and material costs (eg the cost of raw materials, fuel, components and bought-in services) on gross profit share. A rise in real product wages/earnings in excess of any rise in labour productivity and a rise in real material costs in excess of any rise in material productivity[2] will depress profit share and, by the same token, increase wage share. It is possible to allocate the actual change in wage share to movements in real product wages and labour productivity on the one hand (the 'labour cost effect') and to movements in real material prices and material productivity on the other (the 'material cost effect'). Table C4 allocates the actual change in profit share (in percentage points) from a common base year, 1972[3], to these movements in wage (and salary) share and extends the calculations to include other non-wage – non-profit components in value added.[4] (Annex 1 describes the method, the data and the measurement problems in detail.)

---

[1] While there seems little doubt that part of the 1974–75 fall in output below capacity was due to demand deficiency, it is less clear that deficiency of demand was wholly to blame for that and subsequent experience, rather than the existence of supply constraints.

[2] That is, changes in the ratio of the volume of gross output to the volume of material input. In normal circumstances, this ratio probably changes only slowly (see Hill, 1971, Chapter 5).

[3] Owing to large changes in income distribution over this period, year-on-previous-year comparisons would not be meaningful: hence the use of a base year. 1972 is the last year before the marked shift in the UK's terms of trade.

[4] This procedure somewhat understates the full effect of changes in real unit material prices since a proportion of the change in profit share due to changes in non-wage – non-profit components in value added could also be allocated to a 'material cost effect'.

Table C2   Profit Shares in Value Added

	Construction, Gas, Electricity and Water, Transport and Communication		Manufacturing Industry	
	Profit (and other income) Share in Value Added		Profit Share in Value Added	
	Before deducting capital consumption (i)	After deducting capital consumption (ii)	Before deducting capital consumption (iii)	After deducting capital consumption (iv)
1972	37.0	23.4	25.3	18.8
1973	37.4	24.4	25.3	18.9
1974	37.8	24.1	17.1	9.1
1975	34.8	19.8	15.8	7.4
1976	37.9	23.3	16.3	7.7
1977	38.7	22.8	20.2	11.8
1978	38.0	21.3	20.7	12.4

Source: National Accounts, CSO
Notes:
(i) Profit and other income in columns (i) and (ii) include gross profits of companies, income from self-employment and gross trading surpluses of public enterprises, net of stock appreciation.
(ii) Profits for manufacturing industry are gross profits of companies and the trading surplus of public corporations, net of stock appreciation.
(iii) Value added defined consistently with the definition of profits, including or excluding capital consumption as required.

The impact of movements in real material prices, shown in column (iv), was dramatic in 1972−74 − the increase in real material costs accounted for virtually all the fall in profit share (from a 25 per cent to a 17 per cent share). Some of the adverse material cost effect was due to exchange rate depreciation − particularly in 1973 when the effective exchange rate fell by 9 per cent. However there was also a substantial adverse material cost effect between 1973 and 1974, which accounted for 80 per cent of the fall in profit share, at a time when the effective exchange rate fell only slightly − a 3 per cent fall, 1974 on 1973. The fall in the magnitude of the material cost effect after 1974 reflects the fall of real commodity prices on world markets and, since

Table C3   Real Capital Prices and 'Productivities' in Manufacturing Industry, Indices 1975 = 100

	1972	1973	1974	1975	1976	1977	1978
A	106.7	113.2	108.6	100	99.9	99.4	98.4
B	109.1	114.7	109.5	100	99.1	98.2	96.5
C	96.2	103.5	101.9	100	99.1	94.0	97.0
D	98.6	101.2	98.5	100	100.3	97.5	99.5

Source: *National Accounts,* CSO, *Economic Trends*
Series: A – Index of production divided by an index of net capital stock (end year) at 1975 replacement cost
B – Index of production divided by an index of capital consumption at 1975 replacement cost
C – Index of an estimated implicit price deflator for the net capital stock divided by an index of the wholesale price of home sales.
D – Index of the implicit price deflator for capital consumption divided by an index of the wholesale price of home sales

Table C4   Change in the Share of Profits in Value Added by Manufacturing Industry, Percentage *Points*

	Actual change (i) = (vi) + (vii)	Allocated to Change in Share of:					
		Wages and Salaries				Income from Employment (vi) = (ii) + (v)	Other Income (vii)
		Total (ii) = (iii) + (iv)	Labour Cost Effect (iii)	Material Cost Effect (iv)	Employers' Contributions (v)		
1972–73	0.0	+0.3	+1.7	−1.5	−0.1	+0.2	−0.2
1972–74	−8.2	−6.7	+1.3	−8.0	−1.1	−7.8	−0.3
1972–75	−9.5	−7.0	−4.9	−2.1	−2.2	−9.3	−0.2
1972–76	−8.9	−6.4	−2.3	−4.1	−2.4	−8.8	−0.1
1972–77	−5.0	−3.2	+3.8	−6.9	−1.8	−5.0	−0.1
1972–78	−4.5	−3.0	+0.9	−3.9	−1.5	−4.5	0.0

Source: *National Accounts, Economic Trends.* See Annex 1
Notes:
(i) Profits as defined in note (ii) table C2, gross of capital consumption
(ii) Components may not sum to total due to rounding error

end 1976, the combined effect of a strong exchange rate, bolstered by North Sea oil, and an inflation rate higher than that of the UK's main competitors. As a result, the UK's terms of trade have improved, though even by 1978 the adverse shift in real unit material prices accounted for a 4 percentage point fall in manufacturing industry gross profit share from its 1972 level.

The possibly surprising feature of the evolution of real unit product wages – surprising because of the very low rate of labour productivity growth recorded – is that by 1978 they were somewhat lower than in 1972. Apart from the largely cyclical effects in 1974–75, the impact on profit share was therefore slightly favourable (though slightly unfavourable if employers' contributions are taken into account). This general outcome is partly due to the fact that 1972 is not a cyclical peak year: the strong cyclical upturn in productivity 1972–73 (about 8 per cent) exceeded the rise in real product wages (5 per cent). Also important was the impact of Stages I and II of incomes policy applied between July 1975 and July 1977: real product wages, having risen sharply in 1975, fell by 8½ per cent[1] between 1975 and 1977. The subsequent increase in real product wages may of course reflect a rebound from this squeeze on real wages. Taken at face value, however, it is not possible to argue that on balance the growth of real wages has directly squeezed profits since 1972. If the cause of profit's decline is to be attributed to labour costs and, in particular, the influence of trade unions, it would have to be in an indirect sense: for example, through the influence of unions on the inflationary process and thence on excess capacity or through their ability to resist cuts in living standards implied by an adverse shift in the terms of trade[2].

C1.5 SUMMARY AND CONCLUSIONS

The especially poor performance of profitability in the UK in the 1970s – most particularly in manufacturing industry – is largely symptomatic of the prevailing macro-economic problem of 'stagflation' and the rise in real energy prices. The adverse effect of inflation on activity may be regarded as a main reason for the

---

[1] Based on national accounts data.

[2] Sachs (1979) develops this latter idea in his comparative study of labour markets in major OECD countries. He argues that labour market conditions in the United States were conducive to a fall in real wages sufficient to maintain reasonable profitability and, thereby, output growth. This was not however the case in Europe or Japan: profitability fell markedly owing to the failure of real wages to adapt to the lower rate of productivity growth and the terms of trade deterioration after 1972–73. In Sachs' view, these differences in real wage adjustments account for the comparative buoyancy of the US economy after 1975.

persistent fall in output below capacity and, as a result, depressed profitability. Historic cost illusion in pricing policies and/or unexpected increases in costs as inflation accelerated may also have contributed. These difficulties have been compounded by the rise of real energy prices which directly squeezed profits, especially in manufacturing industry, and also added to inflationary pressures.

The recovery of profit share in manufacturing industry from the 1975 output trough reflects the modest recovery of output, the subsequent deceleration of inflation, the containment of the growth of real product wages and the beneficial terms of trade consequences of North Sea oil. At the time of writing (late 1979), this recovery appears unlikely to continue. The loss of competitiveness, the recent strong rise in real product wages and the prospect of a downturn in world trade growth, partly reflecting the second oil crisis of the decade, all augur a fall in profit share.

C2   Causes of the secular decline

While the causes of the more dramatic fall in the level of profit share/profitability in the UK since 1973 seem fairly clear cut, there is no consensus about the causes of the apparent longer term decline since the mid-1950s. This section of the paper considers only those explanations which may be 'tested', if somewhat casually, against readily-available empirical evidence.[1] In brief, these are:

  (a) a fall in the marginal productivity of physical capital;
  (b) a fall in the corporate tax burden;
  (c) a shift in market power from 'capitalists' to 'labour';
  (d) crowding-out by the public sector.

C2.1   A FALL IN THE MARGINAL PRODUCTIVITY OF CAPITAL

The observed increase in the capital-output ratio here and abroad (see Hill, 1979, tables 6.5, 6.6) is not inconsistent with the view that the

---

[1] This criterion is taken to exclude consideration of very general explanations such as 'the gradual disappearance of more profitable investment opportunities' and 'fast changing technologies lowering the profitability of existing capital'. (See eg, Flemming, 1976(a); *Financial Times* leader, 14 December 1978.) Also discounted is Ball's (1978) suggestion that increased international capital mobility may have brought 'UK profit levels down to those of our competitors', which was written before the publication of Professor Hill's work. Two other major theories of distribution – the neo-Keynesian theory (see, eg, Kaldor, 1955–56) and Wood's theory (Wood, 1975) – do not appear to have been subject to rigorous empirical testing (though for an unfavourable assessment of the former see King and Regan, 1976, chapter 6 and Hacche, 1979, chapter 15, esp. pp 293–295).

marginal productivity of capital has declined, leading by one mechanism or another, to a fall in its real return. Although at least one commentator (Clark, 1974, 1978) sees this mechanism as a reflection of a power struggle between employers and unions, the usual explanation is couched in terms of the neo-classical marginal productivity theory of distribution. The basic premises of the theory are familiar and dauntingly at odds with the real world: markets are perfectly competitive, there are diminishing returns to the employment of any one factor of production and there are constant returns to scale. These assumptions ensure that, in equilibrium, factors of production receive their marginal product, thereby exhausting the available output.

Sargent (1968, 1979) and Nordhaus (1974) writing of experience in the UK and US respectively have proposed essentially the same explanation of the alleged decline in the marginal productivity and marginal return to capital. ('Alleged' because we observe average movements whereas the theory refers to the unobserved return and productivity of the marginal investment project.) Sargent and Nordhaus believe that the real post-tax cost of capital has fallen secularly, because of an increasingly more generous tax treatment of company profits and increased post-war optimism reducing risk premiums. This, in turn, has encouraged the substitution of capital for labour in productive processes, implying the adoption of less profitable investment projects at the margin (though, at the same time, increasing the measured growth rate of labour productivity). In such a world, equilibrium is restored when the post-tax real rate of return and post-tax real cost of capital are equal (or their ratio – also known as the valuation ratio or Tobin's q – is unity). Thus a fall in the post-tax real cost of capital leads to a fall in the post-tax real rate of return and, by implication, the pre-tax real rate of return.[1]

This explanation raises at least four questions:
(a) has the real cost of capital fallen?
(b) if so, are the reasons those suggested by Sargent and Nordhaus?
(c) what evidence is there to support the connection between the real cost of capital and capital intensity?
(d) is the elasticity of substitution between capital and labour significantly less than unity?

The fourth question arises if the theory is to explain a fall in profit share in value added as well as the fall in the rate of return. An elasticity of substitution of less than one means that a fall in the

---

[1] Sargent (1979) also proposes two further mechanisms – an increase in real wage growth in excess of labour productivity growth and a rise in real capital prices.

relative price of a factor is less than offset by a rise in the relative
quantity employed, so that its relative share falls.[1] Thus the relatively
rapidly growing factor – capital in this case – will experience a declining
share of income if the elasticity of substitution is less than one.
Moreover, Bronfenbrenner (1960) has argued that unless the elasticity
is well below unity, relative shares will be fairly constant even if the
capital-labour ratio changes markedly. It may be concluded that if the
elasticity of substitution lies in the region of unity, Sargent and
Nordhaus' theory will be unable to explain the fall in profit share,
though it may explain the fall in the rate of return – as the capital-
output ratio rises – if the answer to question (c) is satisfactory. The
following paragraphs look at the available evidence for the UK in
some detail and then, more briefly, for the US.

UK Evidence
(a) A fall in the real post-tax cost of capital?   The estimation of the
real cost of capital is problematic since it requires knowledge of such
imponderables as investors' long run inflation expectations and the
effect of gearing on risk premiums. The common practice of subtracting the current inflation rate from nominal long run interest rates, for
example, is most unlikely to give an accurate picture of the real cost of
long term debt finance if long term expectations of nominal yields and
inflation differ significantly from rates presently observed. Flemming's
(1976(b)) solution is to derive an estimate of the post-tax real cost of
capital from an estimate of the financial valuation of industrial and
commercial companies (the market value of their debt and equity)
since this should reflect, albeit imperfectly, expectations about
inflation and risk.

His method is not, of course, without difficulties; nor is it the only
possible approach. Other methods inevitably yield different answers.[2]
The importance of Flemming's data in the present context is that they
show a secular decline in the real post-tax cost of capital between 1960
and 1969 which is closely matched (apart from cyclical movements) by

[1] This is analogous to the proposition in simple demand theory that total revenues will
fall if price falls and the elasticity of demand is less than one.
[2] For example, a series on the real post-tax 'user' cost of capital (see page 54) calculated
by the Treasury on the assumption that actual and expected inflation rates are equal
shows no perceptible trend during the 1960s cf Flemming's series. A brief review of
measures of the cost of capital is in 'The Test Discount Rate and the Required Rate
of Return on Investment'. *Government Economic Service Working Paper,* No 22,
1979, Annex A. It is also noteworthy that Oulton (1978–9) has calculated a series for
the valuation ratio for industrial and commercial companies quite dissimilar to
Flemming's. Oulton does not calculate separate series for profitability and the cost of
capital.

a consistently defined measure (see Flemming, 1976, (a)) of the real post-tax rate of return for industrial and commercial companies. The valuation ratio – real post-tax profitability divided by the real post-tax cost of capital – has an average value, 1960–69, of 1.2[1] – reasonably close to the theoretical equilibrium value of one, bearing in mind measurement errors and adjustment lags.

After 1969, however, a rise in the cost of capital and a continued fall in profitability have led to a valuation ratio persistently well below unity, having an average value to 1978 of only 0.6. Sargent (1979) contends that this over-shooting was due to other (adverse) factors not stressed by his theory – the state of demand and competition. He also believes that the observed fall in the rate of growth of labour productivity in manufacturing industry since the early 1970s represents 'a reversion to normal after a period of temporary acceleration whose stimulus, a lower real cost of capital, has now been fully absorbed into the system'. It is nevertheless difficult to reconcile the persistent (9 year) substantial excess of the real post-tax cost of capital over the real post-tax rate of return with a theory which suggests a long run valuation ratio of unity, and this may help account for the rather disappointing econometric results for investment functions incorporating the valuation ratio reported by the Bank of England (see C2.1(c) below).[2]

(b) *Why did the cost of capital fall?*   A fall in risk premiums and increased tax allowance on company profits are cited as causes of the falling real post-tax cost of capital. There is little reliable evidence on the question of *risk*. For the earlier period, Nordhaus' explanation looks to the stabilising effect of Keynesian demand management policies leading to 'the dissipation of fear of another Great Depression and the consequent effect on the risk premium on equities'. However, the one traceable study on the latter for the UK (Dimson and Brealey, 1978), based on a comparison of nominal interest rates on Treasury bills and the nominal equity return, suggests that the risk premium was flat between 1949 and 1968. Thus the one piece of available empirical evidence does not support the idea of a trend decline in risk.

---

[1] Based on updated figures consistent with those calculated by Clark and Williams, 1978.

[2] At the time of going to print, the Bank substantially revised its estimates of the cost of capital as a result of data and methodological changes. The trend in the cost of capital measure since 1963, the nice fit up to 1969 between the trend decline in post-tax profitability and the cost of capital shown by Flemming and the overshooting after 1969 are all much less apparent. This warns against drawing strong inferences from data subject to large measurement error.

On the question of *tax allowances,* the relevant theoretical consideration is the effective marginal tax rate (see below). However, Sargent (1968) supports his analysis by reference to the average tax rate on company income and, in particular, to evidence of a 'declining proportion of company income taken in tax'. The theoretical difficulty of using the average tax rate is that it is not necessarily independent of the course of pre-tax profitability or of the capital-output ratio and thus may not be considered an independent reason explaining the fall in the pre-tax rate of return or rise in the capital-output ratio. The average tax rate may be simply expressed as the product of the tax rate and one minus the ratio of allowances divided by the capital stock to profits divided by the capital stock – ie pre-tax profitability. Thus if pre-tax profitability fell for reasons unconnected with the tax regime but the ratio of allowances to the capital stock did not fall proportionately (perhaps reflecting a constant rate of replacement investment attracting tax allowance), the effective tax rate, as observed, would also fall.[1] In short, causation may go either way.

It is also unclear whether average tax rates on company income have, in fact, fallen. Annex 2 summarizes a number of studies addressing this issue. The general impression is one of considerable diversity in choice of relevant taxes and allowances and in industrial coverage. It is thus very difficult to provide a broad summary. Two points are worth making:

(a) The majority of studies covered point to a rise in the average tax rate.

(b) The clear exception to this rule are King's (1975) figures for the UK manufacturing sector (excluding metal manufacturing). King finds that the fall in the effective tax rate was sufficiently marked to leave the real post-tax profit share constant up to 1968 despite the decline in the real pre-tax profit share.

Little can be inferred from these differences without further research. Even then, the theoretical difficulty of using average tax rates remains.

The more relevant theoretical consideration is the influence of the fiscal regime on the marginal investment project via the 'user cost of capital' – the rental which capital goods would attract in a competitive market – and equivalent to the concept of wages as a payment for labour services. In simple theory[2], it is argued that the user cost of capital depends partly on the value of the 'gross/net yield ratio', equal

---

[1] A similar example could be given for an exogenous rise in the capital-output ratio.

[2] What should constitute the effective marginal tax rate (gross/net yield ratio) is in fact a matter of some controversy. Indeed Bean (1979) has suggested that the definitional problem is 'insoluble'.

to one minus the net present value of investment incentives per unit of investment divided by one minus the tax rate on company income. A fall in the ratio indicates that unit tax allowances have risen in relation to the tax rate, reducing the user cost of capital. Gross/net yield ratios presented by Melliss and Richardson (1976) for a mixed project (plant and buildings, national rates) show no clear trend during the decade to 1959. They fell sharply to end 1962 when initial allowances were increased and the writing down allowances for industrial buildings doubled, and have remained broadly *flat* since. On this basis, a trend fall in the user cost of capital would not have been expected, though these results may be sensitive to the authors' assumption that investment is financed from retained earnings or equity, thus ignoring the favourable tax treatment of debt finance.

The conclusion is that the causes of the downward trend in the real post-tax cost of capital, 1960–69, calculated by Flemming are unclear. The possibility remains therefore that the fall was only symptomatic of changes in the expected rate of return rather than part of the explanation of why the rate of return actually fell. The divergence after 1969 is also unexplained by the factors reviewed here.

(c) *Cost of capital, capital intensity and profit share*   The next strand in the Sargent/Nordhaus theory is the effect of a falling real cost of capital on investment/capital-intensity. Models of investment behaviour based on the valuation ratio (Tobin's q) and neo-classical investment functions have a number of similarities and both have a bearing upon the present issue.

There is conflicting evidence on the usefulness of Tobin's q in the UK. The *Bank of England Bulletin* (June 1977, p 157) notes 'To date, the results of econometric work....have not been particularly encouraging....though in some cases q has proved to be just as successful as conventional accelerator models in explaining the behaviour of investment.' (The accelerator model assumes that the relative price of factors of production has no effect on capital intensity). Oulton (1978–79) however contends that, as an explanation of industrial and commercial company investment, q is 'statistically significant and quantitatively important' and 'outperformed other plausible variables'. The reason for this divergence of opinion is unclear, though, as noted previously, Oulton's data on q is quite dissimilar to the Bank's.

On pure neo-classical and related investment functions, earlier researchers (surveyed by Lund, 1976) seem generally to have had more success in establishing a significant role for relative factor prices than more recent UK studies (Doig, 1976; Savage, 1977). Savage, for example, notes 'The performance of the ''pure'' neo-classical model is extremely disappointing and definitely inferior to that of the "pure" accelerator'. Sumner (1979) also concludes that, with regard to the pure neo-classical investment model (a variant of the Jorgenson (1963) model) 'there are strong grounds for its rejection'. Interestingly, Sumner's estimation of a variant of Bischoff's (1971) investment model yields, in some cases, values for the elasticity of substitution in the region of unity which contrasts with values reported by Boatwright and Eaton (1972) in the range 0.47 to 0.65. The latter authors employed the Jorgenson framework.

This very brief survey (a comprehensive review is in Savage, 1978) provides a reasonable indication of the poverty of firm evidence in favour of the neo-classical view of investment behaviour in the UK. In those instances where a significant role has been given to the relative prices of factors of production as a determinant of capital intensity, it is not possible to reject the hypothesis that the elasticity of substitution lies in the region of unity[1], with implications as noted on page 52.

US evidence
The US experience can be discussed more briefly. Here, the evidence of a decline in both profitability and the cost of capital is in dispute. Work by Feldstein and Sumners (1977), Holland and Myers (1978) and Hill (1979) does not support the idea of a secular decline in profitability in the US (though for some contrary evidence see Lovell, 1978). Holland and Myers, who calculate a version of Flemming's valuation ratio, also find no evident trend in the cost of capital since the mid-1950s. The fact that Nordhaus uncovers a falling real cost of capital may be due to his treatment of inflation expectations (see page 52). Against this background, one must be sceptical of Nordhaus' contention that his estimated elasticity of substitution (0.02) played a 'leading role in the tale of the falling share of capital'.

C2.2   A FALL IN THE CORPORATE TAX BURDEN
This theory of the secular decline in profit share, similar, in some respects, to Sargent's, though certainly not based on neo-classical theory, is contingent upon King's (1975) model of corporate taxation and estimates of a falling average tax burden on UK manufacturing

---

[1] Space does not permit a detailed survey of the evidence on substitution elasticities arising from other studies, in particular, of production functions. It is of interest to note however that Anderson (this volume) cites 'substantial evidence' to support an assumption of Cobb-Douglas technology in which the elasticity of substitution is constrained to be unity.

industry. The central hypothesis is that firms in oligopolistic industries seek, in their pricing policies, to maintain a target share of profits *after* tax in value added. Thus, a fall in the effective rate of corporate tax will be passed on in the form of lower prices, giving rise to a fall in pre-tax profit share but a constant post-tax profit share. (As noted previously, King (1975) finds that the post-tax real profit share in UK manufacturing industry, excluding metal manufacturing, remained stable until the late 1960s). Beath (1979) provides econometric evidence supporting this theory of pricing behaviour/secular decline in profit share. It should be emphasized however that there is amongst economists no more consensus about the incidence of corporation tax than there is about the evolution of its effective rate. (On tax shifting, see, eg, Coutts, Godley and Nordhaus, 1978, chapter 5; Agapitos, 1979). There is also the underlying problem of direction of causation (see page 54 above).

C2.3   A SHIFT IN MARKET POWER FROM CAPITALISTS TO LABOUR

The intensification of competition in product markets—as a result of post-war freer trade policies, the general growth of international trade and anti-monopoly/restrictive practices legislation—combined with the (alleged) growing power and militancy of trade unions comprises a third theory of the secular decline in profits. Monopoly profits would be eroded by the intensification of competition; it would also limit the extent to which higher wage settlements, the result of union-pushfulness, could be passed on in prices.

Glyn and Sutcliffe (1972, pp 66-61) propound the view that unions were as the anvil on which increased international competition beat profits, according to their calculations, after 1964[1]:

'...the growth of wages was not all that much higher after 1964 than before.... But in fact we found that as the period went on increases in money wages came to have a bigger and bigger effect in reducing the profit share. Our explanation is that in the early fifties, when international competition was weak, increases in money wages could be easily passed on in higher prices, whereas by the middle and late sixties only a much smaller proportion of wage increases could be passed on. This was despite the reduction in domestic

[1] More precisely, they note that, with regard to the share of profits in company net output, 'a steady downward trend has existed since the early fifties...but since [1964] the steady fall has become an avalanche', p 58.

competition resulting from the increased concentration of UK industry"[1]

An important element in their theory concerns the role of the exchange rate. To suggest that profit margins were being effectively eroded by union cost-push is tantamount to saying that sterling was overvalued. While devaluation might compensate for higher rates of domestic inflation, Glyn and Sutcliffe (pp 166–168) invoke 'real wage resistance' as the main reason why sterling devaluations would not facilitate the long term maintenance of profit margins in the UK (eg because rising import prices following a depreciation would feed into higher wage claims and erode the competitive advantage).

Evidence[2]

(a)   Labour and Material Costs   A squeeze on profits as a result of union cost-push would reveal itself by a growth of real product wages in excess of the growth of labour productivity[3]. (It should be emphasized that the existence of such an adverse 'labour cost effect' is consistent with a number of different theories, one of which is briefly considered below.) As previously argued, however, wage and salary share in value added may also rise if real material prices rise—a possibility which may have very little to do with union militancy/international competition. The following paragraphs therefore attempt to distinguish between these influences.

The analysis concentrates on the manufacturing sector partly for reasons of data availability but more particularly because it is the sector of the economy most obviously open to international competition. Furthermore, real profit share in the miscellaneous category of non-manufacturing industries previously defined (page 45) actually increased, from 11½ per cent in 1955 to 23½ per cent in 1972[4]. Over the same period, real profit share in manufacturing industry (national

---

[1] Ball's (1978) objection to the Glyn/Sutcliffe theory—that union militancy increased in the late 1960s whereas the decline in profits had begun earlier—is therefore somewhat misplaced.

[2] The question of monopoly profits is not considered in detail here. It may be noted however that if the 'post-tax real cost of capital' is taken as an indication of post-tax real 'normal' profitability, the comparison with the post-tax real rate of return as calculated by Flemming (1976(a), (b)) reveals no perceptible trend in post-tax 'supernormal' or 'monopoly' profitability during the 1960s. Nordhaus (1974) reaches a similar conclusion for the US during the post-war period.

[3] Glyn and Sutcliffe (pp 62–64) examine the course of labour productivity growth but do not attempt a direct comparison with the growth of real product wages.

[4] Real profit share increased in each of the main sectors – construction, the public utilities and transport and communication – until 1969 but fell back somewhat thereafter, except in construction.

accounts basis) fell from 28 per cent to 19 per cent. Gross of capital consumption, manufacturing industry profit share fell from 32 per cent to 25 per cent.

Table C5 shows for cyclical (output) peak years since 1955[1] the average annual rates of changes of wage and salary share in manufacturing industry allocated to changes in the relationship between real product wages/earnings and labour productivity on the one hand (labour cost effect) and the relationship between real material costs and material productivity on the other (material cost effect).

Table C5 Average Annual Rates of Change (%) of the Share of Wages and Salaries in Value Added by Manufacturing Industry (net of stock appreciation)

	1955/72	1955/64	1964/72	1960/69	1955/60	1960/64	1964/69	1969/72
Total	0.4	0.2	0.6	0.6	0.2	0.3	0.9	0.1
of which:								
Labour Cost Effect	0.7	0.6	0.7	0.0	1.3	−0.4	0.2	1.6
Material Cost Effect	−0.3	−0.4	−0.2	0.6	−1.2	0.6	0.6	−1.5

Source: National Accounts, Economic Trends, CSO. See Annex 1.
Note: Components may not sum to total because of rounding error.

While the table reveals the existence of an adverse labour cost effect over the whole period 1955–72, this hides a diversity of experience in different periods[2]. In particular, there were strongly adverse labour cost effects in the late 1950s and late 1960s/early 1970s which were partly offset by favourable movements in real material prices. In the 1960s, however, – and contrary to the theory explaining the 'avalanche' in profit share advanced by Glyn and Sutcliffe – real product wages and labour productivity grew at similar rates (about 3½ per cent per annum) – so the increase in wage and salary share in this period is almost wholly attributable to the sustained growth in real material prices. The following paragraphs consider, if briefly, possible explanations of the evolution of labour and material cost effects.

[1] As previously explained, the choice of 1972 – not a peak year – reflects a desire to abstract from the sharp change in the terms of trade in 1973.

[2] Owing to the familiar difficulties of using index numbers over long periods – eg in this context, the influence of structural changes in the manufacturing sector – the figures for the sub-periods are probably more reliable.

Table C6 below gives some clue to the underlying causes of the latter movements. Series A broadly corresponds to the 'material cost effect'. The other three series represent an attempt to construct a series for the real prices of materials purchased by manufacturing industry, roughly distinguishing between 'goods' (materials and fuel) purchased domestically or from abroad (series B) and domestic services (series C) (services cover transport, communication, distributive trades and miscellaneous services). Series D is a weighted average of series B and C and intended to represent average real material prices. A comparison of series A and D suggests that the constructed series are not a bad reflection of the national accounts data: the unreliability of data and method would in any event preclude an exact correspondence[1].

The key feature of table C6 is the contrast between movements in real prices of material and fuel purchases and service purchases. The former are strongly influenced by movements in the terms of trade between manufactured goods and primary products. (According to input-output information for the early 1970s, about 70 per cent of

Table C6   Average Annual Rates of Change (%) in the Real Prices of Materials bought by Manufacturing Industry

	1955/72	1955/64	1964/72	1960/69	1955/60	1960/64	1964/69	1969/72
A	−0.3	−0.4	−0.2	+0.6	−1.2	+0.6	+0.6	−1.5
B	−1.2	−1.6	−0.8	−0.3	−2.2	−0.9	0.0	−2.3
C	+1.3	+1.1	+1.4	+1.5	+0.7	+1.6	+1.4	+1.5
D	−0.2	−0.5	+0.2	+0.4	−1.0	+0.1	+0.7	−0.5

Series A – implied growth of real unit material prices weighted by the ratio of material costs to value added (see Annex 1). National Accounts data (approximately equal to the 'material cost effect' in table C5).

Series B – growth of ratio of prices of materials and fuel purchased by manufacturing industry to the wholesale price of home sales of manufactured goods. (Source: *Economic Trends*)

Series C – growth in ratio of constructed index of prices of services purchased by manufacturing industry to the wholesale price of home sales of manufactured goods (see Annex 1). Source *National Accounts, Economic Trends,* Input-Output tables.

Series D – Weighted average of series B (0.61) and C (0.39); weights based on input-output data. See Annex 1.

[1] Note also that movements of real material prices in series A are weighted by the ratio of material costs to value added, unlike those in series D. Input-output information for the early 1970s suggests this ratio may be close to unity. In principle, series A will also reflect changes in material productivity, unlike series D.

non-service purchases by the manufacturing sector – excluding intra-manufacturing sector sales/purchases – is imported, though this figure includes purchases of foreign manufactured goods.) These terms of trade are known to have moved favourably in the 1950s, but flatten out in the 1960s – a pattern which is reflected in series B, together with the influence of the 1967 sterling devaluation. The (admittedly crude) data on the real price of service purchases reveals the familiar tendency – at least, under a regime of fixed exchange rates – for the prices of manufactured goods to be the least buoyant of prices within the economy (a feature of most OECD countries – see *Inflation, OECD, 1970, p 17*).

One possible inference to be drawn from tables C5 and C6 is that had real commodity prices (in sterling) not moved favourably in the late 1950s and late 1960s, manufacturing industry profit share would have been continually depressed by the movement in relative prices between the manufacturing sector and service sector, as, indeed, did happen during the 1960s. (This assumes that the labour cost effect would have remained the same.) It is possible to interpret such movements as indicative either of the comparatively slow rate of growth of productivity in the service sector[1] or, perhaps more fundamentally, of a mechanism encouraging the re-allocation of resources from the manufacturing sector to the service sector.

Turning to the labour cost effect, the key question is whether the excess rise of real product wages over productivity growth in 1955–60 and 1969–72 can be unambiguously interpreted as the result of union militancy and the intensification of international competition. (Glyn and Sutcliffe themselves would presumably reject that possibility for the former period.) Limitations of space preclude any extensive treatment of this subject; present purposes will be served however if at least one alternative, plausible hypothesis can be entertained. The one in mind is that proposed by, among others, 'international monetarists' who claim that the wage explosion of 1969–70 represented part of the process whereby an international parity of prices and wages was restored following the 1967 sterling devaluation. The impact of incomes policy between 1967 and 1969 delayed the wage adjustment; subsequently wages moved ahead of prices at the same time that the economy was experiencing demand deflation (which would depress profit margins), due to the post-devaluation attempt to 'make room for exports'. (See Meyer, 1973, chapter 2; Ball and Burns, 1976, Laidler, 1976). It may be possible to tell a similar story for the late

---

[1] An interpretation in sympathy with the so-called 'Scandinavian' theory of inflation, originally propounded in a different context by Balassa (1964).

1950s episode – this time representing a (long) lagged reaction to the massive sterling devaluation (30½ per cent) in 1949. (See Hawtrey, 1961, chapter 12; Harrod, 1963, chapter 7; Ball and Burns, 1976).
(b) *International Competitiveness* As mentioned previously, the Glyn/Sutcliffe theory carries the implication that sterling has become progressively over-valued. If UK prices were fully constrained by the forces of international competition, the price competitiveness of UK manufactured goods in foreign markets should, in the long run, remain constant. In these circumstances, a maintained rise in UK unit labour costs in excess of any rise in foreign unit labour costs (both in terms of a common currency) – a loss of relative unit labour cost competitiveness – implies a rate of change in profit share in the UK less favourable than that experienced abroad (whether that movement be an increase or decline in profit share). Since evidence provided by Hill (1979) and King and Mairesse (1978) points to a trend decline in profit share in UK manufacturing industry greater than that experienced by some major competitor countries, the Glyn/Sutcliffe theory necessarily implies that the UK has suffered a trend loss of relative unit labour cost competitiveness.

These propositions about price and unit labour cost competitiveness are both rejected by the evidence:

Table C7 Measures of UK Competitiveness (1975 = 100)

	1961	1962	1963	1964	1965	1966	1967	1968	1969
A	102.7	104.0	105.9	106.9	108.7	111.4	110.8	103.6	103.0
B	116.9	113.2	110.8	111.4	115.5	118.3	113.3	98.7	100.8
C	115.0	113.3	109.9	108.6	113.3	115.3	109.7	94.0	98.0

	1970	1971	1972	1973	1974	1975	1976	1977	1978
A	104.8	106.0	107.6	99.2	98.6	100.0	96.8	103.3	109.3
B	101.8	105.0	103.7	91.6	94.9	100.0	91.9	87.2	93.3
C	101.4	104.3	100.8	88.1	92.4	100.0	93.5	91.6	98.9

Source: IMF

A – export price competitiveness index (the ratio of UK to weighted average export – dollar-prices for major competitors in respect of manufactured goods).

B – normal unit labour cost competitiveness index (index of 'normal' labour costs per unit of output in UK manufacturing industry divided by a weighted average of competitors' normal unit labour costs in manufacturing adjusted for exchange rate changes).

C – Series B, but not 'normalised'.

As can be seen from table C7, although the UK was losing both price and labour cost competitiveness from 1963/64 to 1967, the 1967 devaluation and subsequent depreciations from 1972 led to a substantial increase in both price and labour cost competitiveness over the whole period, though this trend is halted in 1977/78 as a result of the firm exchange rate policy (Brown and Sheriff, 1978, pp 256–258 present similar evidence). Indeed, in many respects, the UK had the appearance (at least until recently) of a cheap-labour economy (see Ray, 1978, pp 73–74).

C2.4 PUBLIC SECTOR CROWDING-OUT

The underlying idea behind crowding-out explanations of the secular decline, extensively developed by Bacon and Eltis (1976/78) is that the expansion of the public sector has, in various ways, reduced productive resources available to the private sector. This pressure on resources raised industrial costs and, given international competition or price controls, led to a squeeze on profit margins. Specific mechanisms that have been proposed include:

(a) the private sector has been robbed of labour (putting an upward pressure on labour costs) by the expansion of public sector employment;

(b) to the extent that public expenditure has not been financed by tax revenues, the public sector has either pre-empted funds from capital markets (so raising the cost of capital to firms) or caused inflation (reducing profits by eg induced activity effects);

(c) the raising of tax revenues to finance public expenditure has either been borne directly by companies (increased effective corporate taxation) or indirectly because of resistance to direct/ indirect tax increases by the workforce, leading to higher wage claims and a Glyn/Sutcliffe type squeeze on profits.

Assessment

There are a number of reasons why the crowding-out hypothesis is not a convincing explanation of the secular decline. As Blackaby (1978 (b), p 649) notes, there seems at a general level of debate to be inadequate distinction drawn between the economic effects of the resources directly used by the public sector and those which it transfers between various groups in the private sector. Transfers themselves need not significantly affect the demand for products in the trading sector; their bearing on the profitability story is more likely confined to indirect effects arising from resentment over the initial redistribution of income within the private sector, typically away from wage-earners. General government's own expenditure on goods and services (which includes expenditures which directly add to demand for goods and capital equipment produced by the private sector) rose as a share of GDP at current market prices from around 20 per cent in 1960 to 23½ per cent in 1973. This share increased sharply over the slump of 1974–75 but subsequently fell back to under its 1973 level by 1978. Echoing Blackaby's sentiments, this seems, on a simplistic basis, hardly sufficient a movement over nearly 20 years to account for the fall in real profit share.

More fundamentally, there is the question of whether the expansion of public sector employment robbed the private sector of labour. The evidence provided by Thatcher (1978) is against crowding-out. He shows that the increase in public sector employment effectively absorbed the increase flow of female labour onto the workforce due to increased participation rates. In contrast, the contraction of employment in manufacturing and production industries since the mid-1960s consisted largely of men.

On the matter of the cost of capital and liquidity, there is no evidence that during the 1950s and 1960s there was any real constraint on the supply of funds to industry. For example, Flemming's measure shows that the average real post-tax cost of capital fell during the 1960s. Furthermore such rises in interest rates as occurred are unlikely to have significantly depressed activity and thus profits in this period. As Savage notes, 'the bulk of research in this country suggests that business fixed investment is not sensitive to changes in the rate of interest' (Savage, 1978, p 87). There may of course have been a rationing of funds to industry (not reflected in the cost of finance) but the Treasury, in evidence to the Wilson Committee (Volume 1, p 52) contends 'all the signs are that industrial borrowing (and especially borrowing from the banks) has been determined by the level of demand'. This accords with the results of attempts to model bank lending to companies in the Treasury (Mowl and Spencer, 1978). As for any adverse activity effects consequent upon inflation generated by increased government spending, simple observation would suggest that these could hardly have been significant until inflation itself accelerated in the 1970s.

These partial observations are supported by the results of simulations of some of the main UK macro-economic models under relatively 'fix-price', fixed exchange rate conditions akin to those prevailing in the 1950s and 1960s (see, eg, the simulations in Laury, Lewis and Ormerod, 1978, and Artis, 1978). Specifically, under these conditions, the initial stimulus to output – and thus profits – of an increase in public spending is not crowded-out to any significant extent by adverse second-round effects. For the 'flex price' world of the 1970s, the issue is of course more contentious and especially important for an economy which is chronically depressed, with the result that budget deficits are large and persistent. There is little consensus amongst economists and their macro-economic models about the magnitude of inflation or interest rate crowding out effects under such conditions.

Turning to the tax question, the problem of whether the effective tax rate on company profits has risen remains unresolved. Thus one is left with the tax-push hypothesis, most favoured by Bacon and Eltis (1978, pp 98–103). Consistently with the theory of the target real wage as an explanation of inflation, there is some support for the idea that the real wage target is struck in terms of post-tax rather than pre-tax income (see, eg, Henry, Sawyer and Smith, 1976). The results of a recent OECD study ('Public Expenditure Trends', 1978) which tested the tax-push hypothesis suggest (p 83) 'that labour unions do attempt to shift income tax increases forward onto higher money wages, and net of tax wage bargaining seems to be a rather common phenomenon in all OECD countries except France'. However, while it is clear that the ratio of total government expenditure (including transfers) to GDP and the effective rate of direct tax on wage and salary earners have increased quite markedly since (at least) 1960, the theory, as an explanation of the secular profits decline, is open to the same objections as those advanced against the Glyn/Sutcliffe theory.[1]

C2.5 CONCLUSIONS

The evidence on theories attempting to explain the secular decline in UK profitability/profit share since the mid-1950s is summarised below.

[1] In a recent exchange with Hadjimatheou and Skouras (1979), Bacon and Eltis have refined their analysis – applied originally to the whole period of 1963–73 (Bacon and Eltis, 1978, p 103) – by contending that their tax-push/frustration theory of profits squeeze helps explain UK experience between 1969 and 1973, especially the 1969–70 wage explosion. Before 1969, workers 'patiently practiced wage restraint and co-operative industries policies... The 'inflation barrier' the workers imposed after 1969 took the form of demonstrations that they had the power to raise money wages extremely rapidly. This obliged governments...to negotiate price and wage controls which were on balance unfavourable to profit share'. This refined explanation is not inconsistent with the evolution of 'labour cost effects' in table C5. As already noted, some economists do not consider the 1969–70 experience as evidence of cost-push inflation, if only because a similar phenomenon is repeated in a number of OECD countries. (See Sachs (1979), pp 274–280 for documentation). Beenstock and Willcocks (1980), for example, note (p 11) that 'it is one thing to argue that within one country 'trade unions implicitly collaborate to force up wage rates', but this kind of conspiracy theory does not extend to the entire world...'

(a) Both the Sargent and King/Beath explanations of the secular decline are advanced on the grounds that the average effective rate of UK corporation tax has fallen. This is open to question – most studies apart from that by King (1975) point, if anything, to a rising effective rate, though, definitions and coverage vary considerably. If further research were to confirm King's view on tax, it remains doubtful, on the basis of econometric research into investment behaviour, whether the underlying mechanism leading to lower pre-tax profitability is 'neo-classical' in nature, as Sargent proposes. Neither is the evidence of forward corporate tax shifting so unambiguous as to provide firm support for the King/Beath theory. Finally, there is the worry that, since the average effective tax burden is not independent of the evolution of pre-tax profitability, causation may go both ways.

(b) The Glyn/Sutcliffe and tax-push Bacon/Eltis theories, which imply that real product wages have grown in excess of labour productivity growth, are not supported by the evidence. Profit share in manufacturing (net of stock appreciation, gross of capital consumption) fell during the 1960s despite the fact that real product wages and labour productivity grew at about the same rate. The same is broadly true of experience between 1972 and 1978. Furthermore, the performance of profit share in UK manufacturing has been less favourable than that abroad despite trend gains in price and unit labour cost competitiveness. While it is true that real wages have, at times, grown faster over the cycle than labour productivity in manufacturing industry (late 1950s, early 1970s) it is not clear that these instances were due to a shift in market power from capitalists to the workers. It should not be concluded from this that organised labour is in no way responsible for the decline in profitability – there are a number of indirect ways in which unions *may* have brought this about[1]. But there is no evidence of any *persistent* direct crowding out.

(c) During the 1960s, the fall in profit share in manufacturing industry can be directly attributed to a rise in the price of services over those of manufactured goods. This is also consistent with the observation that profit (and 'other income')

---

[1] For example, some might contend that real wages should have grown less rapidly than labour productivity when real material costs rose and that unions prevented that adjustment taking place. It has also been argued that union resistance to change is partly responsible for the UK's poor rate of growth of capital productivity.

share in some 'non-manufacturing' industries actually rose over the same period. The rise in relative prices of services may be indicative of a comparatively low rate of growth of productivity or of a market process encouraging the re-allocation of resources away from manufacturing.

(d) There is no support for the view that the growth of the public sector directly 'confiscated' labour resources otherwise available to manufacturers and, by putting upward pressure on wage costs, crowded-out manufacturers' profits.

(e) There is little support for the theory that public sector deficits in the 1950s and 1960s crowded-out private sector activity and profitability as a result of adverse 'second-round' interest rate or inflation effects. For the inflationary 1970s, the issue is far less clear-cut.

This review of the evidence suggests that there has been a low rate of return to the dismal science of explaining secular movements in income distribution. As a valedictory comment, it might be asked whether the effort was worthwhile. First, it is not altogether clear that measured profitability is a particularly valuable concept. It is in no sense a measure of the super-normal 'return to entrepreneurship' which many believe to be the handmaiden of economic growth, since there exists little idea of what constitutes a normal return. Profitability is not a particularly revealing measure of the normal return to capital since 'capital' cannot be defined at all precisely: much of the labour stock, for example, is more akin to a human capital. As for explaining the course of this surplus, once it is accepted that profit is largely a residual outcome of a complex economic system, it would seem particularly fruitless searching for an all-embracing theory. The issue becomes even more complex if the evolution of profits itself affects the workings of the economic system. Somewhat tongue-in-cheek, the diagram below lists some possibilities for the UK. Profits join the roundabout at two points: one – contrary to the evidence – concerning the effect of labour cost pressures, the other concerning the influence of output growth and investment. It would of course be possible to draw in many more lines and boxes. If the result what somewhat messy, it would not be an unfair reflection of our present understanding of the secular decline in profitability.

THE PROFITS ROUNDABOUT

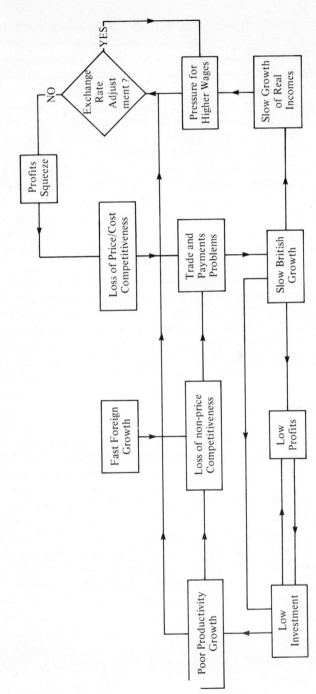

Section D   Consequences of declining profitability

D1   Short-run effects

The short-run issues concern the ability of demand management policies to stimulate the economy and increase employment, given the economy's capital stock. The main question is whether low profitability leads to rigid supply constraints, implying that domestic output will not be responsive to increased demand (which will leak out fully into imports or reduced exports). There are a number of possibilities:

(a) Maynard's (1978) view that, because of the adverse terms of trade movement and real wage resistance, the marginal cost of labour has exceeded its marginal product. Consequently, insufficient profits have been earned to justify an increase in employment;

(b) Ball's (1978) hypothesis that because of eg employment protection legislation, labour has become akin to capital – ie a fixed factor of production. Like investment decisions, employment decisions, especially against a background of low profitability and fragile balance sheets, will be increasingly long term. Thus, the economy's supply response is reduced;

(c) Scott's (1978) theory that there may be 'capital-shortage' unemployment due to (labour saving) rationalisation, itself a reflection of inadequate profitability. Recent OECD calculations ('A Medium Term Strategy for Employment and Manpower Policies' 1978) suggest that unemployment due to an inadequate capital base or labour-saving past investment has risen in all major OECD countries. Such rationalisation may lead to supply bottlenecks despite the apparent magnitude of excess capacity presently experienced;

(d) low profitability may cause short-term financing problems (eg paying for stocks).

There is little firm evidence by which to judge the importance of these factors for demand management. Maynard supports his analysis by empirical work suggesting that, as a result of the commodity/oil crisis, real product wages in manufacturing industry should have fallen by 17 per cent between 1972 Q4 and 1975 Q4 in order to restore the initial relationship between labour demand and supply. Annex 1, employing a different method of estimation, suggests that the equilibrating fall in real product wages, 1972–75 – ie sufficient a fall to maintain the share of wages and salaries in value added – was as little as 3 per cent. (A greater fall than this – perhaps 6 per cent – would have been required to maintain profit share, net of stock appreciation, gross of capital consumption, because of a rise in the share of employers' contributions to national insurance, pensions etc). Since real product wages actually rose (by nearly 8 per cent according to national accounts data) over this period, there nevertheless emerged a large 'real wage gap' (ie between 'equilibrium' and actual real wages) though much smaller, on these estimates, than Maynard's figure implies. While the size of the gap provides some support for Maynard's hypothesis, the central question remains whether the gap could not have been substantially reduced by an expansion of demand, enabling a cyclical recovering of profit share. At present it remains unclear whether the problem was (and is) one of too high real wages or deficient demand. (See, also, Flemming, 1976 (c), Chapter 13, Flemming, 1976 (d); Budd, 1977; Matthews and King, 1977; Corden, 1979; Morley, 1979; Midland Bank Review, Summer 1979, pp 2–3; Sachs, 1979). Finally, even if it is accepted that the economy has become increasingly supply constrained, the distinctive role played by low profitability is still a matter of speculation.

D2 Long-run effects: investment

Low profitability may affect the *volume* of investment in two ways:
  (a) given the cost of capital, low average profitability may be taken as an indicator of low prospective profitability, so reducing the incentive to invest.
  (b) low average profitability may cause financial problems, especially if gearing is already high, effectively raising the cost of capital if external finance is considered more costly than internal finance. This reduces the ability to invest.

The *kind* of investment expenditure may also be affected. Firms may give greater emphasis to replacement investment rather than expansion (especially in risky, innovative activities); the investment may also become labour-saving (so to enhance future cash flow). Generally speaking, however, empirical work at an aggregate level has not supported a direct connexion between investment and profits – the growth of sales and capacity utilisation emerge in many studies as the main determinants. The accepted argument is that these 'real' factors capture the relevant influences on investors' expectations about future profitability. The latter, together with a company's cut off rate (cost of capital plus a risk premium) also emerges from survey evidence to the Wilson Committee as an important element in the investment decision (of large companies at least).

There is far less consensus about the liquidity role played by profits and, in particular, retentions. The Treasury adequately reflected this uncertainty in their memorandum (Investment and Finance for Industry) to the Wilson Committee (Evidence, Volume 1, p 48): 'The importance of the influence of financial factors on investment is harder to establish empirically than the influence of output changes. Much of the econometric research in this area has been inconclusive and considerably varied results have been obtained.'[1] The Treasury goes on to argue that, apart from numerous 'conceptual difficulties of research in this area', the period over which much of this research was conducted – typically, the 1950s and 1960s – was not manifestly one where financial influences were so varied as to have a marked impact on investment. Furthermore, Meeks, in an unpublished paper, has argued that there may have been a change in industrial financial structure because of both the gradual depletion since the war of companies' 'liquidity cushion' – ie their stock of liquid assets – and an unfavourable shift in the relationship between the flow of internal finance and the volume of output. In view of the persistence of company financial deficits, these arguments seem sufficiently compelling to warrant a re-examination of the investment-finance relationship. For the present, the quantitative importance of profit-liquidity factors remains unclear.

[1] A notable exception is the work of Anderson (eg 1979) who, on the basis of a multi-equation model, claims that 'financial factors have a quite natural and significant role in the investment expenditure system'. In some recent Treasury work, Bean (1979) has uncovered significant nominal interest effects on UK manufacturing investment, presumably a reflection of liquidity problems that have emerged with high inflation and high nominal interest rates.

Section E   Policy towards declining profitability

Ideally, an examination of the causes of declining profitability would facilitate a prediction of the future course of profitability and a tailoring of cures to causes. Unfortunately, as far as the secular decline is concerned, it is not possible, on the basis of present evidence, to identify unambiguously the most important causes. The least unhelpful observation would be that the secular decline – most clearly the problem of the UK manufacturing sector rather than the non-manufacturing sector – is not necessarily part of a doomsday machine heralding the collapse of capitalism. This is particularly so if the decline is due to a fall in the corporate tax burden or, more generally, a fall in the cost of capital and/or a market process encouraging re-allocation to other sectors of the economy. The fact that the net rate of return in German manufacturing industry declined at a similar rate to that in the UK, 1955–73, (Hill, 1979, table 6.5) – though admittedly from a much higher level – also suggests that falling profitability is not necessarily a sign of fundamental economic decline.

For the immediate future, the issues are clearer cut though not necessarily more tractable. The reaction of most policy makers in the main industrial countries to the 1979 oil crisis and the resurgence of inflationary pressures has been to deflate. Whether or not such policies will lead to a temporary or prolonged and damaging decline in output and profitability, here and abroad, raises all the current controversies of macro-economic policy. It is obviously impossible to cover these here. It suffices to say that the dichotomy of views between 'monetarists' and 'Keynesians', in so far as these terms identify any particular school, is at base a disagreement about the existence and/or speed of self-righting market processes in the main industrial economies, both collectively and individually.

For those monetarists who believe that the rewards to factors of production are determined – and fairly swiftly so – by the state of technology and movements in relative prices, a policy of disinflation combined with micro-economic 'supply management' suffices as a policy towards declining profitability. Others may have any number of reasons to take a less optimistic view, in particular: the prospect of further increases in real energy prices, the dangers of synchronised deflations in leading economies and, in the UK, the problems associated with free collective bargaining and a weak industrial base. In this view of the world, declining or stagnant profitability may emerge as a long term phenomenon unless institutions can be developed or strengthened reconciling the perceived self-interests of nation states and the indigenous social groups.

Annex 1
Wage share, profit share and real wages

A. Derivation of estimates of material and labour cost effects on profit share

The calculation of the effect of changes in material and labour costs on profit share proceeds in two steps:
- (a) the calculation of the effect of movements in material and labour costs on the wage and salary share,
- (b) the calculation of the effect of changes in wage and salary share and other non-profit income on profit share.

(a) WAGE AND SALARY SHARE IN VALUE ADDED

Denote:

V = value added net of stock appreciation (equal to the value added 'price', p', multiplied by the volume of gross output, o);

B = wage and salary bill (equal to average wages and salaries per head, w, multiplied by numbers employed, l);

G = gross output in current prices (equal to the volume of gross output multiplied by the producer's price, p);

and $b = B \div V$

Using a dot over the variable to denote proportionate growth rates, it follows:

$$\dot{b} \equiv \frac{(1+\dot{B})-(1+\dot{V})}{1+\dot{V}} \tag{i}$$

Multiplying the numerator and denominator of (i) by $1+\dot{G}$ and re-arranging:

$$\dot{b} \equiv \frac{1+\dot{G}}{1+\dot{V}} \left[\left(\frac{1+\dot{B}}{1+\dot{G}}-1\right) + \left(1-\frac{1+\dot{V}}{1+\dot{G}}\right) \right] \tag{ii}$$

For any two periods, t and $t-1$, $1+\dot{V}$ can be broken down into changes in gross output and material purchases (on current account):

$$1+\dot{V} \equiv \frac{p_t o_t - m_t c_t}{p_{t-1}o_{t-1} - m_{t-1}c_{t-1}} \tag{iii}$$

where m and c are the price and volume of materials. Dividing by $p_{t-1}o_{t-1}$ and denoting the share of material purchases in the value of gross output in the preceding period as $y = \dfrac{m_{t-1}c_{t-1}}{p_{t-1}o_{t-1}}$

gives

$$1 + \dot{V} \equiv \frac{(1+\dot{p})(1+\dot{o}) - y(1+\dot{m})(1+\dot{c})}{1-y} \tag{iv}$$

Substituting (iv) into (ii) and noting that $1 + \dot{B} \equiv (1+\dot{w})(1+\dot{l})$; $1 + \dot{G} \equiv (1+\dot{p})(1+\dot{o})$ yields:

$$\dot{b} \equiv \frac{1+\dot{G}}{1+\dot{V}}\left[\left(\frac{\dfrac{1+\dot{w}}{1+\dot{p}}}{\dfrac{1+\dot{o}}{1+\dot{l}}} - 1\right) + \frac{y}{1-y}\left(\frac{\dfrac{1+\dot{m}}{1+\dot{p}}}{\dfrac{1+\dot{o}}{1+\dot{c}}} - 1\right)\right] \tag{v}$$

The first expression inside the square brackets is the 'labour cost effect', being the proportionate growth of real unit product earnings. The second expression is the 'material cost effect', being the proportionate growth of real unit material prices weighted by the ratio of material costs to value added. The scaling factor:

$$\frac{1+\dot{G}}{1+\dot{V}} = \frac{1}{1 - \dfrac{y}{1-y}\left(\dfrac{\dfrac{1+\dot{m}}{1+\dot{p}}}{\dfrac{1+\dot{o}}{1+\dot{c}}} - 1\right)}$$

is an interaction term reflecting (in calculus terms) the product of two differentials—here the changes in b and in the ratio of value added to the value of gross output. For small changes in real unit material prices, b approximates to the sum of the proportionate increases in real unit labour and (weighted) material costs.

For computational purposes, identity (v) can be rearranged from (ii) to give:

$$\dot{b} \equiv \frac{\dot{B}-\dot{G}}{1+\dot{V}} + \frac{\dot{p}-\dot{p}'}{1+\dot{p}'} \tag{vi}$$

That is, the material cost effect calculated here is simply the proportionate increase of the wholesale price less that of the value added price divided by $1+\dot{p}'$.

(b) THE EFFECT ON PROFIT SHARE

Denoting x and z as the shares of profits (X) and non-wage/non-profit income (Z) in value added (all net of stock appreciation), it follows by simple manipulation that the absolute change in profit share dx, is given by:

$$dx \equiv -b_{t-1}\left[\frac{\dot{B}-\dot{G}}{1+\dot{V}} + \frac{\dot{p}-\dot{p}'}{1+\dot{p}'}\right] - dz \tag{vii}$$

B.   Application

SOURCES AND DEFINITIONS

These identities have been calculated for manufacturing industry (1955–1978) based on the latest (1979) national income accounting data, supplemented where necessary (because of revisions or changes in presentation) with data provided directly by the CSO. The national account sources in detail are:

  (i) Wages and salaries in manufacturing industry and number of employees, table 3.3, 1979 BB; CSO.[1]

  (ii) Value added net of stock appreciation in manufacturing industry – table 1.10, 1979 BB; CSO.

  (iii) Index of output of manufacturing industry, 1975 = 100, table 2.2 1979 BB; *Economic Trends Annual Supplement,* 1979, p 73.

  (iv) Employers' contributions, gross profits of companies and trading surplus of public corporations[2], income from self-employment and other trading income, table 3.1, 1979 BB; CSO.

For the output price, the index for wholesale prices of manufactured goods sold at home has been used (Source: *Economic Trends,* August 1979, and *Annual Supplement,* 1979).

PROBLEMS

Difficulties arise on three counts: the definition of the output price, the concept of output and the measurement of the value added price.

THE OUTPUT PRICE

The wholesale price index may not be a good indicator of output prices if, as is often the case in the UK, export prices do not move in tandem with home prices. However, this is probably not a serious problem. The output index is based heavily on the deflated value of deliveries or sales where the deflator is the relevant wholesale price index. In practice, differences between export prices and home prices are not taken into account. Consequently if the measured change in the output price is too low (ie if export prices are rising faster than home prices), real wage growth will be overstated, but so too is productivity growth (since output growth is overstated). Such errors will tend to cancel out in the calculation of labour and material cost effects.

---

[1] Strictly, fees paid to directors should be excluded from wages and salaries.

[2] To derive profits net of stock appreciation, the figure for total stock appreciation has been used though it includes stock appreciation of trivial amount attributable to self-employment income.

THE MEASUREMENT OF OUTPUT

Owing largely to the absence of information on input prices and volumes, most output indices in the UK (with the exception of that for agriculture) are based on other indicators, in particular of the volume of gross output. For manufacturing industry, the indicators are:

	Percentage of weight carried
Quantities delivered or produced	21.7
Deflated value of deliveries or sales	73.8
Number of persons employed	4.5

Thus over 95 per cent of the manufacturing output index is inferred from movements in the volume of gross output. The weighting pattern for individual sectors is based however on value added rather than gross output in the base year, so, assuming material productivity is non-zero, the index is not a precise measure either of 'real product' – value added at constant prices – or the volume of gross output. It is of course quite possible to recast identity (v) in terms of real product. Assuming some growth in material productivity, the labour cost effect would be somewhat less and the material cost effect (confined to movements in real input prices) somewhat greater than implied by (v).

THE VALUE ADDED PRICE

The most serious problems of measurement and interpretation probably arise in defining the index of the value added price – ie an index of value added net of stock appreciation in current prices divided by the index of manufacturing output. Two difficulties are:

(a) the value added price index is a paasche index (albeit chain-linked), being a revenue index divided by a laspeyres volume index. It therefore reflects not only pure price movements but also changes in the quantity weights implicitly applied to the components of manufacturing value added.

(b) probably more serious that (a), at least over short time periods, the data sources for the index of output and value added in current prices are different and possibly inconsistent (value added is based on income statistics).

On (a), two specific difficulties may be mentioned. The weight $\frac{y}{1-y}$ moves from year to year and this may seriously hamper interpretation of annual movements in the material cost effect if y and movements in real material prices are large. This consideration seems particularly pertinent to the 1970s and partly explains the use of a single base year in the calculations in table C4 of the text. The second difficulty is that the ratio of value added to gross output (the value added price divided by the output price) may change not because of movements in real unit material prices but because of shifts in the pattern of production between industries within the manufacturing sector characterised by different value added/gross output ratios. If it is presumed that structural change procedes slowly – which seems reasonable – this consideration counsels caution when interpreting movements in the material cost effect over long periods.

As to (b), if it could be assumed that the residual error for manufacturing industry is a near constant proportion of value added through time, growth rate calculations will not be biased. In any event, the index of the value added price used here is the best that can be constructed with the available national accounts data. One advantage in using this method is that it obviates the need to use input-output information (which is irregular and produced with a considerable lag). More importantly, it is unnecessary to construct indices for input prices especially for bought-in services (which account for about 40 per cent of non-labour direct costs in manufacturing industry – excluding intra-manufacturing industry sales/purchases – according to input-output information 1970–73).

Nevertheless, as a check on the method (see table C6 of the text) a separate input price index has been calculated using a weighted average of the published index for the wholesale price of materials and fuel purchased by manufacturing industry and a constructed index of prices for services: transport and communication, distributive trades, insurance, banking, finance and business services (after deducting the adjustment for financial services) together with other services (all as defined in table 1.10 of the Blue Book). The weights were based on input-output information. These data are rather rough and ready, being subject to various adjustments and discontinuities. Moreover, because the service deflator is derived as a value added price deflator rather than a gross output price deflator it will tend to overstate output price movements when input prices of the service sector are falling relative to the output price (and vice versa). (Note that

$$\dot{p}' \simeq \dot{p} + \frac{y}{1-y} \left(\dot{p} - (\dot{m} - (\dot{o} - \dot{c})) \right)$$. Accordingly, the input price index

is calculated only for the earlier period of study before the major terms of trade movements of the 1970s. The data in Table C6 suggest that the interpretation of the material cost effect proposed here is a reasonable one.

C. 'Equilibrium' real wage growth

The purpose here is to examine briefly the measurement of equilibrium real wages advanced by inter alia Flemming (1976(d)) and in particular by Maynard (1978). Both base their arguments on neo-classical distribution theory which may be briefly stated as follows. A rise in real unit material costs implies a fall in the effective price of output and consequently in the effective marginal revenue product of primary factors of production (capital and labour). Assuming no change in marginal physical productivities of primary factors and a fixed input-output coefficient, the fall in the effective price shifts the demand curve for *both* factors downwards in the same proportion. Equilibrium, in a neoclassical sense, is restored when the real returns to both factors fall so as to maintain their original shares of value added. The required percentage fall in real wages *and* real profits (the latter being the gross rental net of stock appreciation deflated by the output price) is equal to the percentage rise in real material costs weighted by the ratio of material costs to value added.

To demonstrate the latter proposition, it may be noted that, by definition

$$\frac{1+\dot{B}}{1+\dot{G}} \equiv \frac{1+\dot{B}}{1+\dot{V}} \cdot \frac{1+\dot{V}}{1+\dot{G}} \tag{viii}$$

$\dfrac{1+\dot{B}}{1+\dot{G}}$ is 1 plus the rate of growth of real unit product wages, $\dfrac{1+\dot{B}}{1+\dot{V}}$ is 1 plus the rate of growth of the share of wages in value added. If the share of wages in value added is to remain constant, $\dfrac{1+\dot{B}}{1+\dot{V}} = 1$, the rate of growth of real product wages is given by:

$$\frac{1+\dot{w}}{1+\dot{p}}-1 = \frac{1+\dot{o}}{1+\dot{l}}\frac{1+\dot{V}}{1+\dot{G}}-1 = \frac{1+\dot{o}}{1+\dot{l}}\left[1-\frac{y}{1-y}\left(\frac{\dfrac{1+\dot{m}}{1+\dot{p}}}{\dfrac{1+\dot{o}}{1+\dot{c}}}-1\right)\right]-1 \tag{ix}$$

That is real wages can grow at the rate of growth of labour productivity adjusted for the change (fall) in the ratio of value added to gross output due to the change (rise) in real unit material prices. If material and labour productivity growth are both zero, re-arrangement of (ix) gives:

$$\dot{w}-\dot{p}=\frac{y}{1-y}(\dot{p}-\dot{m}) \tag{x}$$

which is (in growth terms) the equality noted above. Analogous
arguments apply to profits.[1]

Equation (x) differs from Maynard's formula for equilibrium real
wage growth. He derives his formula as follows. An initial equilibrium
exists in which the output price is equal to a mark-up (U) on average
unit direct costs—unit labour costs (W) and unit raw material and fuel
costs (M). That is: $p = (1 + U)(W + M)$. In growth terms, assuming no
productivity change, this gives:

$$\dot{p} = (1 - f)\,\dot{w} + f\dot{m}$$

where f is the proportion of total direct costs accounted for by raw
material/fuel costs. The growth in real wages, for small values of $\dot{p}$, is
given by:

$$\dot{w} - \dot{p} = \frac{f}{1-f}(\dot{p} - \dot{m})$$

(Had productivity been allowed to change, labour productivity growth
would be added to the right-hand side and material productivity

growth added into the term $\frac{f}{1-f}(\dot{p} - \dot{m})$).

Maynard's formula differs from (x) because of the weighting
pattern. His formula, in fact, ensures that profit share in gross output
rather than value added remains constant. It may be noted that if
profit share in gross output is constant between any two periods, t and
$t-1$, then the sum of the shares of labour and material costs (C) in
gross output will also remain constant.

$$\frac{B_t}{G_t} + \frac{C_t}{G_t} = \frac{B_{t-1}}{G_{t-1}} + \frac{C_{t-1}}{G_{t-1}} \tag{xi}$$

Dividing through by $\frac{B_{t-1}}{G_{t-1}}$ and assuming no productivity growth of any
kind yields:

$$\frac{1+\dot{w}}{1+\dot{p}} + \frac{1+\dot{m}}{1+\dot{p}}\,\frac{C_{t-1}}{B_{t-1}} = 1 + \frac{C_{t-1}}{B_{t-1}} \tag{xii}$$

Substituting $\frac{f}{1-f}$ for $\frac{C_{t-1}}{B_{t-1}}$ and re-arranging gives Maynard's formula.

[1] An alternative proof would be to note that, in equilibrium, labour would be employed
to the point where its marginal physical product is equal to the nominal wage deflated
by the *value added price*: $\frac{w}{p'} = \frac{w}{p}.\frac{p}{p'}$. ($\frac{w}{p}$ is the real product wage). Differentiating,
holding marginal productivities and the input-output coefficient constant, gives
equation (x).

The implication of maintaining profit share in gross output is that the real normal return to capital (real gross rental) is unaffected by changes in real material prices. If the latter rise, the whole of the burden of adjustment is borne by real wages. Real wages therefore have to fall by a greater proportion than given by equation (x) − so wage share in value added falls and profit share in value added rises. This is easily seen if identity (viii) is rearranged in terms of profit share:

$$\frac{1+\dot{X}}{1+\dot{V}} \equiv \frac{1+\dot{X}}{1+\dot{G}}\frac{1+\dot{G}}{1+\dot{V}} \tag{xiii}$$

If profit share in gross output is fixed, $\dfrac{1+\dot{X}}{1+\dot{G}} = 1$, profit share in value added rises as the ratio of gross output to value added rises (because of a rise in real material prices).

The magnitude of the greater required fall in real wages if real gross rentals are constant, if real material prices rise and if productivity change is zero is, in proportionate terms, simply $\dfrac{f}{1-f} \div \dfrac{y}{1-y}$. This is not an insubstantial amount: on the basis of Maynard's own figures, the factor works out at 1.4 for manufacturing industry in 1971. If real gross rentals are assumed to adjust as well as real wages, this factor would reduce Maynard's figure of the required fall in real wages in manufacturing industry between 1972 Q4 and 1975 Q4 of 17 per cent to 12 per cent.

The calculations based on national accounts data present quite a different picture. For computational purposes equation (ix) above can be rewritten (assuming $\dfrac{1+\dot{o}}{1+\dot{1}} = 1$):

$$\frac{1+\dot{w}}{1+\dot{p}} - 1 = \frac{1+\dot{p}'}{1+\dot{p}} - 1 \tag{xiv}$$

That is, the required fall in real product wages necessary to ensure a constant wage share in *value added* is simply the percentage change in the ratio of the implicit value added price to the wholesale price. For 1972 to 1974, the fall works out at 10½ per cent for real average wages and salaries in manufacturing industry. However, this figure is reduced to 3 per cent, 1972−75, and 6 per cent, 1972−76. The reason for the fall in the magnitude of the figure is presumably the fall on world markets of real commodity prices (apart from real oil prices) after 1974 but the difference between these figures and Maynard's (for end 1972−75) is surprising. Two possible explanations are:

(a) the sharp and maintained rise in energy prices may have encouraged the more rapid adoption of conservation measures – that is, there was an increase in 'material productivity' as a result of the shift in relative prices;

(b) Maynard's figures for input prices relate only to raw materials and fuel – so he presumably ignores substantial purchases of materials from service industries (page 77) and probably overstates the increase in aggregate real material prices.

Annex 2
Average tax rates on company income

This annex briefly surveys published estimates of the effective tax burden on industry. It is confined to studies which extend at least to the 1960s. (For earlier studies, see Budd, 1975).

Flemming

Flemming (1976 (a)), updated by Clark and Williams (1978), calculated the tax burden on the domestic profits of industrial and commercial companies (after deducting stock appreciation and replacement cost capital consumption), where taxes on interest and dividends in the hands of recipients were deducted along with direct company taxes.

Taxes as a proportion (%) of Profits of Non-North Sea Industrial and Commercial Companies

1960	1965	1970	1973	1974	1975	1976	1977	1978
51.3	60.2	66.0	43.2	45.7	57.5	60.8	60.4	59.7

Source: Bank of England
Note: Figures from 1975 take account of stock relief

Their figures show that more than 50 per cent of companies' profits have gone in tax (as defined) with a sharp increase in this burden when the classical corporation tax system was adopted in 1965. (Distributions were not deducted in arriving at taxable profit and income tax was deducted by a company on paying dividends so the latter were double-taxed.) There was a sharp change downwards in 1973 when the UK changed to an imputation system: distributions were still not tax deductible but part of the tax on distributed profits was imputed to the shareholders as a tax credit, reckoned at the basic rate of income tax. But by 1978, the tax burden was still 16 per cent higher than in 1960. (Note, however, that the tax system also impinges on the measure of capital employed: the tax burden in terms of profit is not the same as the tax burden in terms of profitability. See Flemming 1976(a), p 40.)

Price

Unlike Flemming, Price (1978, pp 163–167) works with companies as a whole (industrial, commercial and financial) and excludes net interest payments from his definition of company income. In contrast to the downward trend in the effective burden of company taxation between the mid-1950s and early 1960s (shown in the Richardson Report), Price finds that as a proportion of gross company income (before deducting any 'inflation' adjustments), UK company tax, including that on distribution, increased from 23.5 per cent in 1959 to a peak of 28 per cent in 1968. If taxes paid abroad are taken into account, the corresponding figures are 33 per cent and 38.5 per cent. The effective rate of tax on gross company incomes fell after 1968 but if allowance is made for stock appreciation and capital consumption, the 'true' burden on company incomes rose, once taxes paid abroad are included, from 40.5 per cent in 1959 to 52.5 per cent in 1973. Price regards this as 'perhaps the most accurate indicator available.' However, ignoring taxes paid abroad, his calculations show the effective tax burden on (true) company profits to be the same in 1959 and 1973.

Walker, Glyn and Sutcliffe

Walker (1974, Appendix 1, p xii) and Glyn and Sutcliffe (1972, Appendix E, table E1, p 248) present results for similar industrial groups (large quoted companies in manufacturing, distribution and certain other services in Walker; quoted companies in manufacturing, construction, communication and distribution in Glyn and Sutcliffe) but unfortunately adopt different definitions of company earnings. Glyn and Sutcliffe measure post-tax profitability for total net earnings (gross trading profits plus other (eg overseas) income – gross income – after deducting depreciation at historic cost) before and after deducting stock appreciation whereas Walker shows post-tax profitability (including stock appreciation) for equity earnings only – gross income less all interest payments and depreciation at historic cost. Taxes for Walker include company taxes and any income tax paid on dividends while Glyn and Sutcliffe also include an estimate of income tax on debt interest. Despite these differences, the effective average tax rates on net income including stock appreciation calculated by the authors are fairly similar (both estimates take account of investment grants):

Effective Tax Rates (%)

	Glyn and Sutcliffe	Walker		Glyn and Sutcliffe	Walker
1955	51.2	48.3	1964	45.8	44.8
1956	52.2	50.5	1965	36.8	35.4
1957	52.3	50.5	1966	52.9	53.1
1958	48.6	47.0	1967	46.3	48.6
1959	45.3	42.5	1968	48.9	48.8
1960	44.4	44.9	1969	49.6	48.8
1961	44.8	46.0	1970	47.5	46.8
1962	45.5	45.9	1971	—	43.5
1963	45.0	45.2	1972	—	35.8

Although the level of tax burden is quite different, the trends in both these series are very similar to those described by Price. It seems likely that the latter's comments about the influence of stock appreciation and capital consumption at replacement cost would also apply.

Panic and Close

Similar trends are revealed by Panic and Close (1973, table 1, p 24), whose full results are to be found in Burgess and Webb (1974, tables 4, 5, p 14, 16).[1] Panic and Close deal with quoted companies in UK

---

[1] Burgess and Webb also calculate pre and post-tax rates of return but it is not possible to calculate average tax rates from their published results because of definitional changes.

manufacturing industry and calculate pre and post-tax rates of return on an historic cost basis. The authors define 'net income' to include non-trading income as well as trading profits and did not distinguish between UK activities and those undertaken abroad. Tax for them is simply company taxes and they ignore investment grants. The calculated average tax rates (%) for cyclical peak years are:

1955	1960	1964	1969
34.2	29.6	28.9	40.5

King

Contrasting evidence on the tax question is provided by King (1975). Dealing with domestic manufacturing industry (excluding metal manufacturing) he found that while the pre-tax profit share (gross trading profits less stock appreciation and replacement cost capital consumption divided by such profits plus income from employment) fell secularly, the post-tax profit share remained stable from the mid-1950s until 1968, though falling thereafter. The reason adduced for these divergent trends is that the effective tax burden (which for King excludes both taxes paid abroad and the tax liability of dividend recipients) on gross trading profits as conventionally measured fell secularly to 1973 – the last year covered by his study. The tax burden on 'true' profits (ie conventional gross profits less stock appreciation and replacement cost capital consumption) also fell in line until the mid-1960s but rose somewhat thereafter largely because of the unfavourable tax treatment of stock appreciation at that time.

Effective Tax Rate in Manufacturing Industry*

Ratio of:	1956	1960	1965	1970	1973
Effective tax to gross trading profits	31.0	24.8	15.7	13.0	11.6
Effective tax to gross trading profits less capital consumption less stock appreciation	41.4	31.6	21.4	24.6	24.4

Source: King (1975) p 46   *excluding metal manufacturing

References

Agapitos, G. 'The impact of taxes on price inflation in UK manufacturing industries'; *Bulletin of Economic Research,* 1979.

Anderson, G. 'The financial dynamics of investment expenditure: an empirical study'; paper presented to the economic modelling study group, *London School of Economics,* March 1979.

Artis, M. J. 'Fiscal policy and crowding out'; chapter 8 of *Demand Management,* edited by Posner, M, Heinemann, London, 1978.

Bacon, R. and Eltis, W. *Britain's Economic Problem: Too Few Producers;* second edition, Macmillan, 1978.

Balassa, B. 'The purchasing power parity doctrine: a reappraisal'; *Journal of Political Economy,* 1964.

Ball, R. and Burns, T. 'The inflationary mechanism in the UK economy'; *American Economic Review,* September, 1976.

Ball, R. 'Company profits in Britain'; *London Business School Economic Outlook,* October, 1978.

Barna, T. 'The replacement cost of fixed assets in British manufacturing industry in 1955'; *Journal of the Royal Statistical Society,* Series A, Vol. 120, 1957.

Bean, C. 'An econometric model of manufacturing investment in the UK'; paper presented to the SSRC economic modelling group, *London School of Economics,* March 1979.

Beath, J. 'Target profits, cost expectations and the incidence of the corporate income tax'; *Review of Economic Studies,* July 1979.

Beenstock, M. and Willcocks, P. 'The causes of slower growth in the world economy'; *London Business School,* Economic Forecasting Unit, Discussion Paper No 76, April 1980.

Bischoff, C. 'The effect of alternative lag distributions'; in *Tax Incentives and Capital Spending,* edited by Fromm, G; Brookings Institution, Washington, 1971.

Blackaby, F.(a) 'Incomes policy'; Chapter 8 of *British Economic Policy, 1960–74,* edited by Blackaby, F., Cambridge University Press, 1978.

Blackaby, F.(b) 'General appraisal'; Chapter 14 of *British Economic Policy, 1960–74,* ibid.

Burgess, G. and Webb, A. 'The profits of British industry'; *Lloyds Bank Review,* April 1974.

Boatwright, B. and Eaton, J. 'The estimation of investment functions for manufacturing industry in the UK'; *Economica,* 1972.

Bronfenbrenner, M. 'A note on relative shares and the elasticity of substitution'; *Journal of Political Economy,* 1960.

Brown, A. 'Inflation and the British sickness'; *The Economic Journal,* March 1979.

Brown, C. and Sheriff, T. 'De-industrialisation: a background paper'; in *De-Industrialisation,* edited by Blackaby, F., Heinemann, London, 1978.

Brown, S. 'Cyclical fluctuations in the share of corporate profits in national income'; *Kyklos,* 1978.

Budd, A. 'The profitability of UK industry'; paper presented to Royal Economics Society, conference on profitability, *Sussex University,* September, 1975.

Budd, A. 'The real wages problem'; *Management Today,* November 1977.

Clark, C. 'Inflation and declining profits'; *Lloyds Bank Review,* October 1974.

Clark, C. 'Wages and profits'; *Oxford Economic Papers,* November 1978.

Clark, T. and Williams, N. 'Measures of real profitability'; *Bank of England Quarterly Bulletin,* December 1978.

Corden, W. 'Wages and unemployment in Australia'; *The Economic Record,* March 1979.

Coutts, K. 'Short-run variations in company profits'; *Cambridge Economic Policy Review,* March 1978.

Coutts, K; Godley, W; Nordhaus, W. *'Industrial Pricing in the UK;* Cambridge University Press, 1978.

Coutts, K; Tarling, R; Wilkinson, F. 'Wage bargaining and the inflation process'; *Cambridge Economic Policy Review,* 1976.

Dimson, E. and Brealey, R. 'The risk premium on UK equities'; *The Investment Analyst,* December 1978.

Doig, M. 'Investment and the cost of capital – part two'; *HM Treasury* internal working paper, 1976.

Feldstein M. and Summers, L. 'Is the rate of profit falling?'; *Brookings Papers on Economic Activity,* 1977.

Flemming, J.(a) (with Price, L. and Byers, S.) 'Trends in company profitability'; *Bank of England Quarterly Bulletin,* March 1976.

Flemming, J.(b) (with Price, L. and Byers, S.) 'The cost of capital, finance and investment'; *Bank of England Quarterly Bulletin,* June 1976.

Flemming, J.(c) *Inflation;* Oxford University Press 1976.

Flemming, J.(d) 'Adjust the real elements in a changing economy'; in *Catch '76. . . . ?,* IEA occasional paper, February 1976.

Glyn, A. and Sutcliffe, R. *British Capitalism, Workers and the Profits Squeeze;* Penguin, 1972.

Godley, W. and Nordhaus, W. 'Pricing in the trade cycle'; *Economic Journal,* September 1972.

Godley, W. and Wood, A. 'Profits and stock appreciation'; *Cambridge Economic Policy Review,* February 1975.

Griffin, T. 'The stock of fixed assets in the UK: how to make the best use of the statistics'; *Economic Trends,* October 1976.

Hacche, G. *The Theory of Economic Growth: An Introduction;* Macmillan, 1979.

Hadjimatheou, G. and Skouras, A: Bacon, R. and Eltis, W. 'Britain's economic problem: the growth of the non-market sector?: an exchange'; *Economic Journal* June 1979.

Harrod, R. *The British Economy*; McGraw-Hill, 1963.

Hawtrey, R. *The Pound at Home and Abroad*; Longmans, 1961.

Hibbert, J. Griffin, T. and Walker, R. 'Development of estimates of the stock of fixed capital in the UK'; *Review of Income and Wealth,* September 1977.

Hicks, J. 'What is wrong with monetarism'; *Lloyds Bank Review*, 1975.

Hill, T. *The Measurement of Real Product*; OECD, 1971.

Hill, T. *Profits and Rates of Return*; OECD, 1979.

Henry, S; Sawyer, M; Smith, P. 'Models of inflation in the UK: an evaluation'; *NIESR Review*, August 1976.

Holland, D. and Myers, S. 'Trends in corporate profitability and capital costs'; *MIT*, May 1978.

Jenkinson, N. Appendix to Clark and Williams, 1978, op cit.

Jorgenson, D. 'Capital theory and investment behaviour'; *American Economic Review*, 1963.

Kaldor, N. 'Alternative theories of distribution'; *Review of Economic Studies*, 1955–56.

King, J. and Regan, P. *Relative Income Shares*; Macmillan 1976.

King, M. 'The UK profits crisis: myth or reality?'; *Economic Journal*, March 1975.

King, M. and Mairesse, J. 'Profitability in Britain and France 1956–75: a comparative study'; *University of Birmingham*, Faculty of Commercial and Social Science, Discussion Paper, Series B, No. 53, September 1978.

Laidler, D. 'Inflation in Britain: a monetarist perspective'; *American Economic Review*, September 1976.

Laidler, D. and Parkin, M. 'Inflation: a survey'; *Economic Journal*, December 1975.

Laury, J; Lewis, G; Omerod, P. 'Properties of macroeconomic models of the UK economy: a comparative study'; *NIESR review*, February 1978.

Lund, P; Martin, W; and Bennett, A. 'Price expectations and their role in the analysis of the UK Department of Industry's investment intentions inquiries'; *Journal of Industrial Economics*, March 1980.

Lund, P. 'The econometric assessment of the impact of investment incentives'; in *The Economics of Industrial Subsidies*, edited by Whiting, A, HMSO 1975.

Lovell, M. 'The profit picture: trends and cycles'; *Brookings Papers on Economic Activity*, No 3 1978.

Matthews, R. and King, M. 'The British economy: problems and policies in the late 1970's': *Midland Bank Review*, February 1977.

Maurice, R. (editor) *National Accounts Statistics: Sources and Methods*; HMSO, 1968.

Maynard, G. 'Keynes and unemployment today'; *The Three Banks Review*, December 1978.

'McCracken Report' *Towards Full Employment and Price Stability*; OECD, June 1977.

Meeks, G. 'The dependence of fixed investment on stocks and flows of cash: do firms spend what they earn?; unpublished paper.

Melliss, C. and Richardson, P. 'Value of investment incentives for manufacturing industry 1946 to 1974'; in *The Economics of Industrial Subsidies*, edited by Whiting, A, HMSO 1975.

Meyer, F. *The Functions of Sterling*; Croom Helm, 1973.

Miller, M. 'Can a rise in import prices be inflationary and deflationary'; *American Economic Review*, September, 1976.

Morley, R. 'Profit, relative prices and unemployment'; *Economic Journal*, September 1979.

Mowl, C. and Spencer, P. 'A financial sector of the Treasury model'; *Government Economic Service Working Paper*, No 17, 1978.

Nordhaus, W. 'The falling share of profits'; *Brookings Papers on Economic Activity*, Vol 1, 1974.

Okun, A. 'Inflation: its mechanics and welfare costs'; *Brookings Papers on Economic Activity*, 1975.

Oulton, N. 'Aggregate investment and Tobin's Q: evidence from Britain'; *University of Lancaster*, discussion papers No 3, 1978; No 5, 1979.

Panic, M. and Close, R. 'Profitability of British manufacturing industry'; *Lloyd's Bank Review*, July 1973.

Price, R. 'Budgetary policy'; Chapter 4 of *British Economic Policy 1960–1974*; edited by Blackaby, F, Cambridge University Press, 1978.

Ray, G. 'Comment on technical innovation and British trade performance'; in *De-Industrialisation*, edited by Blackaby, F, Heinemann, London 1978.

Sachs, J. 'Wages, profits, and macroeconomic adjustment: a comparative study'; *Brookings Papers on Economic Activity*, 2: 1979.

Sargent, J. 'Recent growth experience in the economy of the UK'; *Economic Journal*, March 1968.

Sargent, J. 'Productivity and profits in UK manufacturing'; *Midland Bank Review*, Autumn, 1979.

Savage, D. 'A comparison of accelerator models of manufacturing investment'; Discussion Paper No 9 *NIESR* 1977.

Savage, D. 'The channels of monetary influence: a survey of the empirical evidence'; *NIESR review*, February, 1978.

Scott, M. *Can We Get Back to Full Employment?*; Macmillan, 1978.

Sumner, M. 'Investment grants'; paper presented at the 1979 AUTE conference.

Taylor, C. 'Why is Britain in recession?'; *Bank of England Quarterly Bulletin*, March 1978.

Thatcher, R. 'Labour supply and employment trends'; in *De-Industrialisation*, edited by Blackaby, F, Heinemann, London 1978.

Walker, J. 'Estimating companies' rate of return on capital employed'; *Economic Trends*, November 1974.

Williams, N. 'The profitability of UK industrial sectors'; *Bank of England Quarterly Bulletin*, December 1979.

Wood, A. *A Theory of Profits*; Cambridge University Press, 1975.

The effective marginal tax rate on income from capital in the UK

by M A King

This paper is part of the first stage of a project funded by the National Bureau of Economic Research (in conjunction with IFO in Munich and IUI in Stockholm) to compare effective tax rates on capital income in four countries, Britain, the United States, West Germany and Sweden.
I am grateful to M J Naldrett for research assistance.

Summary

The paper presents estimates of the effective tax rate on the return to marginal investment in the UK by the corporate, non-financial, sector in 1978. The effective marginal tax rate – a measure of the wedge between the real pre-tax rate of return on investment and the post-tax rate of return received by savers who provided the finance – depends on several factors. These include: the type of finance employed (debt, new share issues or retained earnings), the physical assets and industry in which investment takes place, the channels through which savings run (for example, personal or institutional saving), the level of pre-tax profitability and the rate of inflation.

As a result of these factors, there exists a distribution of marginal tax rates around the average. The calculations reveal this distribution to be both large and asymmetric – a finding which has clear implications for the gains from tax reform. On the average, the tax system levies at present a marginal effective tax rate on income from capital invested in the corporate sector close to zero. Surprisingly, this average rate is shown to be reduced by an increase in the rate of inflation. This suggests that reform of the tax system designed to alleviate the effects of inflation needs to have regard to the complex inter-relationships between the various taxes and allowances rather than concentrate on a narrow set of provisions, like stock relief.

1   Introduction

The aim of this paper is to provide some empirical estimates of the distribution of marginal tax rates on income from capital in the UK. These are relevant to two policy issues which have attracted attention in recent years.

First, in the wake of the debate on tax reform stimulated by the US Treasury Report Blueprints for Tax Reform (1977), the Meade Committee Report in the UK (1978) and the Report for the Swedish Commission on Taxation by Lodin (1976) economists have been investigating the 'optimal' tax rate on income from capital.[1] The size of the potential welfare gains from moving to the optimum depends upon the effective tax rate presently levied on capital income, and the effective tax rate depends upon a variety of fiscal provisions for savings and investment, the net effect of which we shall try to estimate empirically. A comprehensive income tax would be characterised by a tax rate on capital income equal to that on labour income. This property has been criticised as leading to the 'double taxation' of savings and has been

---

[1]   See Feldstein (1978), Atkinson and Sandmo (1979), King (1980).

used as an argument in favour of an expenditure tax. Under a comprehensive expenditure tax the tax rate on capital income would be zero. The present UK tax system is neither an income tax nor an expenditure tax, but contains elements of both. An interesting empirical question is whether, on average, it is nearer to an income tax or to an expenditure tax.

The second policy issue is that the value of the mean tax rate on capital income may be less significant than the fact that the distribution of tax rates has a very high variance. The tax rate is a measure of the wedge between the real rate of return earned on an investment project and the real rate of return earned by the individual savers who supply the necessary finance. But the size of this tax wedge depends upon whether the savings are chanelled directly from the personal sector to industry or via an institutional intermediary (eg a pension fund or insurance company), the type of financial security in which savings are invested, the industry and type of asset in which the funds are invested, and a number of other factors which will be discussed below. The outcome is that there is a distribution of marginal tax rates on capital income, and we shall be interested not only in the mean but also the shape (the higher moments) of the distribution. Knowledge of the shape of the distribution is important for an assessment of the welfare gains from tax reform.

In section 2 we discuss the methodology of the study. The data used are described in section 3 and the results presented in section 4. The reader should note that this paper constitutes a progress report on the first stage of a project, and that it is hoped to make substantial improvements to both the methodology and data employed here at a later stage.

2   The methodology of the study

To compute marginal tax rates we must define 'the margin'. The margin considered here is the investment decision. The effective tax rate measures the wedge between the return on a marginal investment project and the return on the savings made to finance the project. Consider an investment project which earns p per cent per annum in real terms net of depreciation. In general, the real post-tax rate of return to the individual investors who provide the finance will differ from p (because of taxes) and we denote the return on savings by s. The effective marginal tax rate on capital income is defined as

$$t = \frac{p-s}{p} \tag{1}$$

For a given value of s there is a required rate of return on investment which enables individuals to earn s on their savings. The required rate of return on investment is p and we may describe it as the 'financial cost of capital'. It is a function both of tax rates and the value of s. It is convenient to write both p and s as functions of the nominal interest rate, denoted by r, (for simplicity we shall assume that individuals and firms can borrow and lend at the same interest rate). These functions are

$$s = r(1 - m) - \pi \qquad (2)$$
$$p = MRR - \delta(1 + \pi) \qquad (3)$$

where

MRR = gross marginal rate of return on a project
δ = rate of depreciation in physical terms
π = rate of inflation
m = marginal rate of personal income tax

These equations assume that personal taxes are levied on receipts of nominal income from capital and that in this sense the personal tax system is unindexed. The return on marginal investments projects, p, will be equated to the cost of capital which depends on the source of finance. We shall assume that there are only three sources of finance, debt finance, new share issues, and retained earnings. The formulae for the cost of capital in these cases are given in King (1977, Chapter 8) and the relevant expressions are the following

(a) *debt finance*

$$MRR = \left[\frac{1 - f_2\tau - f_3 g}{1 - \tau} \right] [r(1 - \tau) - \pi + \delta(1 + \pi)] - \frac{\tau af_1}{1 - \tau} \qquad (4)$$

(b) *new share issues*

$$MRR = \left[\frac{1 - f_2\tau - f_3 g}{1 - \tau} \right] \left[\frac{r}{\theta} - \pi + \delta(1 + \pi) \right] - \frac{\tau af_1}{1 - \tau} \qquad (5)$$

(c) *retained earnings*

$$MRR = \left[\frac{1 - f_2\tau - f_3 g}{1 - \tau} \right] \left[\frac{1 - m}{1 - z}r - \pi + \delta(1 + \pi) \right] - \frac{\tau af_1}{1 - \tau} \qquad (6)$$

where

r = nominal long-term interest rate
m = marginal personal tax rate on dividend income
z = capital gains tax rate computed as an 'effective' rate on accrued gains – see King (1977, appendix A and chapter 3)

π = inflation rate (of investment goods)

δ = annual rate of depreciation in physical terms

τ = corporate tax rate

$\hat{\theta}$ = opportunity cost of retained earnings in terms of gross dividends forgone

f_1 = the proportion of investment expenditure which qualifies for an annual depreciation allowance at an *effective* rate of a (when accelerated depreciation cannot be represented as a linear combination of true economic depreciation and 100 per cent first-year allowances, the value of a is itself a function of the statutory depreciation rate and the discount rate).

f_2 = the proportion of investment expenditure which qualifies for 100 per cent depreciation allowances in the first year

f_3 = the proportion of investment expenditure which qualifies for an investment grant at rate g.

Given values for the parameters and for a particular source of finance the above equations determine an implicit functional relationship between p and s. Given that both p and s are linear functions of r then p is itself a linear function of s. This relationship between p and s enables us to answer the following question. What is the relationship between the marginal rate of return to the saver and to the marginal rate of return on the investment financed by his savings? The two differ because of taxes. Inspection of the equations shows immediately that when there are no taxes

$$p = s = r - \pi \qquad (7)$$

Since the relationship between p and s and hence the effective tax rate depends on a large number of parameters describing the different fiscal incentives to investment, tax rates on persons and companies, inflation, the asset in which savings are invested, and the source of finance, we shall consider two ways in which the relevant information may be presented. For any given set of values of the parameters there is a tax schedule which relates the effective tax rate, t, to the pre-tax rate of return, p. The same information may be conveyed in a diagram relating the return to savers to the pre-tax rate of return, and this relationship is linear. We shall present a diagram for such a tax schedule for the 'average' marginal investment project in plant and machinery in the manufacturing sector.

An alternative way of presenting information is to consider the effective tax rate for a given value of the pre-tax rate of return. For this particular value of the pre-tax rate of return we can then calculate the effective tax rate for each of the possible combinations of

(a) source of finance, (b) asset type, (c) industry, (d) category of owner, and (e) inflation rate. I shall present the results below for the distribution of tax rates in the UK for a value of p of 10 per cent per annum.

There is a large number of permutations which we could consider. Denote the effective marginal tax rate by

$$t_{ijk\ell}$$

where

   i = source of finance
   j = asset type
   k = industry
   ℓ = category of owner

In addition the effective marginal tax rate depends upon the rate of inflation. For any given rate of inflation the average marginal tax rate is

$$\bar{t} = \sum_i \sum_j \sum_k \sum_\ell a_{ijk\ell}\ t_{ijk\ell} \tag{8}$$

where $a_{ijk\ell}$ denotes the proportion of total investment expenditure financed by source of finance i in asset type j in industry k financed by the savings of category of owner ℓ. To compute the distribution of marginal tax rates we need information on the proportion of total investment in each of these categories. This means that the number of permutations which we are able to consider will depend on the availability of data on investment. The following permutations are considered

1. *Source of Finance*
It is assumed that there are three sources of finance, (1) debt, (2) new share issues and (3) retained earnings.

2. *Asset Type*
Three asset types are considered, (1) plant and machinery, (2) buildings and (3) stocks (inventories).

3. *Industry*
Three industrial categories are considered, (1) manufacturing, (2) other industrial and (3) commercial.

4. *Ownership*
The personal tax rates used in the calculations should reflect categories of beneficial owners of corporate securities. Four groups of owners are considered, (1) households, (2) tax-exempt institutions (for example,

pension funds and charities), (3) insurance companies, and (4) foreign owners.

For a given rate of inflation the number of permutations (ie effective tax rates) is 108. The distribution was computed for three values of the inflation rate. (1) The actual average rate of increase of the price of fixed investment goods over the period 1960/78 (which was 7.41 per cent). (2) A zero rate of inflation, and (3) An inflation rate of 10 per cent per annum.

In addition to computing the distribution of marginal tax rates it is interesting also to calculate the average marginal tax rates for each source of finance, each asset, each industry, and each category of owner. For example, for the first source of finance the average effective marginal tax rate is given by

$$
t_1 = \frac{\sum\limits_{j} \sum\limits_{k} \sum\limits_{\ell} a_{1jk\ell}\, t_{1jk\ell}}{\sum\limits_{j} \sum\limits_{k} \sum\limits_{\ell} a_{1jk\ell}} \tag{9}
$$

The scope of the study will be restricted to corporate sector investment in the nonfinancial sector. This excludes agriculture, mining and quarrying (including North Sea activities), the financial sector and housing. Of total private sector investment in the industrial and commercial groups which we are considering, the corporate sector accounted for 94.0 per cent.[1] Since companies dominate private investment in these areas we shall proceed on the assumption that the marginal tax rate on income derived from investment in industry and commerce may be derived from equations (4)–(6), and we shall ignore investment by unincorporated enterprises.[2] It would be wrong, however, to conclude that the corporate sector employs the majority of the nation's capital stock. As shown in Table 1, at the end of 1978 43 per cent of the UK capital stock in the form of fixed assets (valued at current replacement cost) was owned by the public sector. Only 35 per cent was owned by the corporate sector, and the remaining 22 per cent by the personal sector. In part these figures reflect also the distribution of the total capital stock by asset. In 1978, 62 per cent of fixed assets comprised dwellings and other buildings, and only 38 per cent was in the form of plant and vehicles. But the corporate sector is dominant in investment in 'industrial' assets, plant, machinery, vehicles and

---

[1] Information kindly provided by the Central Statistical Office.
[2] Unincorporated enterprises are important only in agriculture and housing, and to a much smaller extent in distribution.

inventories, as may be seen from Tables 2 and 3. Our study refers, therefore, to only part of the total level of national saving and investment, but corporate investment in the nonfinancial sector is the most significant component of investment in assets other than buildings.

Capital stock, UK end 1978 (£ billion)

Table 1   Fixed assets at current replacement cost

BY SECTOR		BY ASSET	
Personal	109.8	Vehicles, Ships & Aircraft	31.3
Corporate	174.6	Plant & Machinery	130.6
Nationalised Industries	89.5	Dwellings	153.9
Central & Local Government	126.5	Other Buildings	184.5
TOTAL	500.4	TOTAL	500.4

Table 2 Cross tabulation for plant and machinery		**Table 3** Inventories at book value	
Personal	7.1	Personal	8.7
Corporate	79.1	Corporate	41.7
Nationalised Industries	39.8	Nationalised Industries	3.4
Government	4.6	Government	1.3
TOTAL	130.6	TOTAL	55.1

3   The data

The data requirements for the study are two-fold. First, we need estimates of the proportions of total investment financed by the type of finance i invested in asset j in industry k from the savings of owner ℓ, in other words the $a_{ijk\ell}$. Secondly, we need estimates of the parameters in equations (1)–(6) in order to compute the marginal tax rates for each permutation, the $t_{ijk\ell}$. Unless elsewhere stated the data are for 1978 (tax rates refer to the fiscal year 1978–79). At this point it will be useful to define again the concept of the 'margin' which underlies the calculations of marginal tax rates. We shall consider a small increase in national investment in the same proportion in each asset and industry, and the distribution of marginal tax rates will be computed for this across the board rise in investment. The fractions financed from each source of finance and by each category of owner should ideally be marginal proportions. To calculate these marginal fractions requires an explicit model of corporate and personal portfolio behaviour and in practice we shall resort to the use of average proportions. We shall discuss this further below. As far as tax rates are concerned, we have attempted to compute the marginal values of the relevant tax parameters.

The first step is to compute values for the $a_{ijk\ell}$. At this stage of the project we have not attempted to calculate a cross-tabulation of investment in asset and industry types by either source of finance or category of owner. The proportions of investment in each asset and industry are, therefore, assumed to be independent of the source of finance and category of owner. This implies that

$$a_{ijk\ell} = a_i \; a_{jk} \; a_\ell \qquad (10)$$

The matrix of proportions of investment in each asset and industry by the corporate nonfinancial sector was calculated as follows. A breakdown of investment in each industry by the corporate sector was kindly supplied by the Central Statistical Office. It was then assumed that the proportions of investment by the corporate sector in each asset in a given industry were the same as those for the noncorporate sector. In other words, the division of investment between asset types is assumed to be a function of the industry not the legal form of organisation.[1] The estimated matrix is shown in table 4. One point to note here is that although we have excluded the financial sector, we have included investment in leased assets by companies in the financial sector. These are shown in the industry group 'commercial' although the use of such assets is almost certainly in manufacturing or other industries.

The proportions of investment financed from the different sources of finance were estimated in two steps. First, the ratio of debt to equity was taken to be the average value for 1978 of the market value of the debt-equity ratio for industrial and commercial companies. This was 0.2403, giving a value for the share of debt in total finance of 0.1937. The assumption made here (and it is a strong one) is that the marginal and average debt-equity ratios are equal. To the extent that marginal investments may be financed from debt then the appropriate tax rate will be that for debt finance and not the overall average which is a weighted average of the different sources of finance. Both sets of figures are presented below. The second step is to divide total equity

---

[1] Since the corporate sector dominates the industries we are examining, the bias involved in using industry figures will be very small even if the assumption is wrong.

Table 4   Matrix of Proportions of Corporate Investment by Asset and Industry, UK 1978

Asset	Industry		
	Manufacturing	Other Industrial	Commercial
Plant & Machinery	.3646	.1404	.2326
Buildings	.0623	.0498	.0590
Stocks	.0562	.0031	.0320

Source: own calculations based on *National Income and Expenditure 1979* tables 10.8, 12.2, and information supplied by CSO.

finance between new share issues and retained earnings. Companies raise a much greater proportion of their total equity finance from retained earnings than from the issue of new shares, and the relative magnitudes of the two sources for industrial and commercial companies in the period 1976–79 are shown in table 5. Over that period new share issues accounted for 5.4 per cent of total equity finance.[1] We shall use this figure for the weight of new share issues in equity finance, and so the proportions of investment financed by the three main sources of finance are as shown in table 6.

In order to estimate the weights for different ownership groups we require information on the beneficial ownership of both corporate equity and corporate debt. Unfortunately, we have information only for the former, and we have had to assume that debt and equity are owned in the same proportions by the different types of owner. It is likely, however, that an ownership group will tend to own that security which is the more attractive given the group's tax rates. By ignoring the specialisation of owners in particular securities we shall be over-estimating effective marginal tax rates and the estimates of tax rates presented below will be biased upwards. Statistics on ownership of corporate equity have been collected in various surveys of company registers for the years 1957, 1963, 1969 and 1975.[2] These surveys have attempted, as far as possible, to trace back all nominee holdings to their ultimate beneficial owners. We have used data from the surveys to calculate the proportions of equity owned by the four categories of owner distinguished above, and these are shown in table 7. The trends

[1] This figure is in line with previous UK experience – see King (1977) table 7.3.
[2] See King (1977) Chapter 2 and *Economic Trends,* September 1977 for a discussion of these surveys.

Table 5   Equity finance, UK industrial and commercial companies 1976–79 (£m.)

	New Share Issues	Retained Earnings	$(1) \div ((1) + (2))$
	(1)	(2)	
1976	785	11501	.0639
1977	729	13548	.0511
1978	837	14993	.0529
1979	918	17238	.0506
Average 1976–79	817	14320	.0540

Source: Financial Statistics May 1980 table 9.2

Table 6   Weights for different sources of finance 1978

Debt	0.1937
New Share Issues	0.0435
Retained Earnings	0.7628

Source: own calculations based on table 5 and data supplied by the Bank of England

in share ownership are marked. There has been a sharp decline in the fraction of equity owned directly by the personal sector and increases in the ownership by tax-exempt institutions and insurance companies. The increase in the proportion owned by pension funds has been particularly rapid.

To project these figures to 1978 we start with the share of pension funds. Between the end of 1975 and the end of 1978 the market value of holdings of pension funds increased by 118 per cent (*Financial Statistics,* September 1977, table 8.15, and May 1980, table 8.14). Over the same period the market value of corporate securities rose by 62.1 per cent.[1] This suggests that the ownership share of pension funds rose by 34.5 per cent, and implies a 1978 figure for the proportion of

[1] Information supplied by the Bank of England.

corporate securities owned by pension funds of 29.1 per cent. For insurance companies there are, unfortunately, no data on the market value of holdings and we have estimated a figure of 22.5 per cent. Similarly, for foreign owners an estimate of 6.5 per cent seems plausible. This leaves a residual figure for the personal sector of 41.9 per cent.

Table 7   Beneficial share ownership, UK 1957–78   per cent

	1957	1963	1969	1975	1978 (estimated)
Persons	79.44	71.09	65.95	54.02	41.9
Tax-Exempt Institutions	5.89	9.64	12.64	21.63	29.1
Insurance Companies	9.78	11.34	13.90	18.01	22.5
Overseas	4.89	7.94	7.52	6.34	6.5
Total*	100.0	100.0	100.0	100.0	100.0

Source: own calculations based on King (1977) table 2.4 and *Economic Trends* September 1977 p 100.
*Columns may not sum to total shown becaue of rounding errors.
Notes: Tax-exempt institutions comprise mainly pension funds but include also charities and non-profit making bodies. Persons include unit and investment trusts. The proportions owned by 'other' groups (banks, corporations and the public sector), around 10 per cent of the total, were ignored in calculating the figures in this table. The surveys refer to ownership on December 31 each year except for 1957 when the date is July 1.

The remaining data concern the parameters in equations (1)–(6) which enable us to compute the marginal tax rate for any given permutation of asset × industry × source of finance × owner. Table 8 contains values of both personal and corporate marginal tax rates, and also of the relevant investment incentive and depreciation parameters. The values of the personal tax rates are provisional estimates based on figures for earlier years given in King (1977, Appendix A). Using the figures from table 8 will lead to over-estimates of *current* (1980) effective tax rates for two reasons. First, no account has been taken of the reduction in both the basic and higher rates of tax which came into effect in 1979. Secondly, regional investment grants have been ignored and allowing for these would lower the estimated marginal tax rate.

Table 8   Tax parameters UK 1978

$\hat{\tau}$	0.52			
$\hat{\theta}$	1.493			

	Persons	Tax-Exempt	Insurance Cos.	Foreign
m	0.575	0.	0.24	0.15
z	0.15	0	0.10	0

	Plant and Machinery	Buildings Man./Industry	Commercial	Stocks
f_1	0	0.5	0	0
f_2	1	0.5	0	1
f_3	0	0	0	0
g	0	0	0	0
δ	0.05	0.02	0.02	0
a^1	–	0.04	–	–

Source: own calculations
[1] note that a is redundant when $f_1 = 0$

4   Effective tax rates on capital income in the UK

As we saw in section 2, we may define a linear schedule relating the
real rate of return earned by the saver to the rate of return earned on
the investment which is financed out of the savings. The 45° line is the
no tax or subsidy outcome. When the schedule is above this line there
is a subsidy to capital income, and when it is below the effective tax
rate is positive. In figure 1 we show the schedule for manufacturing
investment in plant and machinery. It lies close to the 45° line and
reflects the fact that the effective tax rate at the margin is close to
zero – in fact for plant and machinery investment in manufacturing
the tax rate is negative, ie a small *subsidy*.

In figure 2 we show the value of the effective tax rate corresponding
to figure 1. For very low values of the rate of return on investment
the tax acts as a large subsidy, but the tax rate converges asymp-
totically to a value of minus four per cent.

It is clear from figure 2 that the precise value of the effective
marginal tax rate depends upon the value of the rate of return on
investment. In Table 9 we show the values of the marginal tax rates
on nonfinancial corporate investment in the UK for a real rate of
return on investment before tax of 10 per cent per annum. Each
column corresponds to a specific assumption about the inflation rate

Figure 1. Rate of Return Schedule for Manufacturing Investment in Plant and Machinery, 1978

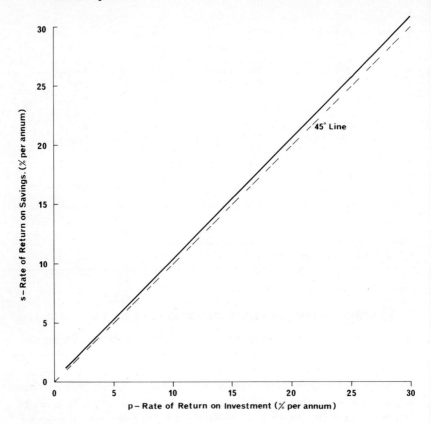

Figure 2. Effective Tax Rate for Manufacturing Plant and Machinery, 1978

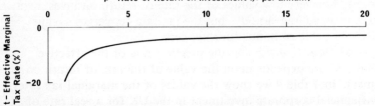

used to compute effective tax rates. Three assumptions are explored; the actual inflation rate experienced over 1960–78, a zero rate of inflation, and a ten per cent rate of inflation. The first row in Table 9 shows marginal tax rates for investment in plant and machinery (including vehicles). This is an average marginal tax rate where the average is taken over industry, source of finance, and category of owner. It can be seen that, as in figure 1, for plant and machinery investment the present tax system provides a subsidy to investment. This is particularly striking when we realise that these figures take into account all personal and corporate taxes together. This means that as far as investment in plant and machinery is concerned, the present system is, at the margin, more favourable to investment than would be an expenditure tax. If a comprehensive expenditure tax were in operation then each entry in the table would be zero, and if a comprehensive income tax on a fully indexed basis was introduced each entry in the table would correspond to an average of marginal income tax rates. It can be seen therefore that only in the case of investment in buildings does the present system approximate anything like an income tax. These figures probably also over-estimate marginal tax rates for reasons discussed in section 3.

The difference in marginal tax rates for industry groups corresponds to the different pattern of investment by asset type. The commercial sector pays higher effective marginal tax rates because of its greater emphasis on investment in commercial buildings. The main differences in marginal tax rates are to be seen in the part of the table which shows these marginal rates for different categories of owner. For pension funds and insurance companies the rates are negative, and in the case of pension funds strikingly so. This means that pension funds receive a very much higher rate of return on their savings than the rate of return earned by companies which invest the finance channelled to them. The opposite is true for the personal sector, although here the effects of the tax system mean that the effective marginal tax rate on income from capital is still very much less than the marginal tax rate which would have been paid by the same people on earned income.

Major differences appear between the effective marginal tax rates for different sources of finance. There is a substantial subsidy to debt finance, and the effect of the UK's imputation system combined with the importance of tax-exempt institutional investors is to increase the attractiveness of new share issues relative to retained earnings.

The overall average marginal tax rates are close to zero. At the inflation rate actually experienced in the period 1960–78 the mean marginal tax rate was only 3.0 per cent. In other words, on *average*

Table 9   Effective marginal tax rates on nonfinancial corporate investment in UK

(per cent)

	Annual Inflation Rate		
	1960–78 Average	Zero	10%
Asset			
1 Plant & Machinery (incl. Vehicles)	−4.08	−2.34	−4.69
2 Buildings	37.41	38.52	37.02
3 Stocks	−4.08	−2.34	−4.69
Industry			
1 Manufacturing	−0.30	1.37	−0.89
2 Other Industrial	3.47	5.07	2.91
3 Commercial	7.71	9.30	7.15
Owner			
1 Persons	32.43	21.04	36.41
2 Pension Funds	−31.73	−14.72	−37.67
3 Insurance Companies	−0.18	2.87	−1.24
4 Foreign	−19.98	−8.17	−24.11
Source of Finance			
1 Debt	−68.05	−34.96	−79.62
2 New Share Issues	0.56	3.28	−0.39
3 Retained Earnings	21.20	14.78	23.45
OVERALL AVERAGE	3.02	4.65	2.45

Source: own calculations

the present tax system almost approximates an expenditure tax as far as new savings and investment are concerned. The major difference between the present system and an expenditure tax is the distribution of marginal tax rates around the mean. With an expenditure tax all income would be taxed at an average marginal tax rate of zero whereas at present there is a wide distribution of tax rates round the mean.

The distribution of marginal tax rates is plotted as a histogram in figure 3. This shows the enormous variation in marginal tax rates, and not only is the variance large but the distribution is also skewed. Some tax rates are in excess of 100 per cent, others are well below minus 100 per cent.

The remaining conclusion to be drawn from Table 9 concerns the effects of inflation. It is often assumed that because the present

Figure 3 : Distribution of Marginal Tax Rates on Capital Income, 1978

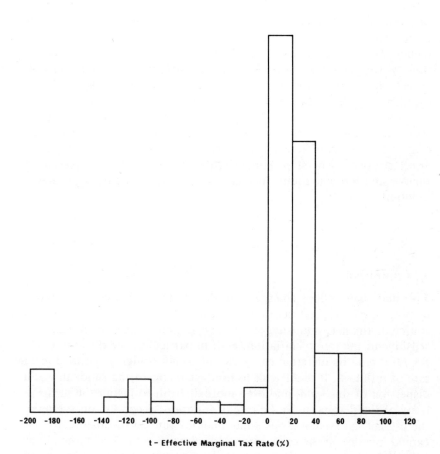

t - Effective Marginal Tax Rate (%)

system of personal taxation is unindexed an increase in the rate of inflation leads to a higher effective marginal tax rate on income from capital. Although this is clearly true for investment financed by savings provided directly by the personal sector, the opposite is in fact true on average. From Table 9 it can be seen that an increase in the inflation rate from zero to 10 per cent almost doubles the marginal tax rate where the personal sector is the beneficial owner. But the opposite is true when income is channelled via pension funds or insurance companies. The overall effect is that the average marginal tax rate is a slightly decreasing function of the rate of inflation. This phenomenon reflects the combination of reliefs for investment and stock relief together with the deductibility of nominal interest payments by the corporate sector, and the fact that a large fraction of the recipients of corporate income pay low or zero tax rates. High rates of inflation exacerbate the tax differential between institutional investment and direct personal ownership. Similarly, the tax differential between debt finance and internal equity finance is greatly increased by high rates of inflation.

5   Conclusions

Two main conclusions emerge from this study. First, there is a wide dispersion of marginal tax rates according to the asset type, industry, source of finance, and category of owner. This dispersion appears sensitive to the rate of inflation, and, in particular, the difference in tax rates paid by different categories of owner is highly sensitive to the rate of inflation. It is difficult to produce a convincing rationale for a dispersion of this kind, and even more difficult to justify the sensitivity of the dispersion to the rate of inflation. Secondly, on average the present tax system levies a marginal tax rate on income from capital invested in the corporate sector close to zero. This means that the reliefs provided at the corporate level and the growth of institutional ownership have converted the unindexed income tax into a system which on average approximates an expenditure tax. High rates of inflation do not increase the average marginal tax rate on income from corporate sector investment. In fact, at present levels they tend to reduce the marginal tax rate. This suggests that when considering policy reforms for alleviating the effects of inflation it is important to consider the tax system as a whole and not to focus exclusively on only one set of provisions, such as stock relief.

References

Atkinson, A. B. and Sandmo, A. 'The taxation of savings and economic allocation'; *University College Discussion Paper*, 1979

Feldstein, M. S. 'The welfare cost of capital income taxation' *Journal of Political Economy*, vol 86, pp S29–S51, 1978

King, M. A. *Public Policy and the Corporation;* Chapman and Hall, London, 1977

King, M. A. 'Savings and taxation'; in *Essays in Public Policy*, eds. Hughes, G. A. and Heal, G. M., Allen and Unwin, 1980

Lodin, S – O *Progressive Expenditure Tax – An Alternative*?; Liberforlag, Stockholm, 1976 (English Edition 1978)

Comment
by J S Flemming

I have for some time argued that the UK tax system approximated
more closely to a messy expenditure tax than to a messy income tax in
that the marginal effective tax rate on income had a large variance
and a very small mean – far below the 30–40 per cent levied on earned
income. It is good to have further confirmation of this position even
if Mervyn King and I as members of the Meade Committee are both
regarded as prejudiced.

The figures presented relate to one particular year (in fact 1978/9);
it would be interesting to have a time series of such computations. The
figures could then be used to assess the alleged fiscal contributions to
the fall in the cost of capital.

The paper emphasises that it is the *effective marginal* tax rate that is
being computed. In two respects this claim is questionable:

(a) Of all the lines in table 9 only one (personal income) relates to
income subject to significantly non-proportional taxation. Thus
the difference between marginal and average rates is likely to be
small.

(b) Deviations from proportionality are liable to arise from the
inability of tax payers to take full advantage of available reliefs
and allowances *at the margin* – yet this problem is assumed
away.

One example of this is the possibility that corporations have
insufficient taxable profits to take full advantage of capital
allowances. The formulae presented assume that all available reliefs
and allowances are effective at the margins. Has this been true in
recent years? Although the growth of leasing has enabled some firms
having no present liability to mainstream corporation tax to finance
investment on terms appropriate to those who do, this process has not
eliminated factors raising both the mean and the variance (yet further)
of the effective marginal tax rate.

Probably more important is the assumption in the construction of
the 'overall average effective marginal rate of tax' that the
composition of marginal and average savings are identical. In
particular the low overall tax rate is due to the roughly equal weight
attached to highly taxed direct personal savings and equally highly
subsidised pension savings. However, there is a limit on the extent of
savings eligible for these subsidies. While doubtless many people do
not exhaust their allowances these intra-marginal savings should loom
larger on average than at the margin.

Taking less important points in the order they occur in the text:
(i) The implication of the introduction – that marginal tax rates are the more relevant to investment decisions – is not self evident. At least it is not self evident that they are the more relevant to the volume of investment.

Taxation has both income and substitution type effects and the average rate determines the former while the marginal rate determines the latter.

This is not a trivial point even if one does not rely heavily on the effects of available retained earnings on investment. One could imagine a divergence between marginal and average rates, a massive marginal subsidy, such that firms basing all their decisions on marginal rates would inevitably go bankrupt (this point is symmetrical with one made by Layard and Nickell (1980) about marginal labour costs).

(ii) Equation (3) does not express p as a function of the nominal interest rate. It would, however, if one added $p = r - \pi$ (as in equation 8.22, p. 241 in King (1977)). Incidentally the term $(1 + \pi)$ is a little bit worrying in that it implies some sensitivity to the time units of the analysis.

(iii) Finance seems to be restricted to long-term debt and equity. Bank borrowing is excluded. This probably simplifies the problem by obviating the need to follow bank interest receipts through to depositors and shareholders, or is it allocated in the same proportion as other interest and dividends? However, the same problem arises in the case of pension funds and insurance companies. Is their intermediary status recognised? The pensions they pay are taxed. Of course if this is to be taken into account so should the tax treatment of contributions. Are these assumed to cancel out? If contributions are deductible against a higher rate of tax than is paid on pensions there is a further subsidy here.

(iv) The assumption (page 100) that corporate debt and equity are held in the same proportions by the four groups of owners is to assume that the tax effects deemed relevant to real investment are irrelevant to portfolio investment! Given the present treatment of capital gains there is no doubt households with their computed 57 per cent tax rate should own equities and gross funds hold debt. This would, of course, reduce the estimated marginal tax rates further.

Finally, I wonder whether an exercise well-designed to exhibit international differences in tax treatments of savings and investment has not been pressed in to service in a context in which significantly different (more behavioural – less descriptive) issues arise.

References

King, M. *Public Policy and the Corporation*; Chapman and Hall, 1977

Layard, P. and Nickell, S. 'The case for subsidising extra jobs', *The Economic Journal*, March 1980

General discussion

The general discussion centred around two themes: the definition of the marginal effective tax rate and the wider ramifications of King's results.

The discussion of 'the margin' was prompted by Flemming's remarks that using the average contribution of pension fund finance as an indication of its weight at the margin would be misleading, it being appropriate to assume that savers would attempt to exhaust this form of subsidised saving before subscribing through other channels. (Taken to the extreme, this argument suggested that the weight of pension funds at the margin should be zero). It was agreed that it was very difficult to define the margin. Much depended on the existence of constraints which prevented savers from taking full advantage of the tax system; some evidence from the United States suggested that they did not. It was also argued that the need to save for precautionary reasons would dissuade individuals from holding the greater proportion of their assets in the form of entitlements to pensions and insurance policies. Thus, at the margin, savings would be placed in a variety of assets. One practical solution to the problem of defining the margin would be to illustrate the sensitivity of the results to a variety of assumptions about the marginality of different forms of finance. It was conjectured that such an exercise would increase further the variation of the effective marginal tax rates around the average.

Various participants considered the possible ramifications of King's figures. The purpose of King's paper – to measure and compare the tax wedge applying to different investors and savers – was agreed to be a narrow one and not easily extended to an assessment of general behaviour. Given that the figures related to only one year, it was difficult to assess the alleged fiscal contribution to the fall in industry's rate of return[1] though the belief was confidently expressed that effective tax rates had declined because of more generous investment incentives and the growth of the institutions. There was some speculation on the possibility that the tax system had contributed towards the under-development of small firms (by penalising personal savings) and to excessive investment in housing as against that in industry.

Other participants were far more sceptical about the implications of King's figures for investment behaviour. Experience led them to

[1] See pp 50–55 of the background paper – *Ed.*

believe that the required rate of return used by companies in their investment appraisals was calculated in a fairly simple and arbitrary manner. It might be based upon an average rate of return expected – though not necessarily achieved – by financiers in the past together with an allowance for risk. Specific investment allowances would be included in the calculations but it would be impractical for companies to allow also for the tax position of their financiers. It was further argued that investment decisions in practice were dominated by considerations of the strategic importance of alternative investments for the growth of a company and its position in the market place. Seeing thus little connection between King's calculations of effective marginal tax rates and actual investment behaviour, some participants thought it premature to conclude, as King himself had done,[1] that the tax system could not be held to blame for levels of investment which may not have matched up to expectations. There was however no dissent from the more general implication of King's results; namely, that the tax system produced wide variations in effective rates of tax and subsidy for which there was little justification.

[1] In his original, but not in the revised, paper – *Ed*.

Cash flow and investment

by G Meeks

I am grateful to the Department of Industry for the provision of data, to the Esmée Fairbairn Charitable Trust for supporting the research, to Andrew Goudie, Gay Meeks and Geoffrey Whittington for helpful comments and to Margaret Clarke for statistical assistance. This paper was prepared for a non-academic audience.

Summary

Some commentators distinguish two channels through which a reduction in profits may influence investment: first, lower prospective profitability in relation to the cost of capital is expected to reduce the *incentive* to invest; and secondly, smaller current profits will constrain the *ability* to finance investment from internal funds. This paper concentrates on the second channel of influence. It first discusses the characteristics of the tax system and of the capital market which could lead to investment being restrained by a reduction in internal funds even if prospective profitability were unchanged (section 1). It then reports, however, that empirical work for Britain in the 1950's and 1960's has not accorded a powerful independent role to profits in explaining fluctuations in investment (section 2); but section 3 shows that circumstances have changed significantly in the late sixties and seventies: cash balances have fallen; the rate of investment which could be sustained using retentions alone has diminished significantly; and the fluctuations in internal funds have followed fluctuations in economic activity less closely than before. Consequently, internal funds may have gained a more important role. This suggestion is put to the test in a preliminary cross-section analysis of the variation of the investment rate across companies (section 4). The results of this exercise favour the qualitative conclusion that companies' investment was influenced by their internal finance in the late sixties and early seventies. The paper then ends (section 5) with a discussion of some of the difficulties involved in interpreting these cross-section results more precisely.

1   Why might retentions constrain investment?

The suggestion that firms' spending on fixed investment is sensitive to the level of their retained earnings finds little favour with the established theoretical schools. Resting as it does largely on the importance of market imperfections, the case for this link is little emphasised by the more diehard of the neo-classical school. Nor are retentions prominent in traditional Keynesian doctrine: as Eatwell (1971) points out, 'a central proposition of the Keynesian analysis...is that... the spending decisions of capitalists (or corporations) on investment goods are not, in a modern capitalist economy with fully developed financial institutions, dependent on past or current real savings.'[1]

---

[1] On the role of capital market imperfections in modifying this basic Keynesian proposition, see Matthews (1959) and Tew (1952)

Nevertheless, the importance of such financial constraints on company spending has been asserted in a number of contexts. They represent one element in the Cambridge Economic Policy Group's notion, implicit in their private expenditure function, that the private sector pretty quickly spends what it earns[1]. They loom large in Kaldor's (1971) argument for tax penalties on dividends aimed at fostering retentions and hence investment. And Bacon and Eltis (1976) place them among the contributors to the investment famine in the UK private sector.

It is of course well known that internal funds have played a dominant role in British companies' financing in recent decades. On the measures used in table 1 long-term external finance has contributed less than 20 per cent of firms' capital spending, an observation at least consistent with the view that there are disincentives to heavy reliance on external funds. One such disincentive has been created by the UK tax system, as King (1977) points out when comparing the tax implications of retentions with those of debt finance: '... given the evidence on the distribution of marginal tax rates of UK shareholders..., a substantial number of shareholders would prefer the firm to use internal finance, *even if* there were no costs attached to a high debt-equity ratio'.

Table 1   Sources of Finance: Quoted Companies in Manufacturing, Distribution, etc., 1949–77.

Sources of funds as a percentage of gross investment in fixed assets plus net investment in current assets plus cash expenditure on takeovers

Long term external funds		17.6
of which:		
Loan	10.1	
Equity	7.5	

Note: The respective sources of funds were expressed as a percentage of the total for each individual year and the years' values averaged.
Sources: NIESR (1956); Royal Commission (1975); CSO (1975); Department of Industry (1971–).

[1] See Cripps, T F, Fetherston, M and Godley, W A H (1974).

Moreover, as Kalecki's[1] principle of increasing risk tells us, there *are* special costs associated with a high debt-equity ratio. According to this account, if future profits are uncertain, firms will be reluctant to commit too much prospective income to regular fixed interest payments on loans lest profits should prove inadequate to finance them. Too high gearing could lead to liquidation in a bad year – a prospect which might not be too daunting if markets for managers and fixed assets were broad and orderly but which in fact will often mean unemployment for the managers; and, since liquidations tend to come in bursts – prompted, say, by a credit squeeze or a fall in activity – then, following the arguments of Minsky and of Roe[2], the markets for the liquidators' specific assets will often collapse, resulting in big capital losses for the owners.

On this account then, debt finance may only permit a limited scaling up of finance from other sources. And some commentators have relied exclusively on this argument to support their contention that private investment has been resource constrained – via the profit squeeze. But of course it doesn't explain why firms avoid new equity issues, which entail no fixed interest commitment but simply grant the subscribers a share of whatever profit or losses occur. It is true that, as table 1 shows, equity issues for cash have typically played a very minor role in companies' expansion[3]. But some explanation is needed of why companies should shun equity issues when they are short of cash to finance attractive investment projects.

Again the tax system is a contributory factor. King (1977) argues that, if external finance is to be used, share issues will be less attractive than new loan stock since in the UK system interest payments are deductible from profit for tax purposes. Apart from this feature of the tax system there are several other reasons why companies might be deterred from new share issues, some of them affecting new loan issues too[4]. One of the more obvious is represented by the transactions costs incurred in an issue – underwriting and registration costs, professional fees, etc. For all but the smallest issues – in 1974 terms, anything over about £1 million – these amount to perhaps 5 per cent of the gross proceeds of the issue:[5] not immaterial, but

[1] See Kalecki (1937)
[2] See, eg, Roe (1973)
[3] In recent years equity issues in exchange for new subsidiaries have been rather more important: see Meeks (1977), Chapter 4.
[4] Baumol's (1965) discussion has been very helpful in what follows.
[5] See Davis and Yeomans (1974).

hardly sufficient by itself to condemn a promising investment. But, in addition, the information on past and expected performance that normally has to be provided in connection with a new issue exceeds that ordinarily required in annual reports; and, apart from the direct costs of assembling this information, there is the possibility that its disclosure to competitors could damage the firm's commercial position. What is more, a management group accustomed to a good deal of autonomy could resent the outside scrutiny associated with new issues – a stronger possibility still if the issue carried with it restrictive provisions. A related point for an owner-controlled company is that a new equity issue might rob an individual or group of control of the firm[1].

A number of other drawbacks of external finance receive attention in the literature. Often uncertainty is the villain of the piece, as it was in the Kalecki argument. To begin with, an issue has to be planned some months ahead, and its proceeds, sensitive as they are to the buoyancy of share prices in a market notorious for its turbulence, may be very difficult to predict (a fall of a quarter in the share price index in six months is not unknown). In other words, when the firm decides whether or not to go to the market, it doesn't know on what terms it may issue shares and so what degree of dilution of the existing equity is entailed. (This is quite apart from the problem that, when the market is depressed, new equity may not be available on acceptable terms for extended periods.)[2] Then again, for an internally-financed project to go ahead it is sufficient that the management should have favourable expectations of its returns, whereas for an externally financed project it is also necessary that 'the market', containing investors less well informed and perhaps more sceptical than the firm's own managers, should concur with these expectations. The new issue means that shareholders have to be induced to increase the firm's representation in their portfolios beyond what they thought desirable at the old price. Some incentive is necessary – hence the drop in price which usually accompanies an issue, and which (as Wood (1975)

---

[1] It used to be thought that this was a consideration confined just to the small family businesses which were relatively insignificant in the economy – in other words that Berle and Means' divorce of ownership from control was for practical purposes complete. But a recent paper by Nyman and Silberston (1978) argues that very many of the largest UK corporations are effectively controlled by small owner – groups – often families with only minority shareholdings but where the majority of share-holders is dispersed and unorganised.

[2] See for instance, the experience of 1973–74 recorded in Midland Bank (1975)

emphasises) involves a capital loss for existing shareholders – a loss which will be more severe, the bigger the issue[1]. Uncertainty also means that, even if firms are prepared to raise new external finance, the amount that they will be willing to raise and the market will be prepared to subscribe is likely to be positively related to the amount of profit (and, other things equal, internal finance) currently being earned. This is for the reasons emphasised in Chapter 12 of the General Theory – in uncertainty current facts exert a special influence over long-term expectations:

'It is reasonable ... to be guided to a considerable degree by the facts about which we feel somewhat confident, even though they may be less decisively relevant to the issue than other facts about which our knowledge is vague and scanty. For this reason the facts of the existing situation enter, in a sense disproportionately, into the formation of our long-term expectations ...' (Keynes (1936) p. 148).

This catalogue of factors favouring internal finance could probably be extended. But how significant an obstacle these various difficulties present to firms contemplating external finance is a matter of dispute. Some accounts scarcely mention them whilst, at the other extreme, Galbraith for instance asserts that 'to minimise dependence on the capital market is a universal planning strategy.'

2   Profits and investment in the fifties and sixties

If internal funds are indeed as significant as Galbraith suggests then one might ask why, in estimates of the investment function for Britain in the fifties and sixties, profits made such a poor showing. For the National Institute reported in 1971 that incorporating profits variables in regressions already containing capacity utilisation and accelerator terms scarcely improved the degree of explanation[2].

One consideration which might help the advocate of profit's importance to reconcile these results with his *a priori* expectation is the state of liquid balances. As the Radcliffe Report pointed out in a discussion of whether monetary restraint would bite, British companies emerged from the Second World War and the late forties flush with money;

---

[1] See also Nickell (1978). It could be objected that increasing the retention ratio in order to raise more internal finance might well depress the share price by just as much as a new issue designed to yield the same sum; and that this might be equally objectionable to shareholders (I am grateful to Roger Witcomb for this point).
[2] See Surrey (1971). Dimsdale and Glyn (1971) provide a cross-section study for this period.

consequently, if desired investment exceeded the sum of retentions and desired external finance, the gap could be filled by running down liquidity stocks – investment would not have to be curtailed[1].

A second possible reason for the weak independent role of profits in the empirical findings is the high collinearity of profit with the physical determinants of investment such as capacity utilisation. The National Institute study reported that profits could be substituted for capacity utilisation in the regression equation with no adverse effect on the fit. This accords with the well-known tendency of profits per unit of output (and *a fortiori* aggregate profits) to rise in the cyclical upswing[2] at the same time as the pressure to invest is increasing. Thus although a shortage of retentions might *potentially* have inhibited investment, in practice it is likely that more internal funds were forthcoming whenever firms wished to increase their investment.

It is not clear, however, that either of these features – generous endowments of cash and sympathetic fluctuations in desired investment and internal finance – has persisted into the late sixties and the seventies. To begin with, as some monetary economists have pointed out,[3] British companies' pool of liquidity has been ebbing away: table 2 shows the continuing decline in net liquidity since 1948.

But also in the last decade or so circumstances have more often arisen where internal funds available for investment have declined at times when sales and the pressure on capacity have been increasing – and sometimes even on the occasions when profitability has been rising. Some of the reasons for this are explained in section 3: in part at least they are associated with the rise from the late sixties in the average inflation rate and in its variance.

3   The level of retentions

Some implications of the very high recent rates of inflation for companies' internal funds can be illustrated using the following symbols:

- A: stock appreciation
- D: depreciation provisions (historic cost)
- i: annual rate of increase of stock values and of fixed asset prices
- L: opening value of short-term loans
- m: life-time of fixed assets

[1] This argument also appears in the US context in Kuh (1963).
[2] See Neild (1963), Coutts, Godley and Nordhaus (1978).
[3] See Bain (1970).

Table 2 Liquid Balances: Quoted Companies in Manufacturing, Distribution, etc., 1948–77.

Marketable securities, tax reserve certificates and net bank balances as a percentage of net assets

1948	17.8
1954	14.1
1964	1.0
1973	0
1977	0

Note: The years chosen are the first year of satisfactory consolidated accounts, three cyclical peak years, and the most recent year for which data were available.
Sources: as table 1.

N: total interest on short-term loans
P: conventional (historic cost) profits
r: rate of interest on short-term loans
R: replacement cost of the fixed assets due for retirement in the current year
S: opening value of stocks
T_a: tax levied on stock appreciation
u: annual rate of growth of real gross fixed investment

If managements wish to maintain their companies' purchasing power when inflation is accelerating, it is not enough that nominal earnings (P) keep pace with the rise in prices, as it can be for wage or dividend recipients. In addition, increases in conventional profits have to match stock appreciation[1], which, assuming that the physical volume of stocks is to be maintained, is:

$$A = iS \qquad (1)$$

This represents the conventional profit which has to be paid out simply to maintain the physical volume of stocks. The proportion of conventional profit preempted on this account is shown by dividing by P:

$$\frac{A}{P} = i\frac{S}{P} \qquad (2)$$

Now, on average, the value of S/P, the stock-profit ratio, for the British quoted company sector is some 2.5; so just 1 per cent inflation in stock values means that 2.5 per cent of the initial conventional profit is pre-empted to maintain stock volumes.[2] And thus, with stocks

[1] Assuming no stock appreciation in the previous period.
[2] This argument is developed in Meeks (1974).

averaging two or three times earnings, earnings must rise by a multiple
of any increase in the inflation rate if disposable profits are to be
maintained even in nominal terms. Moreover, in the late sixties and
early seventies when inflation was gathering pace, the tax system
exacerbated the effect of stock appreciation on firms' funds: conventional profit was still used as a tax base,[1] so in addition to the use of
cash to maintain stocks firms had to find the cash to meet the tax
levied on stock appreciation:

$$\frac{A+T_a}{P} = (1+t)\frac{S}{P}i \tag{3}$$

With a tax rate of 0.4, the multiple therefore grows from 2.5 (ie S/P)
to 3.5 (ie $(1+t)$ S/P). Thus if the rate of inflation rose by 5 per cent
under this regime, conventional profit would have had to rise by 17.5
per cent simply to maintain purchasing power *in money terms*.

Potentially, a similar (though less severe) problem arises over short-
term interest payments (N):

$$N = rL \tag{4}$$

If any increase in the rate of inflation is matched by an increase in the
short-term rate of interest ($\Delta r = \overline{\Delta} i$) the proportion of conventional
profit pre-empted by additional interest payments will be:

$$\frac{\Delta N}{P} = \Delta i \frac{L}{P} \tag{5}$$

As Flemming *et al* (1976) have noted, companies' have lately been
increasing their reliance on short-term borrowing, and average L/P for
the listed company sector stands at around 1.5, so, in parallel with the
stock appreciation argument, for each 1 per cent rise in the inflation
rate, 1.5 per cent of the initial conventional profit will be pre-empted
to meet increased nominal interest payments[2].

Some would argue that this particular problem of interest payments
is not as severe as it first appears. For although a company has indeed
to finance an extra payment of nominal interest, it will have achieved a
corresponding 'gain' from the higher rate of inflation insofar as the
real value of its short-term debt will have been further diminished[3].
And on this argument companies could readily restore their cash flow

---

[1] Until stock relief was introduced in 1974.

[2] There will be a similar type of problem associated with long-term debt. But because of
the long maturity dates, *average* long-term interest rates have been slow to catch up
with inflation.

[3] Looked at from the other side, the lender has received accelerated repayment of his
loan.

by borrowing a further £iL, thus returning to their former level of
capital gearing in real terms. However, this resolution could be
obstructed if, for instance, the rise in interest payments coincided with
a credit squeeze or financial difficulties for the company, either of
which would restrict its access to new short-term finance. Furthermore,
although the company's rise in interest payments is matched on the
income side by the gain from the erosion of debt, still the overall result
will commonly be a rise in the income gearing ratio,[1] a development
which, on the argument of section 1, will often be inauspicious for the
further accumulation of debt.[2]

On the face of it, fixed asset replacement poses a problem similar to
that for stock appreciation. It might be supposed that, because of
rising fixed asset prices, depreciation provisions based on historic costs
would be inadequate to finance fixed asset replacement; part of conventional profit would then be pre-empted for asset replacement, and
'disposable' profit would again be eroded.

The account is rather more complicated, however, when – as in this
paper – attention is focussed on a particular year's cash inflows and
outflows rather than on what funds should be earmarked for the ultimate replacement of the capital stock when it eventually wears out.
For any particular machine – with a lifetime of say twenty years –
funds will be set aside in each year of its lifetime, but only paid out to
replace the machine in the twentieth year. Looked at slightly differently, in any particular year a company will be setting aside money on
all its machines, but only the oldest machines will need to be replaced
in that year. And it could be that the depreciation provisions set aside
in the year exceed the cost of the replacement machines which have to
be installed. An extreme example is provided by a new company which
installs machines which last, say, twenty years: in the first nineteen
years of its existence the company will earmark income for the ultimate
replacement of its assets, but will not have to finance any replace-
ments: the earmarked cash will in the meantime be available to buy
additional machines.

Domar (1953) has provided a formal framework for tracing the
relationship between historic cost depreciation provisions and replacement outlays in a period of inflation and rising real investment. Investment is assumed to grow at a constant rate $(u + i)$ from an initial value,

---

[1] Under conventional accounting, which would not record the gain from debt erosion,
the problem of the income gearing ratio would be more acute.

[2] These arguments apply also to the suggestion that the stock maintenance problem
could be eliminated by taking on short-term debt to finance stockholding.

m years ago, of 1. Thus the current total value of the capital stock (at historic cost) is the sum of the geometric progression:

$$1, (1+u+i), (1+u+i)^2, \ldots (1+u+i)^{m-2}, (1+u+i)^{m-1} \tag{6}$$

$$\text{ie } \frac{(1+u+i)^m-1}{u+i} \tag{7}$$

Depreciation in the current year, provided on historic cost, on a straight line basis, is $(\frac{1}{m})$th of the capital stock:

$$D = \frac{(1+u+i)^m-1}{m(u+i)} \tag{8}$$

The cost of replacing the assets bought m years ago and due for retirement in the current year is:

$$R = (1+i)^m \tag{9}$$

The ratio of replacement costs to depreciation is then:

$$\frac{R}{D} = \frac{m(u+i)\,(1+i)^m}{(1+u+i)^m-1} \tag{10}$$

R/D varies inversely with u, the rate of growth of real investment but directly with i, the rate of inflation in fixed asset prices.

Substitution in (10) of typical values for m, u and i shows the order of magnitude of R/D for the company sector.[1] And it appears that until the early seventies R fell below D: the rate of growth of real investment was sufficient to raise depreciation above replacement costs in spite of some inflation. According to these (admittedly rough) estimates, then, fixed asset replacement did not in the sixties function in the same way as stock appreciation: far from pre-empting part of conventional profit, asset replacement costs typically fell short of companies' (historic cost) depreciation provisions, and part of depreciation was available for net investment.

However, because of the positive relation between R/D and i, the acceleration in the rate of fixed asset price increase from the late sixties means that R/D has been rising, and the surplus of depreciation provisions declining[2]. Indeed, this surplus may well have disappeared by the early seventies and subsequently been replaced by a deficit. Thus although, somewhat surprisingly, the level of historic cost depreciation provisions may well have been sufficient in the sixties to finance replacement and augment disposable profit, still rising asset prices will have contributed, along with the stock appreciation mechanism, to the downward trend in the ratio of internal funds to conventional profit.

[1] See the discussion in Meeks (1974).
[2] This trend has been reinforced by the recent slakening of u.

Figure 1. **Internal finance available for net investment and dividends, as a percentage of the capital stock: U.K. quoted companies in manufacturing, distribution, etc.**

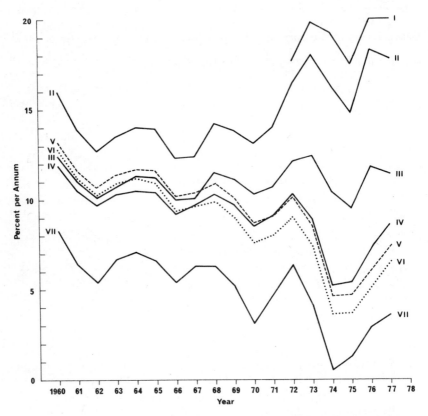

Sources: Department of Industry (1971-). Adjustments for asset revaluation and stock appreciation calculated using Flemming et al (1976) and Central Statistical Office (1979). Basis of, and sources for, line V further discussed in Meeks (1974).

Key: See text.

Figure 1 draws together these and other influences on the level of retentions available for new investment, charting the trends in internal funds for the quoted company sector since the early sixties. It shows estimates of various components of profit as a percentage of the companies' capital (net assets). At one extreme (line II) it gives conventional (historic cost) profits as a percentage of net assets at historic cost; whilst, at the other, it records (line VII) the internal finance

available for net investment plus dividends, this time as a percentage
of the companies' capital revalued in current prices. This latter
measure is the maximum rate at which the companies could expand
their capital if they paid no dividends and relied entirely on internal
finance. What is immediately clear from the diagram is the marked
divergence between lines II and VII, particularly in the seventies. The
intervening lines show how this divergence has come about.

The very top line (I) shows conventional profit before the deduction
of short-term loan interest; line II shows it after this interest. Unfortunately data are not available on short-term interest for years before
1972, but the later years alone illustrate the volatility of this outflow in
a time of fluctuating inflation rates: within just two years (1972–74) it
more than doubles as a proportion of net assets. The second line, the
conventional rate of return, traced an upward movement over the
period, reaching its highest level in 1976. But any upward trend is
eliminated once the denominator, net assets, is valued at current prices
(line III). And the next adjustment, removing stock appreciation from
the profit numerator, turns the trend into a downward one (line IV).
As the argument above suggested, this adjustment suddenly became
much more significant as the inflation rate accelerated in the late
sixties, and stock appreciation reached massive proportions in the price
explosion of the mid-seventies. Moreover, it displays sharp year to year
fluctuations: in 1973, even though conventional profits were rising the
rise did not match the increase in stock appreciation and line IV shows
a decline; in 1977, on the other hand, the reduction in stock appreciation as inflation moderated was sufficient to turn a decline in line III
into an improvement in line IV.

Line V reports the results of applying the 'Domar adjustment'
described above and shows whether the historic cost depreciation provisions set aside in computing profit are enough to finance the estimated cost of replacing the assets due for retirement. At the beginning
of the period the estimates show a surplus of depreciation provisions,
so line V lies above line IV. This situation does not persist, however,
when inflation accelerates, and by the end of the period there is a
deficit: line V falls below line IV.

Lines VI and VII show the effect of deducting long-term loan
interest and tax payments respectively. The decline in VII has been
mitigated somewhat (compared with that in VI) by the reduction in the
effective rate of UK tax on companies' conventional profits.[1] But still
line VII reaches an unprecedentedly low level in 1970 and falls even

---

[1] See King (1975). As the measure in figure 1 includes overseas profits and overseas taxation the reduction is less sharp than for UK profits alone.

further by 1975. In the mid-seventies the rate of growth of capital which could be financed internally were no dividends paid is of the order of half its value ten years earlier.[1]

4   Cash flow and inter-firm differences in the investment rate

Section 1 summarised some of the reasons for expecting investment to be sensitive to the availability of internal finance; and the last section reported that companies' internal finance has been squeezed in recent years. This section develops some empirical work on the question whether in the event this squeeze might have depressed investment: it reports a preliminary attempt to relate inter-firm differences in the investment rate to differences in firms' internal finance, holding other things equal. It presents estimates of a model developed from work on US firms by Meyer and Kuh (1959) which assesses the influence on investment of a number of variables representing the incentive to invest and the ability to invest from internal funds.

In the light of this paper's earlier arguments one would choose to focus on investment net of fixed asset replacement. But unfortunately plausible estimates of *individual* companies' replacement investment cannot readily be derived. Moreover, even if full information were available on which assets a company had retired in a year, there would still often be a problem in identifying which of the new assets went to replace them. Many treatments of asset replacement emphasise the role of technical progress (eg Salter (1969)): the incentive to replace comes

---

[1] In the sixties, the fluctuations in line VII follow the same pattern as those for real rates of return reported in the Bank of England studies (Flemming *et al.* (1976) and Clark and Williams (1978)); but subsequently they follow one another less closely (see figure 2). There are a number of reasons for the difference: figure 1 includes the overseas profits of UK companies, it records tax payments rather than accruals, etc. Figure 1, being concerned with actual cash flow, is more relevant to the ability to invest, the Bank of England studies to the incentive.

One incidental advantage of figure 1's approach is that the resulting numbers are ones which are likely to have impinged forcibly on management since they correspond to the cash flowing into the companies' bank accounts. Managers may not, on the other hand, have been fully aware of the movements in their real rate of return – a point made by Flemming *et al:*

'Many companies may have been unaware of the impact of stock appreciation on profits and have been content if published earnings, expressed as a percentage of capital employed, were broadly maintained' (1976a, p 43). Even if managers were unaware of why it was happening, however, they could not have failed to notice if they were forced (in practice by, for instance, increased stock replacement costs) into overdraft.

Figure 2. Internal finance and the post-tax real rate of return

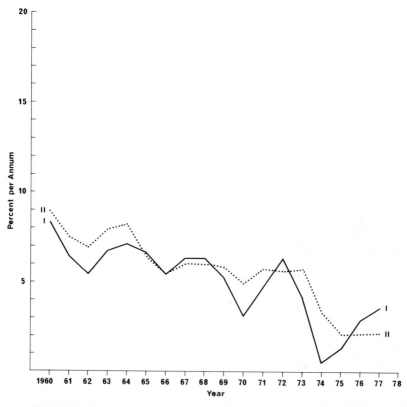

Sources: *I: Figure 1*
II: Clark and Williams (1978)

Key: See text

not just from the physical decay of old equipment but also from the superior efficiency of new; and consequently the distinction between new and replacement investment is blurred. The distinction is therefore abandoned in this model: gross investment is used as the dependent variable[1] and depreciation provisions included as an explanatory variable.

[1] Fixed assets purchased in the course of takeover are excluded. Investment grants netted out of fixed asset purchases in company accounts are added back by the DI as part of their standardisation procedure when preparing the accounts used in this exercise.

Nevertheless, it is recognised that, of two otherwise similar companies, the one with the older capital stock might be expected to undertake more replacement investment. For this reason the model has as one of its explanatory variables an indicator of the age of the company's capital stock, namely the ratio of its accumulated depreciation provisions to its gross fixed assets. This particular measure is clearly imperfect, given variations between companies in accounting policies on depreciation rates, in the proportion of undepreciated land and buildings in total fixed assets, etc. But it is the best available at the company level.

A company producing at or near capacity is more likely to expand capacity in response to an increase in demand (also represented in the model: see below) than one with substantial unused capital equipment. As a second explanatory variable on the incentive side a measure of capacity utilisation was therefore developed for each firm, using a device suggested by Meyer and Kuh. The peak output-capital ratio (sales: gross fixed assets) of each firm during the five years studied was obtained; and the current year's output-capital ratio was expressed as a proportion of this yardstick. The third and fourth variables incorporated represent accelerator effects: the sales level and the increase in sales from the previous year.[1]

Three variables are used to represent the influence of internal finance on the investment decision – two liquidity flows and a liquidity stock. The first is a disposable retentions measure: profit after depreciation, tax, dividends, interest and stock appreciation. This is the variable which has suffered so severely on account of the failure of conventional profit to keep pace with stock appreciation (see above). Unfortunately this variable presents a serious measurement problem: finding an appropriate price index to compute the value of stock appreciation – a problem which is specially acute at the individual firm level. For want of anything better a general (consumer) price index has been used; but to avoid serious error the value of stock appreciation is constrained to be less than or equal to the recorded increase in the nominal value of stocks (ie the actual cash spent on increasing stocks).

[1] Conventional profits were not themselves incorporated in the model because they are correlated with sales on the incentive side and disposable retentions on the finance side: it is likely that their inclusion in the same model as these two would have led to problems of multicollinearity; and also it would have been difficult to distinguish its influence as an incentive factor (reckoned here to be represented by sales) from that as an ability factor. Sales and disposable retentions do not display a very high correlation (see Meeks (1975), table G.I.).

To the extent that managers make allowance for inflation in assessing their current profit[1] this variable may also reflect differences between firms in the incentive to invest.

The second variable on the ability side is current depreciation provisions, the other element of gross savings, apart from disposable retentions. It is a pure liquidity flow variable, being a function only of the capital stock and of the write-off policy.[2] And as Meeks (1974) shows, it has contributed a major proportion of gross savings.

Finally, a liquidity stock variable[3] is incorporated on the grounds mentioned earlier, that large stocks of liquidity may be expected to relax any constraint upon investment that is imposed by a cut in liquidity flows. Thus the basic model may be summarised:[4]

$$I_{hj} = f\,(B_{hj-1}/K_{hj-1},\ U_{hj}/K_{hj-1},\ Y_{hj},\ \Delta Y_{hj},\ R_{hj},\ D_{hj},\ C_{hj-1}) \tag{11}$$

where:

I: Gross investment in fixed assets

B: Accumulated depreciation (indicator of average age of capital stock when divided by K)

U: Sales times minimum capital-output ratio for period (indicator of level of capacity utilisation when divided by K)

Y: Sales

R: Disposable retentions

D: Depreciation provisions

C: Net liquidity stock

K: Gross fixed assets (at historic cost)

e: Error term

h: company

j: current year

The actual version estimated (using multiple linear regression) deflates all the variables except those already so deflated (B, U) with the size

---

[1] However, Panic and Close (1973) suggest that firms typically based their investment decisions on historic cost accounting information in the period under study.

[2] Depreciation provisions and disposable retentions are the two components of cash flow. Any change in the write-off policy would simply alter the allocation of cash flow between depreciation provisions and retentions.

[3] This comprises cash and bank balances plus tax reserve certificates and marketable securities, minus bank overdrafts and loans, dividend, interest and current taxation liabilities.

[4] Current values of the variables are used in all cases except the age indicator and liquidity stocks, where the opening balances are used. These exceptions are made because in both cases investment may be expected to affect directly the closing balances of the respective variables (assuming other things equal). See the discussion below of alternative results when the flows were lagged one year.

measure, gross fixed assets (K). This procedure is designed to mitigate the problems of heteroscedasticity and multicollinearity which are likely to arise when (as in the population used here) the largest company is of the order of 1000 times the size of the smallest. In this ratio form then the model relates investment as a proportion of capital to, for instance, sales, disposable retentions or depreciation provisions as a proportion of the fixed capital stock:

$$\frac{I_{hj}}{K_{hj-1}} = b_o + b_1\frac{B_{hj-1}}{K_{hj-1}} + b_2\frac{U_{hj}}{K_{hj-1}} + b_3\frac{Y_{hj}}{K_{hj-1}} + b_4\frac{Y_{hj}}{K_{hj-1}}$$
$$+ b_5\frac{R_{hj}}{K_{hj-1}} + b_6\frac{D_{hj}}{K_{hj-1}} + b_7\frac{C_{hj-1}}{K_{hj-1}} + e_{hj}$$

(12)

The data used to estimate (12) are derived from a data bank assembled by the author and his colleagues and containing quoted company accounts standardised by the Department of Industry. The coverage of the accounts is the same as for the aggregate quoted figures published in Department of Industry (1971−) and analysed in tables 1 and 2 and figure 1. More information on the coverage of the data bank and its constituent accounts as well as some of the necessary qualifications and caveats can be found in Meeks and Whittington (1976).

The model is estimated for the five years, 1967 to 1971. Earlier years were not used because the sales data necessary for three of the explanatory variables on the incentive side (U, Y, Δ Y) were only disclosed by all companies after the 1967 Companies Act.[1]

The model is estimated separately for 18 individual two-digit industries. Although this causes a proliferation of results and increases the difficulties of presentation, it was thought necessary because so many factors which affect investment, but which cannot readily be measured and incorporated explicitly into the model, are associated with industry − eg the durability of capital equipment and product, production and market structure, trade credit practices. These variables may well affect the extent and speed of response of investment to the explanatory variables actually included; and in fact considerable differences do emerge in the performance of the model for different industries within the same year. In all, then, 90 sets of results are pro-

[1] For 1966, 48.5 per cent of the population studied in the paper published their sales total; 83.8 per cent in 1967; 99.7 per cent in 1968 and 100 per cent subsequently. Where a company has no sales data it is excluded from the computations reported below. This distorts certain comparisons between years when different proportions of the population are included.

vided for the model (5 years × 18 industries). The number of companies contributing to each of these industry-years is recorded in table 3.[1]

Table 4 summarises certain features of the results, reporting the number of industry-years for which the multiple regression coefficient

---

Table 3   Industry Distribution of Companies Included in the Regression Analysis

Industry	No. of Companies
21 Food	30
23 Drink	49
26 Chemicals	49
31 Metal manufacture	43
33 Non-electrical engineering	119
36 Electrical engineering	54
38 Vehicles	31
39 Metal goods, n.e.s.	70
41 Textiles	71
44 Clothing and Footwear	33
46 Bricks, Pottery, etc.	40
47 Timber, etc.	32
48 Paper, printing, etc.	59
49 Other manufacturing	39
50 Construction	57
81 Wholesale distribution	78
82 Retail distribution	82
88 Miscellaneous services	49
Total:	985

Note: Four industries (tobacco, shipbuilding, leather and transport), which contain very few companies were excluded from the analysis, since they would have enjoyed too few degrees of freedom.

---

[1] As this is only a limited preliminary exercise and as each version of the model yields 90 sets of estimates (and hence with seven explanatory variables and a constant term, 720 coefficients per specification), a range of alternative specifications was not estimated. However, one very plausible alternative version of the model was tried which lags the independent variables; for some delay is clearly inevitable between the stimuli to invest, the commissioning of a project, and the purchase of equipment. Accordingly, the model was estimated using all the independent variables but B and C (which represent opening stocks anyway) in a form where they were lagged one year. On an (admittedly crude) comparison, however, this variant performed less well than the 'current' model: R^2 was higher for the current version in 78 per cent of industry-years. In the interests of simplicity, therefore, only the current version is reported in subsequent sections. Little further experimenting with alternative lag structures (a preoccupation of quarterly time series work) was attempted since the available data are annual and the run of years available is very short.

on a particular variable is positive, and in how many cases it is significantly greater than zero at the 5 per cent level.

As table 4 shows, depreciation was accorded a powerful role by the regressions. The coefficient relating investment to depreciation was positive in 84 of the 90 industry-years included; and it passed the test of statistical significance in 61 of these. The detailed results (not reported here) also show that none of the industries or years diverged markedly from this general pattern: in no industry did fewer than two of the five years reveal coefficients significantly greater than zero; and at least 11 of the 18 industries in any year produced coefficients passing this test. In the year of most severe savings squeeze, 1970, every single industry revealed a positive coefficient.[1, 2]

Table 4   Summary of Regression Results for Equation (12), 1967−71

Explanatory Variable	Number of respective multiple regression coefficients that are:	
	Positive	Significantly greater than zero at 5% level
Depreciation provisions	84	61
Net retentions	78	39
Liquidity stock	46	6
Change in sales	63	20
Capacity utilisation	61	11
Sales	54	11
Age of assets	34	2

Note the deflation procedure used in defining the variables and described in the text. The number of samples (ie maximum possible score) is 90.

[1] See the discussion below of why a strong association would be expected when the average level of the independent variable is low.

[2] It has been suggested that the causation does not run from depreciation finance to investment but instead that the current year's investment figure exerts a strong influence over the depreciation provision, since this depreciation figure will include some provision in respect of the current year's investment. In general, however, investment in the current year will have only a very limited effect on the company's aggregate depreciation provision for the year. This is because the depreciation rates most often used in the period were, for instance, only 2 per cent a year in the case of property and 10 per cent in the case of plant (see Institute of Chartered Accountants (1972)). The influence of the current year's investment on depreciation provisions would be greater if depreciation were calculated on a reducing balance basis; bu' straight line method was overwhelmingly dominant at this time (see Institute Chartered Accountants (1972)).

The second liquidity flow variable, disposable retentions, also performed well in the regression analysis, as is shown in table 4. The
coefficient relating investment to this variable was positive in 78 of the
90 industry-years; and was significantly greater than zero in 39 of these
cases.[1] Moreover, the detailed results (not reported) show that there
was a tendency for the role of disposable retentions to be more powerful in years when its typical level was low: in 1970, when the savings
squeeze was more severe (see figure 1), all 18 industries displayed a
positive relationship between the two variables, and in ten the
coefficient was significantly greater than zero. By contrast, in 1967, the
year with the highest retention level of those reported here, the number
of positive coefficients (and of ones significantly greater than zero) was
at its lowest. An analogous result holds for inter-industry comparisons.
The four industries whose investment displayed the greatest sensitivity
to their disposable retentions (according to the rule of thumb adopted
here: most coefficients significantly greater than zero) were all identified in Meeks (1974) as suffering more severely than average from the
stock appreciation mechanism:[2] stock appreciation pre-empted a larger
share of their profit than it did for the aggregate quoted company
sector.

While both the liquidity flow variables were positively and strongly
associated with investment the performance of the liquidity stock
variable did not conform to expectations. The coefficient was negative
in practically half (44) of the 90 industry-years considered; and in only
six of the 90 cases did a coefficient emerge which was significantly
greater than zero at the 5 per cent level (see table 4). In other words
there was little or no suggestion that firms with more liquidity at the
beginning of the year undertook more investment during the year.

Table 4 also summarises the values of the coefficients relating investment to the three variables (apart from the age indicator) which reflect
the incentives to invest: increases in sales, capacity utilisation and the
level of sales. As expected, all were, by and large, positively related to
investment. Too much should not be read into the particular results
for the *individual* incentive variables, since there is some collinearity
between them which creates difficulties for distinguishing the influence
of each and the modelling of their influence is particularly rough and

---

[1] Since considerable error may have been introduced by the use of a general price index
when estimating this variable (see above), its explanatory power is all the more
striking.

[2] These results are consistent with the suggestion made below that a strong and positive
relation between saving and investment will be detected for years or industries where
internal finance is in short supply and is an operative constraint on investment.

ready. All three were included in order to represent as fully as possible the influence of demand factors whilst using the limited information available at the company level. The aim was to hold things as near equal as possible when assessing the role of the finance variables rather than, as in some studies, to test the physical and financial variables as competitors or to compare the performance of different physical variables.

Finally, table 4 reports the performance of the variable which proxies for the average age of the firm's capital stock. It seemed possible that the processes of decay and obsolescence would stir companies whose capital stock was relatively old to invest more heavily in replacement equipment. In the event, the relationship between gross investment and the age proxy was more often than not negative (in fifteen industry-years the coefficient was significantly less than zero; and in only two cases was it significantly greater). If this proxy is to be trusted, the results suggest that companies with younger equipment typically invested more heavily.[1]

5   The significance and limitations of the regression results

The results favour the qualitative conclusion that investment has been influenced by companies' internal finance in the late sixties and early seventies: the depreciation variable, which represents both the major component of internal finance (the ability to invest) and the one free

---

[1] There are many respects in which this empirical work has been modelled on that of Meyer and Kuh; and, although their results related to another country (the US) and a different period (the late forties), they are often similar to those reported here. They accord in particular in finding a relatively weak association between investment and liquidity stocks (albeit differently defined) and an often negative association between investment and the indicator of the capital stock's age. However, the most significant similarity for the special issue at stake here – the role of the savings squeeze in restraining investment – was their general opinion that the 'conclusions...converge in their emphasis upon the importance of internal liquidity [flows]' (p 190). But the results presented here considerably strengthen the basis for such conclusions. The partial correlation coefficient between investment and depreciation was significantly greater than zero at the 5 per cent level in 12 of 72 industry-years in Meyer and Kuh's study, whereas the parallel result in this analysis held for 61 of 90 industry-years. And their partial correlation between investment and profits, which, in years of low inflation and stock appreciation and of consequent close association between profits and retentions, corresponds reasonably with the disposable retentions result provided here, passed the same test in 17 of 75 industry-years compared with 39 out of 90 here.

of any element of the incentive to invest, was strongly and positively associated with investment spending. It would, however, be premature to infer more precise conclusions from the results – for instance on the form of the relationship between cash flow and investment or on a quantitative estimate of the relationship. This is because a number of problems of interpretation remain.

The first problem concerns the crude form of relationship specified between cash flow and investment. The model adopted here implies that £x of cash flow are sufficient to elicit £1 of investment, but are not necessary: if £x of extra internal finance are earned, investment will rise by a pound; but, according to the model, a pound increase in investment might equally be elicited by a rise in sales with finance unchanged. An alternative specification would make retentions a necessary but not a sufficient condition of investment: the desired level of investment would be established on the basis of the physical variables (incentives) but would be undertaken only if certain financial conditions were satisfied.[1] That retention finance may have this restraining rather than an active role is suggested by two features of the present results. First, the coefficients for different years of the same industry are pretty unstable; and, secondly, the positive association between investment and internal finance is noticeably more marked in years and industries when such finance was in relatively short supply. These features are consistent with the view that it was the physical variables which determined desired investment; but that actual investment was in some industry-years constrained by finance – with the result that the 'true' relationship between desired investment and the physical variables was not reflected in the coefficients actually estimated, whilst the observed relation between investment and finance changed from year to year according to whether or not finance was exerting a restraining role.

Considerations of this sort have led some commentators to suggest that internal funds will affect not the desired capital stock but the speed of adjustment from the actual to the desired capital stock.[2] The effect of a savings shortage might then be to delay but not to cut investment. This suggestion is very plausible at the aggregate level for a closed economy. However, two qualifications are worth mentioning. First, at the micro level, a firm which hesitates to invest to meet the

---

[1] J G Meeks (1974) discusses possible inter-relations of necessary and sufficient conditions in economic causation.
[2] See Coen (1971).

growth of its market may find that a competitor who is not experiencing cash flow difficulties undertakes the investment instead, with the result that the investment opportunity has escaped the first firm by the time its cash flow recovers. This process would then lead to cuts in investment for some firms; though, as investment would be redistributed to its competitors, aggregate investment would be unaffected. But then again, the same process could develop at the national level for an open economy. Suppose that the growth of a particular international market meant that both home and overseas producers could profitably expand their capacity, but that home producers faced a cash flow problem – for reasons peculiar to the home economy. If the home producers held back, the foreign ones which were unaffected by liquidity problems might well supply the investment warranted by the market's growth. This redistribution of investment would then mean a cut for the home economy (though not for the world).

There are two other international aspects of the investment decision which add further complication. First, multinational production means that foreign companies with plants in Britain and British companies with plants overseas may have injections of cash available from their overseas operations should domestic cash flow be restricted at a time when domestic investment prospects are favourable. The potential significance of this mechanism is illustrated by the fact that, according to our preliminary estimates, the top 100 members of the Department of Industry quoted company population derived some 25 per cent of their profit from overseas in 1976 (this percentage having risen from 15 per cent in 1968). Within the economy those companies which have access to this source of internal funds may gain from a redistribution of investment at the expense of companies confined to the home economy.[1]

This suggests the second complication introduced by international factors: the possibility of footloose multinationals switching investment from one country to another in response to differences in local profit rates. For firms serving international markets, the considerations when assessing the incentive to invest in Britain may include not just whether investment in Britain offers a historically high return and one well in

[1] Just as there can be injections into the UK of cash flow from foreign divisions of the multinational, so also of course there can be leakages. And investment in a foreign country which would have been restrained for lack of domestic internal finance might be saved by retentions generated in the UK.

excess of the cost of capital but also whether it exceeds the rate obtainable from an overseas location.[1]

These international complications apart, the cross-section regression estimates might be subject to a further difficulty arising from persistent differences in performance between firms. It could be argued that these measures of statistical association do not represent the impact of one variable upon the other for the representative firm but rather reflect the fact that some firms will always score more highly on most of the variables, 'dependent' and 'independent', than their less proficient brethren. Thus, on this account, a high performance firm will persistently be more profitable, extract more output from its capital stock, and expand its capital stock faster than the average firm in the industry; but the inter-firm differences in these variables may be no guide to the individual firm's investment behaviour over time. One of this paper's findings is consistent with this view, namely that firms with an older capital stock tend to invest less heavily than average.[2] But the association that is less readily explained away along these lines is that between investment and depreciation provisions: it is not at all clear why a more proficient firm should have higher depreciation provisions in relation to its capital stock. Nevertheless, this general objection to the cross-section approach cautions against slipping too readily from cross-section results to conclusions for changes over time.

Because of the many difficulties of interpretation, then, while this preliminary study does point to the qualitative conclusion that investment was influenced by companies' internal finance in the late sixties and early seventies, it makes no claim to establish a quantitative measure of the impact of cash flow.

---

[1] And on the evidence of the McCracken Committee (1977) Britain would not emerge very favourably from such a comparison.

These two international complications raise questions for exchange rate policy. For an increase in the exchange rate creates a double incentive for UK companies to switch investment abroad: it makes overseas production more competitive with British on international markets; and it also means that a given sum of sterling retentions would finance more investment abroad in relation to investment in Britain. Moreover, totally indigenous producers suffer the same disincentive to produce in Britain whilst enjoying no insulation from cash flow difficulties when the high exchange rate depresses profits earned from domestic production.

[2] And the weak relation between investment and cash balances may be partly because more proficient firms tolerate less slack in managing their cash balances.

References

Bacon, R. and Eltis, W. *Britain's Economic Problem: Too Few Producers;* Macmillan, 1976.

Bain, A. D. *The Control of the Money Supply*; Penguin, 1970.

Baumol, W. J. *The Stock Market and Economic Efficiency*; Fordham U. P., 1965.

Berle, A. A. and Means, G. *The Modern Corporation and Private Property*; New York, 1932.

Central Statistical Office. 'Structure of company financing'; *Economic Trends.* September, 1975.

Central Statistical Office. *National Income and Expenditure*; HMSO, 1979.

Clark, T. A. and Williams, N. P. 'Measures of real profitability'; *Bank of England Quarterly Bulletin*, December, 1978.

Coen, in Fromm, ed., *Tax Incentives and Capital Spending*; Brookings, 1971.

Coutts, K., Godley, W. and Nordhaus, W. *Industrial Pricing in the United Kingdom*; Cambridge U. P., 1978.

Cripps, T. F., Fetherston, M. and Godley, W. A. H. 'Public expenditure and the management of the economy'; Appendix, *Ninth Report from the Expenditure Committee.* HMSO, 1974.

Davis, E. W. and Yeomans, K. A. *Company Finance and the Capital Market*; Cambridge U. P., 1974.

Dept. of Industry. *Business Monitor, M3: Company Finance*; 1971-.

Dimsdale, N. H. and Glyn, A. J. 'Investment in British industry – a cross-sectional approach'; *Bulletin of Oxford Institute of Statistics*, 1971.

Domar, E. D. 'Depreciation, replacement and growth'; *Economic Journal*, 1953.

Eatwell, J. L. 'On the proposed reform of corporation tax'; *Bulletin of Oxford Institute of Statistics*, 1971.

Flemming(a), J. S., Price, L. D. D. and Ingram, D. H. A. 'Trends in company profitability'; *Bank of England Quarterly Bulletin*, March, 1976.

Flemming, J. S., Price, L. D. D. and Byers, S. A. 'The cost of capital, finance and investment'; *Bank of England Quarterly Bulletin*, June, 1976.

Galbraith, J. K. *The New Industrial State*; London: Andre Deutsch. Revised Edition, 1972.

Institute of Chartered Accountants. *Survey of Published Accounts, 1970–71*; London: Institute of Chartered Accountants, 1972.

Kaldor, N. 'The economic effects of alternative systems of corporation tax'; Evidence in the *Report of the Select Committee on Corporation Tax*, House of Commons Paper 622. HMSO, 1971.

Kalecki, M. 'The principle of increasing risk'; *Economica*, 1937.

Keynes, J. M. *The General Theory of Employment, Interest and Money*; Macmillan, 1936.

King, M. A. 'The UK profits crisis: myth or reality?'; *Economic Journal*, 1975.

King, M. A. *Public Policy and the Corporation*; Chapman and Hall, 1977.

Kuh, E. *Capital Stock Growth: A Micro-Econometric Approach*; North Holland, 1963.

Matthews, R. C. O. *The Trade Cycle*; Cambridge U.P., 1959.

McCracken Committee. *Towards Full Employment and Price Stability*; OECD, 1977.

Meeks, G. 'Profit illusion'; *Bulletin of Oxford Institute of Statistics*, 1974.

Meeks, G. *The Profits and Growth of U.K. Companies*; Ph.D. Thesis, University of Edinburgh, 1975.

Meeks, G. *Disappointing Marriage: A Study of the Gains from Merger*; Cambridge U.P., 1977.

Meeks, G. and Whittington, G. *The Financing of Quoted Companies in the United Kingdom*; Background Paper No 1, Royal Commission on the Distribution of Income and Wealth. HMSO, 1976.

Meeks, J. G. 'INUS conditions in economics'; Mimeo, Cambridge, 1974.

Meyer, J. R. and Kuh, E. *The Investment Decision*; Harvard U.P., 1959.

Midland Bank. 'Another poor year for new capital issues'; *Midland Bank Review*, 1975.

National Institute of Economic and Social Research. *Company Income and Finance; 1949–53*, 1956.

Neild, R. R. *Pricing and Employment in the Trade Cycle*; Cambridge U.P., 1963.

Nickell, S. J. *The Investment Decisions of Firms*; Cambridge U.P./Nisbet, 1978.

Nyman, S. and Silberston, A. 'The ownership and control of industry'; *Oxford Economic Papers*, 1978.

Panic, M. and Close, R. E. 'Profitability of British manufacturing industry'; *Lloyds Bank Review*, 1973.

Radcliffe Report. *Committee on the Working of the Monetary System*; Cmnd. 827. London: HMSO, 1959.

Roe, A. R. 'The case for flow of funds and national balance sheet accounts'; *Economic Journal*, 1973.

Royal Commission. *Report No 2 of the Royal Commission on the Distribution of Income and Wealth*; HMSO, 1975.

Salter, W. E. G. *Productivity and Technical Change* (second edition); Cambridge U.P., 1966.

Surrey, M. J. C. *The Analysis and Forecasting of the British Economy*; N.I.E.S.R., 1971.

Tew, B. 'The finance of investment'; *Oxford Economic Papers*, 1952.

Wood, A. J. B. *A Theory of Profits*; Cambridge U.P., 1975.

Comment
by G Wenban-Smith

General

Dr Meeks' paper sets out to re-examine the question of whether the
volume of liquid assets available to a firm has any influence on its
current fixed investment expenditure. The apparently obvious
proposition that purchases of capital goods depend on the volume of
available cash has proved hard to verify in previous econometric
analyses of the company sector, possibly because in aggregate time
series data, profits, cash flow and output have tended to move
together. Dr Meeks argues that a number of factors, including changes
in inflation and investment rates, may have interrupted the earlier
contemporaneous movement of profits and output and that cross-
section analysis may show up more clearly the different effects of sales
(accelerator principle), profits, and liquidity or cash flow on
investment plans.

Firms need to invest to maintain the capital stock. Additional
investment will be required to expand capacity in the face of
anticipated rising demand. The accelerator principle has been used
with some success in the past to 'explain' net investment, and a recent
example of this is the equation derived by Bean (1979) in which fixed
investment expenditures have been fitted to past volumes of output via
a complex lag structure. While no one would claim that output, or
even expected output, is the only influence on investment decisions,
the role of other factors such as cash flow in determining investment
has never been clear. Firms presumably would not spend money on
investment goods for which they had no use, however much spare
liquidity they had. We may therefore be looking for an asymmetric
relationship in which shortages of internal finance restrict investment
temporarily, or even defer it indefinitely, but surpluses do not
necessarily imply expenditures. Aggregate data may not be suitable for
looking into this kind of question, since large divergences between the
supply of funds and current (as a proxy for expected) output are
perhaps more likely to be observed at the company level.

The reason that cash flow effects may be more easily identified in
recent data is that inflation may have broken the link between output
and the volume of cash flow, so that output effects may no longer
hide the influence of liquidity. The first way in which this might
happen is that directors may not be prepared to tell shareholders that
stock appreciation, which is included in conventional profits under

historic cost accounting, is not available for distribution as dividends or expenditure on investment. The greater awareness of the effects of inflation which developed in the seventies and the change to current cost accounting will to some extent have reduced (though not eliminated) the risk of this happening. Higher interest charges on loans to cover higher nominal stockholding costs might also have the effect of reducing the amount of cash available for investment, especially if they were accompanied by reduced availability of credit. The Domar replacement cost-depreciation provision relationship must be extremely complex in a world of quickly changing prices, and anyway, appeared to have only a small effect as calculated by Dr Meeks for the period he was interested in. These inflation effects, if valid, would have been much more marked in the seventies, (not covered by Dr Meeks' calculations). In view of the changes which have taken place since 1971, the last year of his data, Dr Meeks' findings may not be directly relevant to policy in the eighties.

Empirical results

Going on to the empirical work, the first problem, which is common to all investment analyses, is that information is only available for gross investment, which includes expenditure on assets to maintain the capital stock at its given capacity. This is often allowed for in time series work by introducing ($\delta \times$ capital stock in the previous period) on the right hand side of the equation, as an estimate of replacement investment. (δ = rate of depreciation of the capital stock.) In aggregate, replacement investment is estimated (by the CSO perpetual inventory model) to be around half of gross investment, and somewhat more in some industries. In individual firms, however, the proportion is likely to be rather variable from year to year, which may make the interpretation of empirical work more difficult. It may be argued that the volume of replacement investment is influenced to some extent by the same factors which determine net investment; the two should still be modelled separately however, because of probable differences in their reaction to changes in economic conditions.

  The lack of specific modelling of the variables according to expected behavioural rules in Dr Meeks' analysis means that the values of the coefficients cannot be easily interpreted by reference to the structure of the equation. The meaning attached to the coefficients is not clear, and the results have been discussed only in terms of the significance of the variables and their sign, not their size. If the model were specified as one in which the optimal size of the capital stock is determined using the accelerator principle, and in which the path of adjustment to the optimal capital stock is dependent on the cash flow variables then the coefficients could be used to derive the associated elasticities. A further problem is that the treatment of heteroscedasticity does not appear to have been verified by the appropriate tests (see Johnston 1972, p 214); and, while the appropriate size deflator is assumed to be the level of the capital stock, it does not look as though the original model has been deflated throughout. With this treatment it is not possible to go back to the original equation to obtain an analysis of variance.

The concise presentation of the results makes it difficult to get an idea of how far different behaviour was observed in different industries, and although significant and positive coefficients are desirable, the complete regression results are needed to assess their importance. A particular worry about the success of the depreciation provisions as an explanatory variable is the probability of some accounting identity being involved. For example, Dr Meeks posits a behavioural relationship:

$GI_t = \ldots . + b_6 D_t + \ldots .$; but there is also a definitional relationship:
$D_t = a_1 GI_t + a_2 GI_{t-1} + \ldots .$,

where a_1 is the proportion of gross investment written off in the current year, a_2 is the proportion written off in the second year, and so on. This simultaneity suggests that cross-section analysis is not entirely suitable for this subject, a proposition borne out by the complete absence of influence of the sales variables. The real problem, I think, is that decisions about investment involve expectations about the future and dynamic interaction between the variables. Static analysis cannot be used to investigate these. Planned investment expenditure must be related to projected sales and/or profits (apart from monopolistic barriers to entry, etc. considerations); cash flow factors are likely to affect the timing of actual investment expenditures in the short-term, and possibly achieved volumes of investment in the longer run, and these dynamic influences cannot be identified in cross-section data.

Ideally, it would be most fruitful to use disaggregated time series data for the analysis of the effect of liquidity on actual investment expenditures. Possibly, some use could be made of the techniques of pooling cross-section and time-series data. Amongst the additional factors to be borne in mind when analysing data from the seventies would be the well known use of investment to defer tax payments (because expenditure on capital goods can be set against taxable profits) and the increase in the practice of leasing. The latter is especially important in some industries (eg chemicals, food, drink and tobacco), and needs to be taken into account in a broad framework of investment, finance, and tax liability considerations. Leasing may become increasingly significant for technical reasons too.

In conclusion, Dr Meeks' results are interesting in that they suggest that liquidity has a discernible effect on the volume of investment. Further work involving the use of a more sophisticated model, and an extension of the sample period to more recent years might add further to our understanding of this aspect of company behaviour.

References

Bean, C. 'An econometric model of manufacturing investment in the UK'; *Government Economic Service Working Paper*, No 29, 1979

Johnston, J. *Econometric Methods;* Second Edition, McGraw-Hill, 1972.

Investments and profits in the industrial and commercial sector

by G J Anderson

This paper is the result of bringing together several different strands of research pursued by the author which have each benefitted from the helpful comments of several people. Special mention should be made of the SSRC Economic Modelling and Economic Theory Study Groups and Workshops at Birmingham, LSE, Manchester and Southampton.

Summary

Much controversy surrounds the role of profits and finance in models of investment behaviour partly because most existing models, if they accommodate financial factors at all, do so through the inclusion of real interest rates. The model presented in this paper, relating to the industrial and commercial sector, allows financial factors to play a more explicit role in the investment expenditure process. It consists of several equations and identities cast in nominal terms and its central features are an investment expenditure equation depending upon output and financial variables and equations determining the internal financing decision (profit retentions) and the external financing decisions (loans and share issues).

The model is still in the development stage and exhibits some shortcomings in failing to capture adequately some short run cyclical behaviour. However its long run features, being relatively stable, provide some insight into the relationship between investment expenditures and tax and interest payments, output and other financial variables. One of the more important findings is that while profits have a significant impact on the flow of investment expenditures, this impact is relatively small compared with a change in profits associated with a change in output. This would suggest that investment would be more successfully stimulated by policies which increased aggregate demand (and hence output) than by merely attempting to raise overall profitability.

1 Introduction

The relationship between investment and profits has long been a contentious issue in the applied econometric literature on the subject. Most empirical studies of aggregate investment expenditures view the investment decision in a single equation framework (notable exceptions to this being Eisner and Nadiri (1969) and Dhrymes and Kurz (1965)) imposing a relationship between investment and profits *a priori* via the choice of the underlying technological relationship to be used in the theoretical formulation. Such an approach does not afford the opportunity of assessing the empirical validity of such a relationship which would contribute to the resolution of some of the issues.

In a series of papers (Anderson (1980) (1980a) (1980b) (1980c) (1980d)), the author has developed a model of the investment expenditure/financing behaviour of the Industrial and Commercial Sector of the United Kingdom in a framework which facilitates the analysis of the impact of profits. Whilst the model is not yet complete, it is felt that it provides some insight to the complex relationships that are embedded, and to some extent hidden, in the more usual approaches. This is because in conventional neo-classical models (with a few exceptions) any impact that profits have is indirectly captured via the relative price term rather than explicitly modelled.

Section 2 of this paper discusses the relationship between the model herein presented and those to be found in the extant literature. The structure of the model is described in Section 3 and its properties are discussed in Section 4, together with its implications for the investment/profits relationship. Some conclusions are drawn in Section 5.

2 Theoretical Framework

Most studies of investment in the neo-classical framework are based upon a Cobb Douglas production function having a long run equilibrium gross investment expenditure equation of the form:[1]

$$I(t) = \frac{(\delta(t) + g(t))\, \alpha(t)\, p(t)\, Q(t)}{(1 + g(t))q(t)\, (\delta(t) + r(t) - \dot{z}(t))\, \dfrac{(1 - v(t))}{(1 - u(t))}} \qquad 2.1$$

In this formulation I is gross investment expenditures in real terms, p: price of output, Q: level of output, δ: capital deterioration rate, g: output growth rate, α: the capital factor share, r: the market rate of interest, $\dot{z}$: an adjustment factor transforming the market rate of interest to the 'real' rate, q: the price of investment goods, v: the discounted value of tax savings due to investment incentives expressed as a proportion of the price of capital goods, u: the corporate tax rate, all of these prevailing and having been expected to prevail at period t.[2]

---

[1] This may be obtained by observing that the equilibrium condition for capital stock is that the marginal productivity of capital equals the real user cost of capital $\dfrac{c(t)}{p(t)}$. From a Cobb Douglas production function, $Q(t) = AE(t)^{1-\alpha(t)} K(t)^{\alpha(t)}$ (where E(t) represents the stock of labour) the equilibrium capital stock may be obtained as $K^*(t) = \alpha(t)\, \dfrac{p(t)}{c(t)}\, Q(t)$. In long run constant relative price growth equilibrium (growth measured in terms of output), $Q(t) = (1 + g) Q(t - 1)$ and capital stock in the previous period would have been at the equilibrium value for that period. Hence equilibrium gross investment is given by $I(t) = K^*(t) - K^*(t - 1)(1 - \delta)$ which by substitution yields 2.1 where the other terms in the expression make explicit the influence of various factors in the opportunity cost of capital term c(t).

[2] See for example Jorgenson and Stephenson (1967) (1967a), Hall and Jorgenson (1967) (1969) (1971), Jorgenson and Seibert (1968), Bischoff (1971) and Ando et al (1974).

What is important for the issues at hand is that in much of the extant literature $\delta(t)$ and $\alpha(t)$ are assumed constant for all t. Whilst much has been said of the former assumption,[1] little has been said of the latter with regard to its empirical validity. To fix ideas, Chart 1 indicates the profile of gross profits per unit of revenue for the period 1964 Q1 to 1977 Q2 for the Industrial and Commercial Sector. Fluctuations due to seasonal variation have been eliminated by basing the diagram on fourth order moving averages of an index of profits per unit of output using 1964 as a base year of 1. An index is used rather than actual values since no quarterly series of gross revenues is available for the sector and the calculations are based upon an index of gross revenue for the sector calculated by the author (see Appendix 1). For comparison an index of investment expenditures per unit of output is also provided on the same basis. As may be seen from the chart there is a marked similarity between the two profiles, peaks and troughs of the profit share series preceding the investment series by between three and six quarters. Other series such as net of tax profits and net of stock appreciation profits display the same characteristics, the essential point being that the share of profits does not appear to be constant over time, indeed it appears that the variation in these series is relatively systematic.

In a state of equilibrium, which may be defined as a situation in which expectations about the time paths of the variables in 2.1 are fulfilled and have been so for a considerable period of time (and for simplicity in which $\dot{z}(t) = 0$), 2.1 may be re-arranged as:

$$q(t)I(t) = \alpha(t)p(t)Q(t)(1 - u(t))\frac{(1 + g(t)/\delta(t))}{1 + g(t)} \qquad 2.2$$
$$+ q(t)I(t)v(t) - r(t)q(t)(1 - v(t))K(t)$$

where K(t) is a measure of the capital stock. Since in equilibrium q(t) will be such that $q(t)(1 - v(t)) K(t)$ is equal to the nominal value of the companies' total assets, it may be shown that 2.2 reduces to an equation which states:

$$q(t) I(t) = PR(t) + EF(t) \qquad 2.3$$

where PR(t) represents profit retentions and EF(t) represents new external finance and q(t) I(t) represents gross investment expenditures. Furthermore when g(t) = 0, EF(t) = 0 (see Anderson (1980a) for details). The equation has in effect been translated into a nominal

[1] See Feldstein and Foot (1971), Eisner (1972), Feldstein and Rothschild (1974) and Jorgenson (1974).

Chart 1: Indices of Profit Rate and Investment Rate per Unit of
Output (1964 = 1) for Industrial and Commercial Companies.

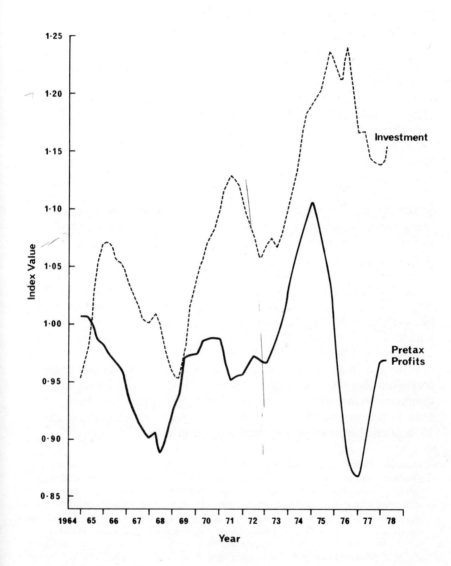

expenditure framework[1] and simply states that in long run equilibrium the sources and uses of funds will be equal. The essence of the model upon which this work is based is its description of the interplay between these sources and uses of funds.

The effect of financing on investment decisions

The way in which expenditures on investment goods are constrained in 2.3 is through the availability of internal and external finance. These two sources of finance are not independent in the sense that for a given rate of interest the amount of external finance is limited by the sector's ability to service the debt and this in turn is constrained by the appropriation of profits to dividend and interest payments and profit retentions respectively. It is via these constraints that factors such as taxation and interest charges have their impact. This highlights another feature of the model. What is critical for actual investment expenditure is effective tax and interest rates which are most accurately reflected by actual tax and interest payments rather than the nominal rates used in more conventional analysis. In as much as there is avoidance and evasion of payments or delays in payment the use of nominal prevailing rates is inappropriate.

From the preceding discussion if follows that an important aspect of the model is an explanation of the financing variables. Chart 2 will help to fix ideas in this regard since it indicates the time profile of the relative shares of the alternative sources of long term finance in the industrial and commercial sector. The exact definitions of the categories will be outlined in the next section. Broadly speaking, long-term finance may be divided into profit retentions, loans and share issues for cash. As may be seen, internal financing has been the dominant source of funds over the period, providing, on average, just over 70 per cent of the finance used, though, from mid-1972 to early 1975, loans began to play a more significant role.

---

[1] Working in terms of nominal rather than real values has a number of advantages. It avoids expressing dependent variables as non-linear functions of other dependent variables in the model and conveniently sidesteps some tricky statistical issues associated with such a structure. Aside from this practical advantage, it may be argued that all the signals that are received and transmitted and the responses to those signals are perceived in current value terms. Translation into real values involves assumptions that the statistically constructed price vectors involved in the translation are those perceived by the decision makers which may not be supportable in the short run (see Deaton (1978)). Working in terms of nominal expenditures avoids this problem whilst preserving the model's ability to capture the testable predictions of economic theory. It does however present the possibility of some statistical problems concerning heteroskedastic error processes, which in fact fail to arise (see Anderson (1980a) (1980b)).

Chart 2 : Relative Proportion of Profit Retentions, Loans, and Share Issues as a Source of New Finance in Industrial and Commercial Companies (based on four quarter moving average).

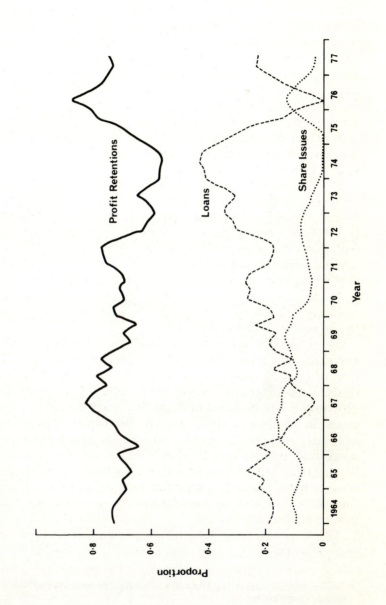

Economic theory is remarkably barren on the issue of what
determines the structure of financing; indeed there is a substantial
body of literature associated with the seminal work of Modigliani and
Miller (1956) which suggests that as far as the cost of capital is
concerned the structure of finance is of no consequence. King (1977)
has shown that the necessary and sufficient condition for this result is
that the prices of goods purchased now by shareholders for delivery at
any time contingent upon a given state of the world are independent of
the firm's structure of finance. It can be shown that various conditions
such as the existence of bankruptcy or the lack of sufficient markets to
span the set of contingencies will violate this independence condition
and the wealth of literature on 'Modigliani-Miller' type theorems[1] are
in effect constructions to this end.

So far as modelling the financial equations is concerned, reliance has
been placed upon the modification of a basic model attributable to
Lintner (1956) for the internal financing decision (see Anderson
(1980b)) and upon a 'two stage financing requirement/gearing' model
outlined in Anderson (1980c) for the external financing decision. The
internal financing decision of firms has attracted a considerable
applied literature in the wake of Lintner's work[2] though to the
author's knowledge the external financing decision has attracted
relatively little attention (which may be a reflection of its relative
importance as a source of finance!).

One strand that should be acknowledged is on the profitability of
alternative sources of finance. The proposition in dispute is that
internal financing, in not being subject to the discipline of the market,
tends to encourage less efficient use of funds. Support for the
proposition is to be found in Baumol *et al* (1970) and to a qualified
extend in Whittington (1973) whereas the contrary view is to be found
in Brealey *et al* (1977).[3] At best the issue can only be said to be
unresolved, opening up a Pandora's Box of side issues such as: do
firms finance expenditures on a piecemeal basis?; in which case are
some projects wholly externally financed and some wholly internally
financed?; if so what has happened to the notion of opportunity cost
in such behaviour?

As will be seen from the structure of the model to be presented in
this paper, the market does seem to exercise a discipline but the

---

[1] See for example Archer and D'Ambrosio (1967), Diamond (1967), Nickell (1978),
Stiglitz (1969) (1974).

[2] See for example Dhrymes and Kurz (1963), Fama (1974), Fama and Bibiak (1968),
Feldstein (1970), Fisher (1970), Turnovsky (1967) and King (1977) for a review.

[3] See also Friend and Husic (1973) Racette (1973) and reply by Baumol *et al* (1973).

direction of causality is somewhat different. The contention here is that greater profitability, resulting in an expansion of dividends, encourages firms to expose themselves to the market via issuing shares for cash. This is presumably so because, at that stage, firms are able to back up claims for the future prosperity of the company with a suitable recent record of profitability. Such a story is consistent with the predictions of a developing literature on the role of dividends as a signalling instrument (see Bhattacharya (1979) and Ross (1977)).

Together with the investment expenditures equation and various identities implicit in the model these equations form the basis of a description of the investment and financing decisions of the Industrial and Commercial Sector which will be described in the next section.

3 The Model

Table 1 presents a listing of the model with attendant identities. Whilst full details of the development of the stochastic equations are available in the papers by the author cited above, a brief description of the theory underlying them follows in order to clarify the mechanics of the model.

3.1 LONG AND SHORT RUN INFLUENCES

Fundamental to the structure is a partition of the various sources of expenditure and finance into long and short run factors. This is because a basic premise in the modelling process is that the time path of the variables of interest characterise a set of responses to disequilibrium states which are characterised by inequality between the *long run* expenditure and financing variables.[1] Since in theory[2] the sources and uses of funds account is always balanced, identifying equilibria requires prior separation of short and long run influences. In this respect two accounting identities are of importance.

The first, the Appropriation Account, indicates equality between the sum of gross trading profits, rent and non-trading income and income from abroad and the sum of dividends, interest payments, profits due abroad, taxes on income and profit retentions. This account represents the result of the internal financing decision: the split of profits, after having satisfied various obligations, between dividend disbursions and saving. The impact of profitability is effectively channelled through

---

[1] Work by Davidson *et al* (1978), Hendry and von Ungurn Sternberg (1979) and Hendry and Anderson (1977) is characteristic of such an approach and has its roots in the work of Phillips (1954) (1957).

[2] In practice because of errors in data collection the account has a balancing item reflecting the sum of the errors.

Table 1 The Model Structure

Equation 1. Investment Expenditures

$((1 + .644L^2)(1 - L) + .626L + .338L^7 + .628L^9) IIC_t =$

$+ (7.080L(1 - L^4)L^2 + 9.256L^7 + 9.834L^8) OICP_t - 440.478$

$+ ((.028L - .062L^4)(1 - L) - .075L^6)INF_t - (462.981 + 212.244L)(1 - L)CTAX_t$

Equation 2. Profit Retentions

$((1 + .160L^2)(1 - L) + .750L)PR_t = (.717(1 - L^2) - .278(1 - L)^2L)GPNT_t$

$+ (.569 + .660L^2 + .237 L^5)ING_t + .154(1 - L)L^3 IVS_t$

$+ .637(1 - L^4)L CTAX_t - 167.093 SND_t - .889 OIP_t$

Equation 3. Loans

$((1 - .147L^3)(1 - L) + .382L - .157L^5)LNS_t = (1.882L^2(1 - L) + 1.745L^4)SHD_t + (-.299L^2(1 - L^2) - .376L^5)UKT_t$

$+ (-.124L^2(1 - L) + (.059 + .198DCCC)L^3)INFC_t - 1626.657(L - L^2)CTAX_t$

$- 110.007DUMI + 315.779 DCCC$

Equation 4. Share Issues

$(1 + .386L^4 + .458^9 - .227L^2(1 - L^3))SHD_t = .154 (L + L^2 + L^3 + L^4)DPOS_t + (-.025(L - L^3) + .067(1 - CTAX_t)L^4$

$+ .067(1 - CTAX_t)L^6)INF_t + ((-.359 + .809L^2)(1 - L^3)$

$- .402(2 - L^2 - L^5)L)OIP_t + 3.154L^4(1 - L)^4OICP_t + 35.785DUM2$

$GPNT_t = GP_t + NTI_t + IA_t - PDA_t - UKT_t$

$DPOS_t = GPNT_t - PR_t - OIP_t$

$FI_t = PR_t + IG_t + OCT_t + LNS_t + SHD_t - SA_t$

$ING_t = IIC_t - IG_t - OCT_t$

$INFC_t = (IIC_t - FI_t)(SDY_t - TBY_t(1 - CTAX_t))$

Table 1:
LEGEND (All variables relate to Industrial and Commercial Companies and are in current values unless otherwise stated).

IIC: Gross Investment Expenditures
PR: Profit Retentions
LNS: Loans and Mortgages
SHD: Share and Debenture issues for cash
OICP: Output
FI: Long Term Finance for Investment
GPNT: Gross Profits net of taxes
ING: Investment expenditures net of grants and other capital transfers
IVS: Increase in the value of stocks and work in progress
OIP: Interest payments on loans and mortgages
UKT: U.K. Tax payments
INFC: A measure of the riskiness of the financing burden
SDY: Share Dividend Yield
CTAX: Corporation Tax Rate
DPOS: Dividends paid on shares
GP: Gross Trading Profits
NTI: Non-Trading Income
IA: Income from Abroad
PDA: Profits Distributed Abroad
IG: Investment Grants
OCT: Capital Transfers
SA: Stock Appreciation
TBY: Treasury Bill Yield
DCCC: Competition and Credit Control Dummy (zero/one)
DUM2:   Dividend Restraint Dummy (zero/one)
SND: Steel Nationalization Dummy (zero/one)
DUMI: Temporary instability dummy, (zero/one)
L: The lag operator such that $Lx_t = x_{t-1}$, $L^2x_t = x_{t-2}$ etc.

this account and a satisfactory description of it is necessary in order to understand the nature of this impact.

The second identity relates to the Sources and Uses of Funds Account and states that there is equality between the sum of Profit Retentions (or Saving), Investment Grants, Loans, Shares Issues for Cash and Net Income from Overseas and the sum of Gross Domestic Fixed Capital Formation, Increases in the Value of Stocks and Work in Progress and the Net Acquisition of Financial Assets. Because of errors in reporting and data collection this account in practice carries a balancing or unidentified item. A fuller description of these accounts is available in CSO (1977) and in a much abridged form in Anderson (1980d).

As for the long run aspects of behaviour, it is assumed that on the expenditure side these are captured by Investment Expenditures and

Stock Appreciation and on the sources side they are captured by
Investment Grants (including other capital transfers), Profit
Retentions, Loans and Mortgages and Share and Debenture Issues for
Cash. This is very much an *ad hoc* separation in the sense that there
are undoubtedly as many short run elements in these variables as there
are long run features in the Net Acquisition of Financial Assets (which
includes Changes in Cash and Current Balances) and the Unidentified
Item which, by their exclusion from consideration, are deemed to be
purely short term financing variables. Similarly, it presupposes that the
long run element in the Increase in the Value of Stocks and Work in
Progress is characterised by Stock Appreciation, physical changes in
stocks representing purely short run phenomena and not posing a long
run financing problem.[1]

However, given this rather *ad hoc* separation, the long run financing
shortfall is defined as:

$$INF_t = IIC_t - IG_t - PR_t - LNS_t - SHD_t + SA_t \qquad 3.1$$

and in its various guises it serves to drive the model through time
causing the expansion of expenditures and attenuation of financing
when it is less than zero and the attenuation of investment and the
expansion of finance when it is greater than zero. Since, given the
Sources and Uses of Funds identity (ignoring the unidentified item),
this variable may be equated with changes in cash and current balances
plus physical changes in stocks, it has the alternative interpretation
that when firms are liquid they will expand expenditures and attenuate
new finance and vice versa when they are illiquid.[2]

The financing shortfall variable plays an important role in the
investment equation where it reflects the relative price effects normally
represented in investment equations by the term $p(t)/c(t)$ obtained by
rewriting 2.1 as:

$$I(t) = \frac{(\delta(t) + g(t))}{1 + g(t)} \frac{\alpha(t)\, p(t)\, Q(t)}{c(t)} \qquad 3.2$$

In addition it reflects variability of the share of profits $\alpha(t)$. The scale
effects $(((\delta(t) + g(t))Q(t)/(1 + g(t))$ in 3.2 above) are captured in the
nominal expenditure formulation by the inclusion of the value of
output as a separate argument in the equation.[3] Such a formulation

---

[1] An interesting discussion pertinent to this issue is given in King (1975).

[2] This interpretation permits drawing the analogy between the role of this variable in
the investment equation discussed below and the work on liquidity effects in
investment functions by Coen (1971).

[3] This does present some difficulties as acknowledged in Anderson (1980a) footnote 4,
and results in the inclusion of a constant term in the equation which turns out to be
of the expected sign and magnitude.

may be interpreted as accommodating the effects of a putty-clay technology where relative prices are allowed to have a slower dynamic impact on capacity because of the fixity of factor proportions associated with extant capacity stock. It is of interest to observe that the implicit long run adjustment coefficient on scale effects is .982 and the corresponding coefficient on the financial factors (relating to the impact of relative prices) is .044. This is much in accord with a putty-clay technology and provides a clue as to why the impact of profits on investment expenditures has been so difficult to capture. Since changes in profitability are simply the result of changes in relative prices and productivity which have such a small (though none-the-less significant) impact on investment expenditures it is not surprising that evidence of a relationship between investment and profits has been difficult to obtain.

3.2 INTERNAL FINANCING

The internal financing decision is represented by the profit retentions equation which has resulted from a modification of the familiar partial adjustment – equilibrium dividend payout ratio model. In the usual approach, target dividends are proportionate to some measure of profits, with slow adjustment to the target resulting in the transitory components of profits being retained. In this model, retentions are proportionate to investment expenditure flows and interest payments in the long run, whilst changes in the value of stocks and work in progress, gross profits net of taxes and tax rates are found to have a transitory effect upon the relationship. Given the not unreasonable assumption of proportionality between dividend disbursements and interest payments it is possible to show that this is consistent with the long run structure of the Lintner model whilst permitting investment expenditure flows to have an influence on the decision in the short run.

Such a formulation is consistent with, though does not constitute irrefutable support for, worlds in which the constant capital stock deterioration assumption is invalid, in which there was not perfect sub-stitution between the equities of firms[1] and in which the Modigliani-Miller theorem is invalid. It also highlights the dynamically simultaneous character of the investment and financing decision in that, over time, investment expenditures influence the retentions behaviour and, via the financing shortfall variable, retentions influence the flow of investment expenditures.

---

[1] See Nickell (1978) for the implications of such a situation and evidence cited in Wood (1975) for the presence of the 'clientele' phenomenon characteristic of such a situation.

3.3 EXTERNAL FINANCING

The external financing decision is characterised by two equations, the Loans equation representing the acquisition of loans, mortgages and hire purchase agreements and the Share issues equation representing the issue of shares and debentures for cash. The distinction is based upon the priority that a particular financing instrument has in being serviced out of a firm's activity and thus relates to the degree of risk associated with the particular instrument of debt. In this context it will be convenient to consider Loans and Share issues as non-risk and risk finance respectively.

The equations are based upon the notion of a stable ratio between risk and non-risk finance (bearing a close resemblance to the gearing ratio commonly discussed in the financial accounting literature) that is a simple function of a measure of the degree of risk. The degree of risk is in turn related, at the micro level, to the threat of bankruptcy which may be loosely defined as the firm being unable to meet its fixed interest charges. Several factors will impinge upon this condition: for example, the magnitude and stability of gross profit flows, the growth rate of the firm's net revenues, the market environment that the firm enjoys and the nature of the capital stock that the firm employs in terms of its closeness to the final product (this is allied to the 'Austrian' notion of the roundaboutness of capital).

At the aggregate level, difficulties arise in attempting to capture many of these features. Firstly, there is a problem of measuring the notion of risk. Secondly, there is a problem of discriminating between supply and demand responses to changing levels of risk. The market evaluation of risk is represented here by the difference between the tax adjusted yield on equities and some safe yield (say that on bonds). Whilst this is an imperfect measure, it does present a practical solution to the problem. In addition it was found to work very well in conjunction with a measure of the degree of liquidity – the now familiar financing shortfall variable. Thus the risk measure used was the product of the sector's financing shortfall and the market's evaluation of risk.

Given this measure, it is not clear what its impact will be since borrowers' and lenders' attitudes will differ. *Ceteris paribus*, borrowers will be disposed towards a higher debt/equity ratio given higher levels of risk because of the higher cost of risk finance. On the other hand, lenders will be disposed toward lower debt/equity ratios which would make the so-called 'riskless' return on their loans more secure. The introduction of Competition and Credit Control policy, signalled in the model by a dummy variable entered in its own right and applied to the risk variable, served to indicate that supply considerations predominated over the sample period except during the period of the policy when borrowers' attitudes had a significant impact. This also lends support to the institutional structure implicit in the model which characterises suppliers of loans as being unwilling to lend to firms whose gearing diverges to a significant degree from the appropriate norm. Thus the gearing ratio operates in the loans equation, requiring that the necessary risk finance be acquired before new loans are obtained.

The impact of taxation and tax payments is also a complex question. King (1974) discusses the theoretical framework of the financing choice based upon the tax determined opportunity cost of alternative sources of finance. Unfortunately, announced rates are not effective rates and changes in tax structure change the risk associated with a given gross income stream. Thus whilst an increase in taxation increases the relative attractiveness of loans (interest charges on loans being tax deductible) it is more likely to decrease attractiveness in terms of lenders' risk and to reduce demand for finance in general because of the income effects.

Since the gearing and associated risk effects are captured in the loans equation, it remains for the share issues equation to accommodate the 'scale' or 'financing requirement' effects. As may be recalled from equation 2.3 external financing is primarily associated with expansion investment. Thus it is to be expected that share issues will be predominantly related to growth signals as perceived by the aggregate of agents. In the context of the model, these signals stem from three major sources: the time path of dividend distributions, changes in the sector's revenues and persistent financial shortfalls. The latter two need little explanation though some brief discussion of the dividend disbursion signal may be appropriate.

Most of the theoretical literature seems to point to their being no reason to distribute dividends at all, primarily because of the tax advantages of retaining earnings or debt financing (see King (1974), (1978)). However, the role of dividends as a signalling instrument in indicating improvements in future income flows would suggest an expansion of the risk finance base (ie shares) in order that the gearing ratio be maintained. Hence a positive relationship between share issues and dividends is observed which runs counter to the traditional view of dividends being treated in a similar fashion to interest rates. However, if the firm expands dividend disbursements and the market revalues its shares accordingly, share issues will be positively related to dividends since it will be most inexpensive to issue new shares when dividends are high (see Wood (1975) p.59). This view should be distinguished from that expounded in work by Baumol *et al* and Whittington cited earlier since the contention here is that greater profitability encourages firms to expose themselves to the discipline of the market rather than vice versa.

4   Results

4.1   GENERAL

The equations were estimated using single equation instrumental variable techniques and the estimates together with associated statistics are provided in Appendix 2. The problem of identification in models developed in this fashion is discussed in Anderson (1980d). It suffices to say that the model satisfies the identification criteria proposed in the literature (see Hatanaka (1975)). A difficult aspect of piecemeal dynamic simultaneous equation modelling is the development of sensible distributed lag functions associated with the exogenous variables in the system. This arises because the dynamics in each equation are formulated without reference to those on other equations; hence there are no restrictions imposed to ensure that the dynamic structures are compatible. Such a procedure could well lead to a model which is dynamically unstable in the sense that the adjustment path of the endogenous variables is divergent rather than convergent.

An approach to checking the model for this problem is to calculate the control solution of the model and compare it with the realised values of the endogenous variable. The control solution uses the actual values of the dependent variables at the beginning of the estimation period as starting values and then uses the realised values of the exogenous variables but the computed values of the lagged endogenous variables to predict the path of the endogenous variables over the estimation period. The comparison of the control solution and realised values of the endogenous variables is a strong test of model specification being very much like a prediction test over a number of time periods, each prediction being conditioned upon previous predictions rather than realised values of the endogenous variables.

Graphs 1 to 4 present comparisons of the Realised and Dynamic Control Solutions of variables representing investment expenditures, profit retentions, loans and share issues. It is clear that the long run features of the theory underlying the data generation process are accommodated quite well by the model. Indeed one feature that has been notable throughout all the stages of the development of the

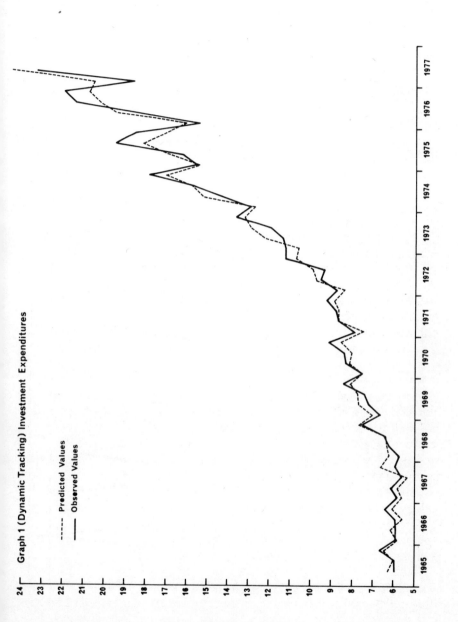

Graph 1 (Dynamic Tracking) Investment Expenditures

---- Predicted Values
—— Observed Values

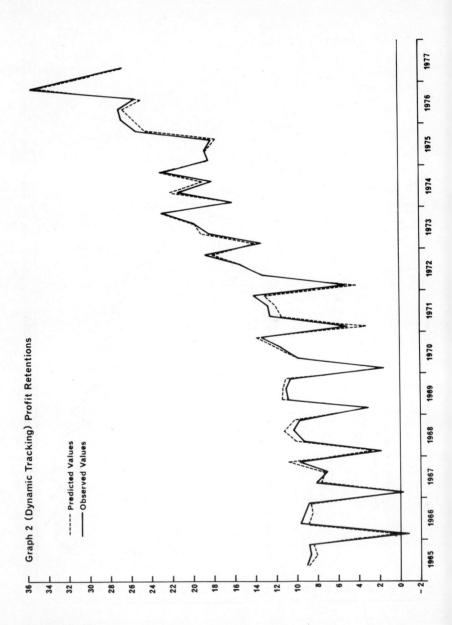

Graph 2 (Dynamic Tracking) Profit Retentions

----- Predicted Values
——— Observed Values

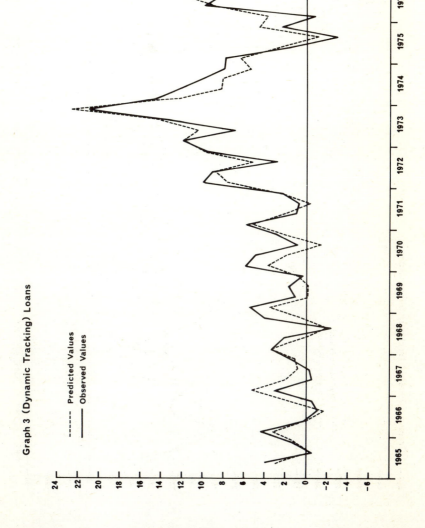

Graph 3 (Dynamic Tracking) Loans

----- Predicted Values
—— Observed Values

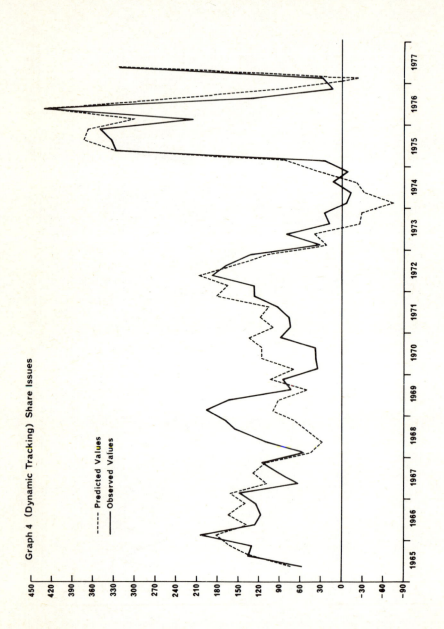

Graph 4 (Dynamic Tracking) Share Issues

Table 2 Long run model properties

	IIC	PR	LNS	SHD	DPOS	SND	CNST	OICP	UKT	IG	SA	OIP	GP	DCCC	DUM1	DUM2		
Sample Averages	991.655	1160.3	438.638	114.931	359.986	1	1	112.959	254.8	80.5517	353.114	377.971	2144.06	1	1	1		
	1.721	-.075	-.075	-.075	0.0	0.0	440.478	19.09	0	.075	-.075	0.0	0.0	0.0	0.0	0.0	IIC	Long Run Structure*
	-1.465	.750	0.0	0.0	0.0	-167.093	0.0	0.0	0.0	-1.465	0.0	-.889	0.0	0.0	0.0	0.0	PR	
	-.076	.075	.3	-1.668	0.0	0.0	0.0	0.0	-.376	.076	-.076	0.0	0.0	315.779	110.007	0.0	LNS	
	-.08	.08	.08	1.924	-.616	0.0	0.0	0.0	0.0	-.080	.080	0.0	0.0	0.0	0.0	35.785	SHD	
	0.0	1.0	0.0	0.0	1.0	0.0	0.0	0.0	-1.0	0.0	0.0	-1.0	1.0	0.0	0.0	0.0	DPOS	
						10.134	-237.537	10.295	-.108	.128	-.039	-.015	.069	33.141	11.545	4.008	IIC	Long Run Reduced Form**
						-202.995	-463.988	20.109	-.212	-1.703	-.077	-1.215	.135	64.735	22.552	7.829	PR	
						377.378	759.981	-32.937	-2.117	3.200	.108	.783	1.225	748.915	260.897	71.17	LNS	
						58.163	126.269	-5.477	-.160	.447	.063	.086	.223	-53.180	-18.526	12.975	SHD	
						202.995	463.988	-20.109	-.788	1.703	.077	.215	.865	-64.735	-22.551	-7.829	DPOS	
						.010	-.240	1.173	-.028	.010	-.014	-.006	.149	.033	.012	.004	IIC	Long Run Elasticities***
						.175	-.377	1.958	-.047	-.118	-.023	-.396	.249	.056	.019	.007	PR	
						-.860	1.733	-8.482	-1.230	.588	.087	.674	5.988	1.707	.595	.162	LNS	
						-.506	1.100	-5.383	-.354	.313	.195	.283	4.166	-.463	-.161	.113	SHD	
						-.564	1.289	-6.289	-.558	.381	.076	.226	5.153	-.180	-.063	-.022	DPOS	

Legend: See Table 1; CNST is the constant term

Notes:

*   The Long Run Structure describes the set of simultaneous relationships between the endogenous and exogenous variables that pertain after all transitory influences have worked their way through the model.

** The Long Run Reduced Form describes the dependence of the variables explained by the model upon the variables assumed exogenous to the model.

***The Long Run Elasticities relate to the ceteris paribus proportionate response of a dependent variable to a given proportionate change in the exogenous variable.

model is the stability of the long run structure (see for comparison Anderson (1979)). However, it is clear that the model has failed to capture some of the short run cyclical behaviour over the sample period. The manner in which the control solution oscillates around the realised values suggests that the mis-specification has resulted in a model which is dynamically unstable and the results of work reported elsewhere support this conclusion.[1]

The instability property only has a significant impact over an extended prediction period and does not offer a good reason for ignoring the conclusions that may be derived from the long run structural form of the model. Table 2 presents the long run structure of the model in terms of its structural form, reduced form and long run elasticities based upon sample means. Aside from the implications that the long run structure has for issues such as the empirical validity of the Modigliani-Miller theorem (discussed in Anderson (1980d)), it does have much to say concerning the relationship between investment expenditures, profits, taxation and the various sources of finance.

The first observation to make is that profits do not enter explicitly into any of the structural equations in the model (apart from the relevant identities) in the long run. The various strands of theory upon which the model has been based have not indicated that gross profits should enter any of the equations and as a consequence it is not surprising that explicit relationships between investment and profits have been hard to come by empirically in a single equation context. Notice however that the profits variable plays an important role in determining all of the endogenous variables when its impact is worked through the structural form of the model. In a similar manner dividends, interest payments and tax payments do not have a direct influence on investment expenditures but have an indirect impact through the simultaneous structure of the model. It is the extent to which variations in these variables induce variations in the effective constraints on investment, ie via the availability of finance for investment expenditures, which determines their impact upon the path of investment expenditures. On the other hand the value of output, whilst having a direct influence on the investment expenditures, does not appear to have a 'structural influence' on any of the financing equations. However, it may be observed from the reduced form coefficients that its indirect

---

[1] Anderson (1980d) indicates that the loans and share issues equations are the most likely source of instability. Since these equations are still not yet fully developed in that the single equation prediction properties are unsatisfactory it is hoped that this particular problem will be resolved in the near future.

impact is substantial, especially on the internal financing decision and the acquisition of loans.

At this stage it is appropriate to mention the dummy variables used in the model. Three important factors which have affected the aggregate have been accommodated by dummy variables. The first, steel nationalisation, resulted in the nationalised part of iron and steel manufacturing and distribution being omitted from the aggregate after July 1967. This had a major impact on the internal financing decision of the aggregate and as a consequence upon all the other equations in the model (note that the dummy variable was insignificant in each of the other equations). It resulted in a switch into internal financing and out of loan financing at the time as well as a reduction in the overall level of the operations. The second factor, the Competition and Credit Control Policy of the early seventies,[1] had its major impact on the loans behaviour of the sector and has already been mentioned in that context. It is worth noting that the policy had little relative influence on the flow of investment expenditures, its primary impact being on changes in the value of stocks and work in progress, an aspect of behaviour not yet incorporated in the model. Since the main impact of the policy as far as the sector was concerned was to increase its ability to obtain finance, the results do lend support to the view expressed by the CBI in evidence to the Wilson Committee[2] that shortage of finance was not an effective constraint on investment behaviour. The third factor, the introduction of dividend restraint over the periods 1967 Q4 to 1969 Q2 and 1972 Q4 to the end of the estimation period, appears to have provided a positive incentive for the sector to issue shares for cash. A fourth dummy, used to accommodate some instability in the model generated by the loans equation, does not yield a great deal of explanatory power and is still under investigation.

4.2   ESTIMATED ELASTICITIES

4.2.1   *Taxation*

The structure of the model is more easily related to economic theory by comparing the elasticities implied by the estimates with those predicted by the theory. Before dealing with those relating to profits, revenues and output, brief consideration will be given to some of the other results thrown up by the model. Turning firstly to taxation, it can be shown that if the underlying technology were Cobb Douglas

---

[1] See Spencer and Mowl (1978), Blackaby (1980).
[2] See CBI (1977).

(and substantial evidence exists for such a proposition[1]) the elasticity
of investment expenditures with respect to a change in the level of
taxation may be written in terms of the proportionate value of tax
incentives (TI) as:

$$E_{I,UKT} = \frac{-TI}{1-TI}$$

The estimate for the sample period $-.028$ implies a tax incentive value
of the order of $.027$ which is much lower than the average of the
values of tax incentives computed in Mellis and Richardson (1976).
This may be accounted for in many ways, but obvious possibilities are
that announced rates of taxation are not effective rates of taxation
and that the value of incentives is not fully anticipated because of
inadequate profits or the application of a particularly high discount
rate to these factors. The much larger negative elasticity of loans with
respect to tax payments reflects the role that taxation plays in reducing
the sector's ability to make interest and dividend payments in spite of
making tax deductible loans a relatively more attractive financing proposition. Also in this regard, it is interesting to note that Investment
Grants which may be considered as negative taxation have a much
weaker effect than do tax payments.

4.2.2 Stock appreciation and interest payments
Stock appreciation, in increasing the financing burden of companies
without increasing realisable profits, stimulates a slight attenuation of
investment expenditures. Again based upon an underlying Cobb
Douglas technology, the elasticity of investment expenditures with
respect to interest payments may be shown to be:

$$E_{Ir} = \frac{-r}{\delta + r}$$

Accommodating dividend payments as part of the interest payment
burden results in an estimate of this elasticity as $-.01$. It is interesting
to observe than an increase in interest payments brings about an
expansion of loans and share issues to partially accommodate the
resultant cut back in internal financing. This estimate of the elasticity
implies that the capital stock deterioration rate is almost 100 times the
real rate of interest which is only plausible if the real rate of interest
were close to zero given conventional notions about capital stock
deterioration.

---

[1] See for example Griliches (1967), Griliches and Ringstad (1971), Mizon (1977), Sargan
(1971) and Zarembka (1970).

4.2.3 *Profits and output*

In considering the relationship between investment and profits a view must be taken as to what is happening to the value of output. As Anderson (1980a) points out, there is a particular relationship between the output variable and the constant term in the investment equation. This implies that the elasticity of investment expenditures with respect to the value of output should always be considered in conjunction with the constant term. Naturally it should also be considered in conjunction with a view of what is happening to gross profits. This highlights one advantage of modelling in this framework; namely that all of these influences are separately modelled.

The usual assumption of a constant capital factor share implies that a proportionate change in output will yield the same proportionate change in profits. Taking this to be the case, the elasticity of investment expenditures with respect to output may be calculated as 1.082, which can be compared with the value of 1 implied by a Cobb Douglas technology.[1] The correspondingly calculated elasticities of profit retentions, loans, share issues and dividends are respectively 1.83, − .761, − .117 and .153. These estimates indicate that, given a *ceteris paribus* increase in output, there would be a switch into internal financing and away from external financing accompanied by a minor expansion in dividend disbursements.

These results relate to an increase in profits brought about by an expansion of output. The effects of increased profitability may be analysed by looking at the elasticities with respect to gross profits alone. Being partial elasticities, those with respect to gross profits alone are based upon output being constant and hence relate to an increase in profitability. In this context a substantially different picture may be observed. An increase in profitability only brings forth a modest proportionate increase in investment (.149) and has a much greater impact on dividends (5.15) and an expansion (relatively) in external financing as opposed to internal financing with elasticities for loans and share issues of 5.99 and 4.17 respectively compared with a profit retentions elasticity of .249. This change in profitability has a very natural interpretation in terms of economic theory in being similar to a change in relative prices making capital goods relatively cheaper.

---

[1] Throughout the development of the model and with each specification entertained, this elasticity has always been computed as greater than one (though never significantly so given the standard statistical tests). If it is greater than one it could well be a result of the capital deterioration rate being an increasing function of the output capital stock ratio. This most plausible assumption can be shown to lead to a minor increase in the elasticity of investment with respect to the level of output of the order indicated above. Unfortunately the data is indecisive on this issue.

Hence expansion is observed in all the financing variables as investment expenditures respond to the change in relative prices in favour of capital goods.

5 Conclusions

Before drawing conclusions, some qualifications are apposite. Aside from the fact that the external financing sector is still in the process of development, there are many relationships in the model still to be accommodated. From a policy standpoint the relationship between tax rates, profits and the effective tax bill would be of great importance. In terms of economic theory the link between market rates of interest and profitability would provide an extra dimension to the model. Of most importance for the investment/profits nexus is the way in which gross profits and revenue relate to one another and obviously this requires modelling the wage bill, pricing and output decisions. Clearly with these developments incorporated the model would provide a most powerful tool of economic analysis.

The stable features of the model are essentially the long run results. As for the shorter run aspects of the model it may be observed from Table 1 that changes in policy variables such as tax rates, dividend restrictions, credit control policies all have impacts on the investment expenditure flows aside from the effects they have on the realised financing flows. Changes in corporation tax rates have an effect on internal and external financing decisions and investment expenditures, independent of the effect that the consequent changes in the flows of tax payments may have. These may be interpreted as announcement effects and all have the expected signs given such an interpretation. However it would be a mistake to attach too much importance to these transitory features of the model until the short run dynamic stability properties of the model are clarified.

On the role of profits in the investment decision the model captures an important relationship for which little support has been found in the literature hitherto. Profits have a significant impact on the time path of investment expenditures through the way in which they influence the financing decisions of firms. This role is limited when compared with the impact of a change in profits which is associated with a commensurate change in output and simply reflects the 'relative price' nature of a change in profitability as compared with the scale effect of a change in output. This does suggest that effective demand management, if such a thing exists, would have more important consequences for the stability of investment flows than would a policy of stimulating profits.

This view is supported by the apparently inelastic response to tax payments observed in the model which runs counter to the popular conception of the impact of taxation, certainly as expounded by the CBI. This is partially due to the very low rates of taxation enjoyed by companies, given the tax deductibility of interest payments, stock appreciation, etc. It may also be the case that the company sector is not so effectively taxed as other sectors of the economy. It would be a mistake to assume that such a small response to taxation would prevail at higher rates of effective taxation but it does appear that in the long run the level of investment expenditures is relatively immune to fairly substantial increases in the level of taxation given present levels of tax payments.

Appendix 1

DATA DETAILS

Most of the financial data is culled from amended versions of Tables 134, 142 and 144, *Economic Trends Annual Supplement* 1977, the amendments being a result of the misprints in these tables which result in the usual identities not holding.[1] Treasury bill yields and Dividend yields were obtained from quarterly averages of the monthly data offered in Table 153 of the same volume. Problems exist with obtaining a measure of Output at current prices for Industrial and Commercial Companies. Work elsewhere (Anderson 1980), suggests that output in Manufacturing and Service industries is not an adequate proxy for Output in Industrial and Commercial Companies especially if recent years (1975 onwards) are included in the data set used. As a consequence some attempt has been made to construct an index of output which is more closely connected with that of Industrial and Commercial Companies.[2] For various reasons it is not yet possible to subject the new measure of output to the tests in Anderson (1980) though the results obtained in this paper lead one to suspect that the new measure would provide an adequate indicator of output in industrial and commercial companies. Basically the index is a weighted average of various indices of the form

---

[1] I am grateful to the CSO for helping to clarify these errors. Details are available from the author on request.

[2] I am grateful to the Department of Trade and Industry for supplying me with various details of sales and volume indices which have enabled me to construct the new series.

$$OICP_t = (317\ OM_t + 64.1\ OC_t + 104\ OR_t - 18.87OMET_t^*)/466.23$$

where OM = Manufacturing Output index; OR = Construction
Output index; OR = Retail Trade Volume index; OMET* = 0.0 up to
1967 (3) and = Ferrous Metal Output index thereafter. The weights
were calculated from the *Monthly Digest of Statistics* and *Economic
Trends* 1977 *Supplement*, the weight on OR_t including a Wholesale
Trade weight (i.e. it is presumed that the Wholesale Trade index would
be the same as the Retail Trade index).

Appendix 2

INVESTMENT EXPENDITURES BY INDUSTRIAL AND COMMERCIAL
COMPANIES

$$((1 + .644L^2)(1-L) + .626L + .338L^7 + .682L^9)\ IIC_t =$$
$$(7.53) \qquad (7.85) \quad (2.35) \quad (4.70)$$
$$+ (7.080(1-L^4)L^2 + 9.256L^7 + 9.834L^8)OICP_t - 440.478$$
$$(3.95) \qquad\qquad (3.58) \qquad (5.94) \qquad\qquad (7.34)$$
$$+ ((.028L - .062L^4)(1-L) - .075L^6)INF_t - (462.981$$
$$(2.07) \quad (4.14) \qquad\qquad (4.82) \qquad\qquad (1.48)$$

$$+ 212.244L)(1-L)CTAX_t$$
$$(1.03)$$

$\bar{R}^2 = .92$ Standard Error 39.381   D.W. 2.29

Residual Correlogram $\chi^2(8) = 5.28$

Prediction Test

Period		Observed	Predicted
1976	3	275.00	248.04
1976	4	51.00	37.26
1977	1	− 534.00	− 239.10
1977	2	471.00	425.48

Forecast Equation Standard Error 39.76

$\chi^2(4)$ Prediction Test 7.59

PROFIT RETENTIONS BY INDUSTRIAL AND COMMERCIAL COMPANIES

$$((1 + .160L^2)(1—L) + .750L)PR_t = (.717(1—L^2) — .278(1—L)^2L)GPNT_t$$
$$\quad(1.96)\qquad\qquad(9.40)\qquad\qquad(26.40)\qquad\quad(5.75)$$
$$+ (.569 + .660 \ L^2 + .237 \ L^5)ING_t + .154(1—L)L^3 \ IVS_t$$
$$\quad(4.97)\ \ (6.31)\quad\ \ (2.74)\qquad\qquad(2.77)$$
$$+ .637(1—L^4)L \ CTAX_t — 167.093 \ SND_t — .889 \ OIP_t$$
$$\quad(4.06)\qquad\qquad\qquad(4.88)\qquad\qquad(3.80)$$

$\bar{R}^2 = .99$ Standard Error 56.82   D.W. 2.09

Residual correlogram $X^2(8) = 3.01$

Specification Test $X^2(10) = 7.99$

Prediction Test:

Period		Observed	Predicted
1976	3	−157.00	−223.05
1976	4	997.00	1025.60
1977	1	−394.00	−479.96
1977	2	−497.00	−513.28

Forecast Equation Standard Error 57.49

$X^2(4)$ Prediction Test 3.88

LOANS TO INDUSTRIAL AND COMMERCIAL COMPANIES

$$((1—.147L^3)(1—L) + .382L—.157L^5)LNS_t =$$
$$\quad(2.06)\qquad\qquad(6.33)\ \ (2.69)$$
$$(1.882L^2(1—L) + 1.745L^4)SHD_t + (−.299L^2(1—L^2)—.376L^5)UKT_t$$
$$\quad(5.91)\qquad\qquad(8.24)\qquad\qquad(5.59)\qquad\qquad(4.66)$$
$$+ (−.124L^2(1—L) + (.059 + .198DCCC)L^3)INFC_t$$
$$\quad(3.72)\qquad\qquad(1.70)\ \ (2.73)$$
$$—1626.657(L—L^2)CTAX_t$$
$$\quad(1.80)$$
$$—110.007DUMl + 315.779 \ DCCC$$
$$\quad(1.91)\qquad\quad(4.50)$$

$\bar{R}^2 = .84$ Standard Error 164.2   D.W. 2.36

Residual Correlogram $X^2(8) = 7.63$

Prediction Test

Period	Observed	Predicted
1976 3	− 174.00	117.31
1976 4	531.00	554.47
1977 1	− 678.00	− 697.57
1977 2	212.00	384.42

Forecasting Equation Standard Error 167.19

$\chi^2(4)$ Prediction Test 4.13

SHARES ISSUED BY INDUSTRIAL AND COMMERCIAL COMPANIES FOR CASH

$$(1 + .386L^4 + .458^9 - .227L^2(1-L^3))SHD_t =$$
$$\quad (3.09) \quad (3.54) \ (3.85)$$
$$.154 (L + L^2 + L^3 + L^4)DPOS_t + (-.025(L-L^3) + .067(1-CTAX_t)L^4$$
$$(7.15) \qquad\qquad\qquad\qquad (2.75) \qquad\qquad (2.01)$$
$$+ .067(1-CTAX_t)L^6)INF_t + ((-.359 + .809L^2)(1-L^3)$$
$$(2.27) \qquad\qquad\qquad (3.56) \quad (5.60)$$
$$-.402(2-L^2-L^5)L)OIP_t + 3.154L^4(1-L^4)OICP_t + 35.785DUM^2$$
$$(6.54) \qquad\qquad\qquad (4.06) \qquad\qquad\qquad (4.49)$$

$\bar{R}^2 = .90$ $\qquad$ Standard Error 30.89 $\qquad$ D.W. 2.38

Residual Correlogram $\chi^2(8) = 5.77$

Specification Test $\chi^2(11) = 20.87$

Prediction Test:

Period	Observed	Predicted
1976 3	129.00	293.67
1976 4	13.00	120.55
1977 1	27.00	9.41
1977 2	323.00	361.88

Forecast Equation Standard Error 24.09

$\chi^2(4)$ Prediction Test 66.30

References

Anderson, G. J. 'Unobservables and the use of overlapping measures as proxy variables'; *Review of Economic Studies,* p.371–384, 1980

Anderson, G. J. 'A new approach to the empirical investigation of investment expenditures'; *University of Southampton* Department of Economics Mimeo, 1980a Forthcoming in Economic Journal, 1981

Anderson, G. J. 'The internal financing decisions of the industrial and commercial sector: a reappraisal of the Lintner model of dividend disbursions'; *University of Southampton* Department of Economics Discussion Paper No. 8003, 1980b

Anderson, G. J. 'The external financing decisions of the industrial and commercial sector'; *University of Southampton* Mimeo, 1980c

Anderson, G. J. 'Investment expenditures and finance in the industrial and commercial sector of the U.K. economy: an empirical study'; Paper presented to *Association of University Teachers of Economics,* Durham, 1980d

Anderson, G. J. 'The financial dynamics of investment expenditures: an empirical study''; Paper presented to S.S.R.C. *Economic Modelling Group,* 1979

Ando, A. K., Modigliani, F., Rasche, R. and Turnovsky, S. J. 'On the role of expectations of price and technological change in an investment function'; *International Economic Review.* p. 384–414, 1974

Archer, S. H., D'Ambrosio, C. A. *The Theory of Business Finance: A Book of Readings;* Macmillan, New York, 1967

Baumol, W. J., Heim, P., Malkiel, B. G., Quandt, R. E. 'Earnings retention, new capital and the growth of the firm'; *Review of Economics and Statistics,* vol. 52, p.345–355, 1970

Baumol, W. J., Heim, P., Malkiel, B. G., Quandt, R. E. 'Efficiency of corporate investment: reply'; *Review of Economics and Statistics,* p.128–132, 1973

Bhattacharya, S. 'Imperfect information, dividend policy and the bird in the hand fallacy'; *Bell Journal of Economics,* p.259–270, 1979

Bischoff, C. W. 'The effect of alternative lag distributions' in G. Fromm (ed) *Tax Incentives and Capital Spending;* Brookings Institution, North Holland, 1971

Blackaby, F. T. *Demand Management: The British Economy 1960–1974;* C.U.P./National Institute, 1980

Brealey, R. A., Hodges, S. D. and Capron, D. 'The return on alternative sources of finance''; *Review of Economics and Statistics,* p.467–477, 1977

Central Statistical Office. *Financial Statistics Explanatory Handbook,* 1977.

Coen, R. M. 'The effect of cash flow on the speed of adjustment' in *Tax Incentives and Capital Spending,* G. Fromm (ed) Washington: The Brookings Institution, 1971

Confederation of British Industry. *'Industry and the City: The C.B.I's Evidence to the Wilson Committee'',* 1977

Davidson, J. E. H., Hendry, D. F., Srba, F. and Yeo, S. 'Econometric modelling of the aggregate time series relationship between consumers' expenditure and income in the U.K.;' *Economic Journal,* vol. 88, p.661–692, 1978

Deaton, A. S. 'Involuntary saving through unanticipated inflation'; *American Economic Review* 67, p.899–910, 1977

Dhrymes, P. J., Kurz, M. 'Investment, dividend and external finance behaviour of firms'; in *Determinants of Investment Behaviour* edited by R. Ferber NBER Columbia University Press, New York, p.427–465, 1967

Diamond, P. 'The role of the stock market in a general equilibrium model with technological uncertainty'; *American Economic Review,* vol. 57, p.759–76, Sept, 1967

Eisner, R. 'Components of capital expenditures: replacement and modernisation versus expansion'; *Review of Economics and Statistics,* vol. 54, p.297–305, 1972

Eisner, R. and Nadiri, M. I. 'Investment behaviour and neo-classical theory'; *Review of Economic Statistics,* vol. 50, p.369–82, 1968

Fama, E. F. 'The empirical relationships between the dividend and investment decisions of firms'; *American Economic Review,* vol. 64, p.304–318, 1974

Fama, E. F. and Bibiak, H. 'Dividend policy: an empirical analysis;' *Journal of the American Statistical Association,* p.1132–1161, 1968

Feldstein, M. S. 'Corporate taxation and dividend behaviour'; *Review of Economic Studies,* vol. 37, p.57–72, 1970

Feldstein, M. S. and Foot, D. 'The other half of gross investment: replacement and modernization expenditures'; *Review of Economics and Statistics,* vol. 53, p.49–58, 1971

Feldstein, M. S. and Rothschild, M. 'Towards an economic theory of replacement investment'; *Econometrica,* vol. 42, p.393–423, 1974

Fisher, G. R. 'Quarterly dividend behaviour' in Hilton K. and Heathfield D. ed *The Econometric Study of the U.K.;* Macmillan London, 1970

Friend, I. and Husic, F. 'Efficiency of corporate investment'; *Review of Economics and Statistics,* p.122–127, 1973

Griliches, Z. 'Production functions in manufacturing: some preliminary results'; in *The Theory and Empirical Analysis of Production,* N.B.E.R. p.275–332, 1967

Griliches, Z. and Ringstad, V. *Economies of Scale and the Form of the Production Function;* Amsterdam, North Holland, 1971

Hall, R. E. and Jorgenson, D. W. 'Tax policy and investment behaviour'; *American Economic Review,* vol. 57, p.391–414, 1967

Hall, R. E. and Jorgenson, D. W. 'Tax policy and investment behaviour: reply and further results'; *American Economic Review,* vol. 59, p.388–401, 1969

Hall, R. E. and Jorgenson, D. W. 'Application of the theory of optimal capital accumulation'; in Fromm G. ed. *Tax Incentives and Capital Spending,* Washington, 1971

Hatanaka, M. 'On the global identification of the dynamic simultaneous equations model with stationary disturbances'; *International Economic Review,* vol. 16, p.545–554, 1975

Hendry, D. F. and Anderson, G. J. 'Testing dynamic specification in small simultaneous systems: an application to a model of building society behaviour in the U.K.'; in *Frontiers in Quantitative Economics,* vol. III, M. Intriligator (ed) North Holland, p.361–383, 1977

Hendry, D. F. and von Ungern Sternberg, T. 'Liquidity and inflation effects on consumer expenditure'; *London School of Economics Mimeo,* 1979

Jorgenson, D. W. 'The economic theory of replacement and depreciation'; in W. Sellikaerts, Ed, *Essays in Honor of Jan Tinbergen,* North Holland, Amsterdam, 1974

Jorgenson D. W. and Siebert, C. D. 'A comparison of alternative theories of corporate investment behaviour'; *American Economic Review,* vol. 58, No. 4, p. 681–712, 1968

Jorgenson, D. W. and Stephenson, J. A. 'The time structure of investment behaviour in United States manufacturing 1947–1960'; *Review of Economics and Statistics,* vol. 49, p.16–27, 1967

Jorgenson, D. W. and Stephenson, J. A. 'Investment behaviour in manufacturing industry 1947–1960'; *Econometrica,* vol. 35, p.169–220 1967a

King, M. *Public Policy and the Corporation;* Chapman & Hall Ltd., 1977

King, M. 'The United Kingdom profits crisis: myth or reality?'; *Economic Journal,* vol. 85, p.33–54, March, 1975

King, M. 'Taxation and the cost of capital'; *Review of Economic Studies,* vol. 41, No. 1, p.21–35, 1974

King, M. 'Profits in a mixed economy'; Inaugural Lecture, *University of Birmingham,* 1978

Lintner, J. 'Distribution of incomes of corporations among dividends, retained earnings and taxes'; *American Economic Review,* vol. 46, p.97–113, 1956

Mellis, C. R. and Richardson, P. W. 'Value of investment incentives for manufacturing industry 1946–1974'; in *Economics of Industrial Subsidies,* HMSO. Whiting (ed), 1976

Mizon, G. E. 'Inferential procedures in nonlinear models: an application in a U.K. industrial cross section study of factor substitution and returns to scale'; *Econometrica,* vol. 45, No. 5, p.1221–1242, 1977

Modigliani, F. Miller, M. H. 'The cost of capital, corporation finance and the theory of investment'; *American Economic Review,* vol. 48, p.261–97, 1958

Nickell, S. J. *The Investment Decision of Firms;* Cambridge University Press, 1978

Phillips, A. W. 'Stabilisation policy in a closed economy'; *Economic Journal,* vol. 64, p.290–323, 1954

Phillips, A. W. 'Stabilisation policy and the time form of lagged responses'; *Economic Journal,* vol. 67, p.265–277, 1957

Racette, G. A. 'Earnings retention, new capital and the growth of the firm: a comment'; *Review of Economics and Statistics,* p.127–128, 1973

Ross, S. A. 'The determination of financial structure: the incentive signalling approach'; *Bell Journal of Economics,* p.23–40, 1977

Sargan, J. D. *Qualified Manpower and Economic Performance;* Layard P. R. G. et el, Allen Lane, The Penguin Press, p.146–204, 1971

Spencer, P. and Mowl, C. 'A financial sector for the Treasury model: part 1, the model of the domestic monetary system'; *Government Economic Service Working Paper,* No. 17, 1978

Stiglitz, J. E. 'On the irrelevance of corporate financial policy'; *American Economic Review,* vol. 64, No. 6, p.851–866, 1974

Stiglitz, J. E. 'A re-examination of the Modigliani-Miller theorem'; *American Economic Review,* vol. 59, p.784–93, 1969

Turnovsky, S. J. 'The allocation of corporate profits between dividends and retained earnings,; *Review of Economics and Statistics,* vol. 49, p.583–589, 1967

Whittington, G. 'The profitability of retained earnings'; *Review of Economics and Statistics,* p.152–160, 1972

Wood, A. *A Theory of Profits;* Cambridge University Press, 1975

Zarembka, P. 'On the empirical relevance of the C.E.S. production function'; *Review of Economics and Statistics,* vol. 52, p.47−53, 1970

Comment[1]
by J Hibberd[2]

1 Introduction

Gordon Anderson has written an interesting paper on the role of
profits in the determination of company investment expenditure. It is
part of a long-term project to estimate a consistent simultaneous model
of company behaviour. This simultaneous approach is particularly to
be welcomed. For too long, perhaps, researchers have concentrated on
single equation techniques despite tacit or explicit acknowledgement
that investment is but one of many decisions taken by a company,
each of which interacts with the others. It may be that the persistent
failure of researchers to obtain significant effects from profitability, or
indeed other financial factors, in UK studies of investment stem from
a failure to conceive company behaviour in its entirety.

His approach contains a number of innovative features. Foremost
among these is his concentration on the various accounting identities
underlying company operations and his efforts to isolate from these
those factors which are appropriate to companies' long run equilibrium
behaviour. Anderson then attempts to synthesise a behavioural model
based on the interaction of these factors. This seems to me a particularly promising avenue for future research and it is perhaps only
surprising that it has not been more widely investigated before.

All this is to endorse Anderson's strategy in a general sense. But
when it comes to the detail of his work on the investment expenditure
relationship and the role of profits I believe there are sufficient doubts
to urge a cautious interpretation of his results. Two particular aspects
of the work concern me. First is the attempt to anchor the model
relationship in a Jorgensonian neo-classical theoretical framework. It
will be argued below that such an approach fails to encompass the
basic problems which Anderson is, at least implicitly, addressing.
Second, there are doubts concerning the dynamic stability of the
investment equation which suggest that, as yet, *no* long run properties
can reasonably be adduced from the estimated system. I deal with
these in Sections 2 and 3 respectively. Section 4 contains some
observations of a more general nature while Section 5 presents a
summary and conclusions.

[1] This comment includes points additional to those made at the time of the seminar. I
have therefore invited Dr Anderson to make a formal reply (page 193). — *Ed.*
[2] The author acknowledges the permission of his department to publish this comment
which does not however necessarily represent the views of HM Treasury.

2   The Jorgensonian framework and financial constraints

As Anderson acknowledges in an earlier paper which he cites
(Anderson 1980a), the nominal investment expenditure paradigm used
in his research is unusual. It is unusual because economists usually
conceive investment as a real phenomenon. Anderson argues however
that '. . . . this does not deny the existence of a nominal expenditure
analogue to the real investment decision'. This analogue is derived in
his paper for the Jorgensonian investment demand function (through
equations 2.1, 2.2 and 2.3) and in that form provides the theoretical
rationale for his own investment relationship. It shows that in long run
equilibrium nominal investment is equal to the sum of retained
earnings and new external finance:

$$qI = PR + EF \qquad\qquad 2.3$$

where q is the price of new investment goods and I is the volume of
investment. An alternative statement of the same relationship is that
sources and uses of funds are equal and the essence of Anderson's
work is 'its description of the interplay between these sources and uses
of funds'.

I do not deny that a nominal analogue to the Jorgenson real
investment demand equation exists; the important point is that within
that theoretical model it is of no operational significance. Jorgenson's
theory is based on the notion of an optimal capital stock derived from
present value maximising behaviour of firms operating in perfectly
competitive markets subject to the production function constraint[1].
The latter is a technological relationship between physical inputs and
output and implies factor demand equations expressed in real terms
with real (or relative) prices as the fundamental arguments. Any
disparity between internal funds available and the nominal value of the
desired investment goods is obviated by the underlying assumptions of
(a) a perfect capital market; (b) all agents acting under perfect
certainty and (c) no risk of bankruptcy. These assumptions *preclude*
any notion of financial factors imposing constraints on firms
behaviour. But Anderson appears to assume otherwise when he writes:
'The way in which expenditures on investment goods are constrained in
2.3 is through the availability of internal and external finance'. That
proposition represents an inappropriate interpretation of 2.3 in neo-
classical theory since no such constraint is recognised.

---

[1] In fact the theory is derived for an individual firm. To apply the theory across a wide
collection of industries or even the whole economy raises serious and well known
aggregation problems. But it is usual in the literature to 'look these problems squarely
in the face and move on.'

Parenthetically, one might note other well known problems with the Jorgenson investment demand function, as represented in equation 2.1 of Anderson's paper, which would lead to a very different nominal investment relationship. First it is incomplete. Analogous to desired investment demand is desired labour demand (assuming two factors of production) which, given the production function, determines the level of output (which is endogenous). The factor demand equations should then simply be functions of the prices of output, labour and capital services. But to be fair, this simultaneity issue is more frequently ducked than dealt with in the literature. Second, the assumption of Cobb Douglas technology is highly restrictive and I am less confident in the empirical support for it than Anderson.

None of this is to argue that financial constraints do not exist. Instead it is to emphasise that their origins lie in a fairly comprehensive set of market imperfections which render the Jorgenson model inappropriate. Foremost among these are (i) uncertainty and risk (ii) incomplete contingent commodity markets (iii) factor market imperfections and (iv) transactions and adjustment costs. Indeed it is interesting to observe that one market with which Anderson is concerned, the stock market, is virtually incidental to neo-classical production theory. Thus Leland (1974)[1] has written:

'Neo-classical production models have not needed stock markets because profit maximisation provides a complete description of firm behaviour under certainty. Stockholders are invoked to justify profit maximisation, but thereupon are hastily retired from the scene. Indeed, the existence of the stock market has been somewhat embarrassing, since traditional economic models are complete without it'.

Nor do I wish to decry a nominal investment expenditure relationship as such. But I would point out that the existence of these imperfections imply very careful consideration of the objective functions of firms and the precise nature of the constraints they face. Thus if the justification for the nominal paradigm (apart from econometric convenience) is, as Anderson asserts, that firms receive and transmit signals in nominal terms and conceive their responses also in current value terms, then we need a behavioural theory of the firm consistent with that assertion. (Strangely, the assertion itself is relegated to footnote status despite it being a singular departure from most economic theories of the firm.)

Of course some of these problems have exercised economists for many years and have proved fairly intractable. It would be churlish to

[1] This reference is cited from King (1977), p 127

criticise Anderson for not having solved them in his present research. That is not my main intent. It is instead to contend that the problems of company behaviour, particularly with regard to the interaction between financial factors and firms' expenditure decisions, is so complex that we shall continue to rely on fairly *ad hoc* models to capture their impact. Anderson's model may be one such worthy of further investigation. But it is an *ad hoc* model and Anderson cannot look to the Jorgenson neo-classical approach to underpin his model in the way he does both in the present paper and in earlier work (Anderson 1980(a)).

Nonetheless Anderson's model appears at first sight to fit the data extremely well and I now turn to a more detailed consideration of its properties.

3   The model and its long run properties

Two relationships are central to its construction. The first is an identity for the appropriation account and represents the result of the internal financing decision. In Table 1 of Anderson, this identity is represented by two equations (I use his notation). The first defines gross profit net of tax. The second states that the sum of dividends paid and profit retentions must be equal to gross profit net of tax and interest payments.

(i) $GPNT \equiv GP + NTI + IA - PDA - UKT$

(ii) $DPOS \equiv GPNT - PR - OIP$

These can be combined to give an appropriation account identity:

(iii) $DPOS \equiv GPT - PR - OIP - UKT$

where GPT is gross trading profits before taxes plus non trading incomes plus net property income from abroad.

The second key relationship concerns the long run sources and uses of funds. Here Anderson is forced to make fairly arbitrary but nonetheless reasonable distinctions regarding the appropriate long term magnitudes in these accounts. The relevant equation is

$$FI = PR + IG + OCT + LNS + SHD - SA$$

where FI is long-term finance available for investment.

At any time these magnitudes will not be in equilibrium and actual investment will need to be attenuated or expanded depending on whether desired gross investment expenditure is greater than or less than the finance available. This shortfall is defined as:

$$INF = IIC - FI = IIC + SA - PR - IG - OCT - LNS - SHD$$

and, as Anderson says, drives his model through time.[1]

The key feature of this structure which distinguishes it from other econometric studies of the role of profits in investment demand is, as Anderson notes, that profits 'do not enter explicitly into any of the structural equations in the model (apart from the relevant identities) in the long run'. *Prima facie*, this result follows from his careful consideration and isolation of the long run financing factors underlying firms' behaviour and the modelling of their simultaneous interaction. Together they imply that the notion of gross profit as such is an inappropriate variable in the explanation of investment. Instead profits must be viewed in conjunction with alternative sources and competing uses of funds. But two caveats need to be entered against these findings both of which suggest that they should be treated cautiously. The first concerns omitted structural equations from Anderson's model. These are considered in Section 4 below. The other concerns doubts regarding the dynamic stability of Anderson's estimated model which preclude confident conclusions on its long run properties. It is to this point that I now turn.

The precise details of Anderson's econometric estimates are presented in Appendix 2 of his paper. They reflect the approach to dynamic modelling advocated by Hendry *et al.*[2] The equations fit impressively as evidenced by Graphs 1–4 of Anderson's paper which present the results of a dynamic tracking test of the complete system ie a comparison of the actual paths of the relevant variables with the control solution of the associated equations. As Anderson explains the control solution uses 'the actual values of the dependent variables at the beginning of the estimation period as starting values and then uses the realised values of the exogenous variables but the computed values of the lagged endogenous variables to predict the path of the endogenous variables over the estimation period'.

Though this is a severe test of the model specification, it is not perhaps the most severe test since it is entirely confined, as I understand it, to within sample estimating experience. A more rigorous test would be to terminate the estimation at some earlier date, and use the equation to explain post sample values of the endogenous variables. It would be interesting to see the results of such tests.

---

[1] Anderson misses out the term for other capital transfers in his equation 3.1 though they are mentioned in the text and, possibly, conflated with the term for investment grants.

[2] See Davidson, Hendry, Srba, Yeo (1978); Hendry and Mizon (1978); Hendry (1979)

Anderson notes that there is evidence of instability in the system because of the tendency for the control solution to oscillate around the realised values 'although long run tracking performance appears highly satisfactory'. This instability is ascribed by Anderson to probable deficiencies in the loans and share equations. I have not been able to conduct tests of stability of the integrated system but have investigated the dynamic properties of the individual equations. This analysis points to the investment equation as being the cause for concern.

The investment equation from Appendix 2 implicitly contains additional lagged dependent variables in the finance shortfall variable, INF. Solving out these lags and combining them with the directly estimated lag coefficients on investment, IIC, gives the following difference equation:

$$1 - 0.402L + 0.672L^2 - 0.644L^3 + 0.062L^4 - 0.062L^5 + 0.075L^6 + 0.338L^7 + 0.682L^9)IIC = (7.08L^2 - 7.08L^6 + 9.256L^7 + 9.834L^8)\ OICP + (0.028L - 0.028L^2 - 0.062L^4 + 0.062L^5 - 0.075L^6)\ X - (462.981 + 212.244L)\ (1-L)\ CTAX$$

where $X = INF - IIC = SA - PR - IG - OCT - LNS - SHD$

Evaluation of the lag polynominal on investment[1] indicated four pairs of imaginary roots two of which have moduli greater than unity. These are shown below:

Roots of Equation	Modulus
$-0.5872 - 0.7227i$	0.9312
$-0.5872 + 0.7227i$	0.9312
$-0.1268 - 1.0234i$	1.0313
$-0.1268 + 1.0234i$	1.0313
$0.9568 - 0.3488i$	1.0184
$0.9568 + 0.3488i$	1.0184
-0.8530	0.8530
$0.3847 - 0.8295i$	0.9143
$0.3847 + 0.8295i$	0.9143

The implication of imaginary roots with absolute value greater than unity is that the associated dynamic structure is unstable.

The results of a comparable exercise on the remaining equations of the model are presented in the Annex. There are no problems with any of these equations.

---

[1] The evaluation used a programme devised by Stephen Phillips in the Treasury. It incorporates an algorithm devised by Numerical Algorithm Group Ltd.

The implications of this instability for the individual lag weights in the implied rational lag on output, evaluated between lag quarters 0 and 60 and 165 and 198 are shown in Figure 1A[1]. The cumulative response is shown in Figure 1B. The instability is quite pronounced even over a comparatively short period and gets progressively worse the longer the period of evaluation. (The rational lags on the other variables in the equation exhibit similar properties.)

Clearly the equation never converges to the steady state once it has been given an exogenous shock and it seems impossible that the equation can be a reasonable representation of the underlying investment process. As a result I cannot share Anderson's opinion that the instability 'does not offer a good reason for ignoring the conclusions that may be derived from the long run structural form of the model'. In the case of the investment equation, the long run structural form merely describes some hypothetical equilibrium relationship which can never be achieved once the system is shocked. This feature of the model must cast serious doubt on its long run estimated coefficients and I doubt that, as yet, any sensible long run conclusions can be derived from the structure.

4   Other comments

This section briefly records some more general comments on Anderson's model. First, my doubts concerning the implications of dynamic instability for the long run structural properties are compounded by the incompleteness of Anderson's model. I know that he is well aware of these omissions and that he has plans to encompass them in future research. It would therefore be inappropriate to make too much of them in this comment and I mention them only as factors which when integrated can be expected to alter the estimated coefficients and/or structure of the system. They include the employment demand, inventory demand, and pricing functions. The latter in particular may have considerable significance. For example, Wood's theory of pricing suggests that firms may *set* prices with the objective of raising sufficient internal funds to finance desired investment. Such a theory may have different implications for the structure than, say, a cost mark-up model. But until these aspects are investigated we should perhaps beware confident assertions on the long run impact of financial factors on company behaviour.

---

[1] This evaluation used the RATLAG programme devised by Peter Richardson of HM Treasury

Figure 1A: Lag Weights on Gross Output in Investment Equation

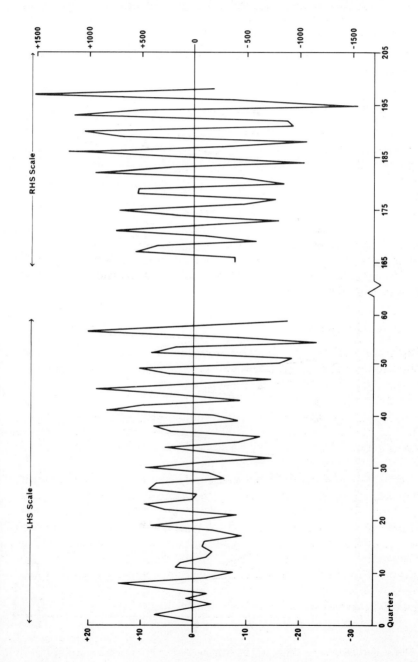

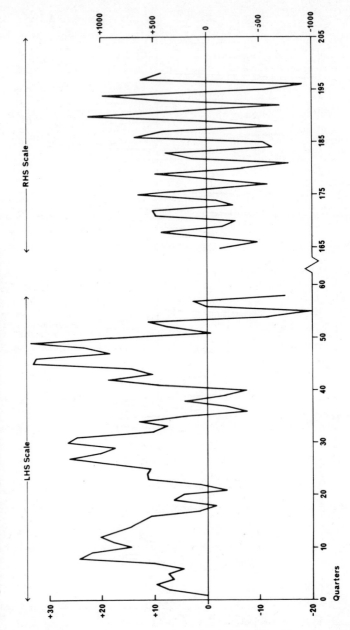

Figure 1B: Cumulative Lag Weights on Gross Output in Investment Equation

Second, I was surprised to see little reference to the role of expectations in company behaviour. In a world of uncertainty, expectations of output, profits etc will loom large in company decision-making. It may be argued that the complex dynamic structures estimated by Anderson are convolutions of expectations and adjustment lags. But it would nonetheless be interesting to see the model extended by more explicit consideration of expectations mechanisms.

Third, as a matter of principle, the restriction of identical lags and long run coefficients on prices *and* output in the current price output term should be investigated. This principle also extends to any other variable which is a compound of many variables.

Finally, it seems potentially fruitful to consider the separate demand and supply structures underlying the reduced form equation for loans and mortgages. It may be that firms have never effectively been constrained by the supply of bank lending. In this case, Anderson's model would be little altered, if at all. But the implicit assumption of perfect capital markets should nonetheless be examined.

5   Conclusions

To conclude, I repeat that Anderson's attempt to develop a simultaneous model of company behaviour is laudable. In particular I believe that his detailed attention to the underlying accounting identities may provide a valuable insight to behaviour. There remains much work to be done however. The theory seems inadequately specified and there is a serious question mark concerning the stability of the system. There are also a number of areas in which the model should be extended. Future research must look to these issues as Gordon Anderson himself acknowledges. I look forward to seeing the future results of his work.

Annex: Stability of profit retentions, loans and new share issue equations

The tables below show the roots of the lag polynomials on the dependent variables in their respective equations.

Roots of profit retention equation	Modulus
$-0.1376 - 0.5345i$	0.5519
$-0.1376 + 0.5345i$	0.5519
0.5253	0.5253

Roots of
loans equation

0.8664	0.8664
− 0.4669 − 0.5009i	0.6848
− 0.4669 + 0.5009i	0.6848
0.3427 − 0.5186i	0.6216
0.3427 + 0.5186i	0.6216

Roots of share
issues equation

0.5384 − 0.7273i	0.9049
0.5384 + 0.7273i	0.9049
− 0.7203 − 0.6077i	0.9424
− 0.7203 + 0.6077i	0.9424
− 0.9247	0.9247
0.8553 + 0.3946i	0.9401
0.8533 − 0.3946i	0.9401
− 0.2090 + 0.8526i	0.8779
− 0.2090 − 0.8526i	0.8779

References

Davidson, J.; Hendry, D.; Srba, F.; Yeo, S. 'Econometric modelling of the aggregate time-series relationship between consumers' expenditure and income in the UK'; *Economic Journal*, Dec 1978

Hendry, D. and Mizon, G. 'Serial correlation as a convenient simplification, not a nuisance'; *Economic Journal*, Sept 1978

Hendry, D. 'Predictive failure and econometric modelling in macro-economics: the transactions demand for money'; in *Economic Modelling*, ed Ormerod, P., Heinemann, 1979

King, M. *Public Policy and the Corporation*; Chapman and Hall, 1977

Leland, H. 'Production theory and the stock market'; *Bell Journal of Economics and Management Science*, 1974

Wood, A. *A Theory of Profits*, Cambridge University Press, 1975

Rejoinder
by G J Anderson

I am most grateful to Jim Hibberd for his comments; some observations are appropriate in response. First, his concern over the use of the neo-classical formulation in the introduction highlights an inadequacy of the exposition in that it is not intended to 'anchor the model relationship' in a Jorgensonian framework. The intention was to show the relationship between the long run structure of that model and the one developed in the paper.

It is my belief that any new empirical work should relate to the extant literature and it is possible to do so in the present context only in the long run. The model most commonly used in the investment literature is the neo-classical model and its relationship to other models is well understood. Parenthetically, I disagree that firms are not constrained in the Jorgenson model since, given constant returns and the exogenous determination of output and prices, factor rewards exhaust the total product and the amount of finance available for investment expenditures is naturally constrained by the technologically-determined factor share.

With regard to the second criticism, it should be noted that it is only appropriate to consider the stability of a system of equations one equation at a time if all the matrices of coefficients on the endogenous and lagged endogenous variables in the system are uniformly triangular. Clearly this is not the case in the present model. More generally, the procedure used by Jim Hibberd places an overly restrictive requirement on a dynamic, simultaneous equation model.

Nonetheless, Hibberd's observation does indicate another potential source of the model's acknowledged instability which will be investigated in the future. However, there is no reason to believe that, because equations are individually unstable, they cannot be a reasonable representation of the underlying data generation process.

194 Papers Four & Five

General discussion

The general sentiment of those participating in the discussion of the two papers was that realised profitability and cash flow were important influences on investment decisions, though several doubts were expressed concerning technical aspects of the analysis presented by Meeks and Anderson.

Meeks' paper was particularly concerned with the existence of factors – such as transactions costs of new share issues, tax arrangements, and uncertainty – which led to a 'discontinuity in the supply of funds schedule'. In other words, the perceived cost of finance rose disproportionately at the point where retention finance was exhausted. Meeks' views were supported by a number of participants. Experience suggested to them that considerations of gearing and interest cover were important influences on investment behaviour. While there was no question that external finance was available to sizable companies, the greater cost of such finance in comparison to that of internally generated funds did inhibit the volume and timing of investment expenditure. Particular emphasis was laid upon the uncertainty of investment decisions, especially when markets were not growing quickly. In such circumstances, the availability of internal finance, now or in the future, was a very important influence on confidence of the investor. Cash shortages would lead to a failure of confidence and deferment of investment, if not actual cancellation of projects.

While there was thus some endorsement for the view that the availability of internal funds had an important influence on the perceived cost of investment finance, some participants were less confident that the econometric studies had faithfully captured that influence. Meeks himself was worried lest his cross section results reflected only variations in general performance between firms rather than the influence of financial factors on investment: high performance firms, for example, may simply be more profitable and expand their capital base more quickly than other firms. This worry, shared by others, could be overcome, it was suggested, by modelling explicitly the distribution of variation in the technique of production between firms. The use of cross section data was nevertheless thought to be promising since it might well contain information which was not available in time series data. In future work, Meeks was encouraged to exploit some of the recent developments in the theory of specification searches, in particular the work of Leamer.

Two further technical points were raised concerning Meeks' paper. It was suggested that there was a danger of simultaneous equation bias affecting the true significance of the net retentions variable which Meeks had noted performed well in the regressions. Net retentions were defined as profits after depreciation, tax, dividends, interest and stock appreciation. The econometric problem arose from the fact that the use to which the residual funds could be put was restricted to investment in either physical assets or financial assets. Given the danger of some bias, the use of a more sophisticated econometric technique – such as instrumental variables – was suggested to the author. A second set of worries concerned the significance of the depreciation variable, a point also raised by Mrs Wenban-Smith in her formal comments. It was argued that the direction of causation might well run from investment to depreciation provisions: the composition of capital assets, and therefore their rate of obsolescence, would vary between firms and this would be reflected in their depreciation policies.

Some technical doubts were also raised over Anderson's paper. A fundamental criticism was that his model failed to capture properly the constraints which external borrowing placed upon investment decisions. While the existence of a 'discontinuity in the supply of funds schedule' was not in dispute, it was argued that Anderson's model was deficient in failing to incorporate the conditions, in terms of prices and quantities, on which firms could borrow. It was suggested that equation 2.3 was no more than an incomplete identity and therefore did not help in an understanding of investment behaviour. In the discussion which followed, the validity and significance of this criticism were not established, though it was admitted that the model did not include explicit terms for the cost of finance.

A second set of issues concerned the equation for loans. It was agreed that the ability of the loans equation to track the extreme observations in 1973–74 was heavily dependent upon the use of a complex dummy variable which was intended to isolate the effects of competition and credit control policy introduced in 1971. A second worry was that the equation reflected an assumption of gearing in terms of flows rather than of outstanding stocks of equity holdings and bank finance. Gearing in terms of stocks had developed rather differently from that in terms of flows in recent years as a result of the increasing dependence of industrial and commercial companies on bank borrowing. It was agreed that it was theoretically more respectable to formulate the gearing in terms of stocks rather than

196 Papers Four & Five

flows but that the presence of a distributed lag in the loans equation might capture some features of stock adjustment, albeit imperfectly. A more satisfactory treatment of external financing decisions and, indeed, of prices and output were matters which would be considered in the future development of Anderson's model.

A final, more general, query concerned Anderson's conclusion that a spontaneous increase in profits was much less effective in raising investment than was a rise in output and profits together. Anderson drew the conclusion that demand management policy was to be preferred on these grounds to a policy directed specifically at profitability. Against this, the point was made that output itself would depend on the evolution of profitability and to look simply at the partial response of investment to increased profits, without regard to the wider macro-economic consequences for output, could well be misleading. A spontaneous increase in industrial profitability would, for example, improve our international cost and price competitiveness, stimulating foreign demand and thus domestic output. Output increases would further increase profitability and investment, the latter by the usual accelerator process. If the economy was supply-constrained by low profitability – as Professor Maynard believed – these second-round influences of increased profits on investment via higher output, could be extremely important – far more important, in fact, than the partial responses calculated by Anderson.

Factors affecting profitability and employment in UK manufacturing industry, 1960–1978

by G W Maynard

Summary

The paper is presented in the form of a note for discussion and seeks
to analyse in broad terms the various factors which have formed the
pattern of employment and profitability experienced in the UK manufacturing sector over the last twenty years. In doing so, the author
draws heavily from earlier articles by himself and Professor Sargent.
The two main factors identified as contributing to the decline in profitability are firstly a labour sector seeking to increase its income share
and maintain or improve real wages and secondly government policy
which sought to promote full employment and economic growth by,
inter alia, investment incentives in the form of tax allowances.

A framework for the discussion is set by decomposing the rate of
return on capital into the share of income taken by profits and the
capital-output ratio; that is, the inverse of capital productivity. The
latter term is equivalent to the capital-labour ratio divided by labour
productivity. By examining the trends in these variables it is possible to
'explain' the decline in the rate of return on capital. The fact that
labour productivity and manufacturing output increased during the
years 1960–72 but fell in the mid 1970s suggests that different factors
were operating on the profit rate in these two periods and thus they
are analysed separately.

The earlier period was marked by a significant increase in the
capital-labour ratio and the author suggests changing factor prices
brought about by trade union bargaining power and acquiescent
government policy as the major cause. This policy provided tax allowances on investment and had the dual effect of lowering the cost of
capital and stimulating the substitution of capital for labour. At the
same time, excess demand pressure in the labour market maintained by
full employment policies led to real wage increases which further
stimulated capital-labour substitution. An over-valued exchange rate
together with rising relative labour costs could explain some of the fall
in profitability but this view is discounted as, from 1966, relative
labour costs in the UK have been on a downward trend, at any rate up
to the end of 1976. Moreover, implicit in the view that a lower
exchange rate would have been associated with greater real competitiveness is the assumption that labour would have accepted a decline in
income share. But the author suggests that trade union pressure to
preserve or increase real wages and income shares is the major factor
behind falling profit rates and profit shares. Although government
policy of subsidising investment persuaded firms to continue investing
in the face of declining returns, the continuing rise in the capital-

labour ratio and the rigidities in the labour market contributed to lost employment opportunities.

The years 1973–77 were differentiated from the earlier phase by a fall in output and employment and the pronounced collapse in profit share and profit rates. This section of the paper focuses on the effect that increases in the cost of raw materials and fuel inputs, especially oil, have on the profitability of employing labour. In brief the rise in energy prices reduced labour's marginal revenue product. Although recognising the imprecision of such estimates, the author argues that a substantial fall in own product wages was needed to keep them in line with the fall in the marginal revenue product of labour and thus the demand for labour. In fact, between 1973–75 own product wages rose rather than fell so that employment and profitability fell. It is estimated that because of these factors both real and nominal profits fell, the latter by as much as 30 per cent. During 1976 the growth in money wages was slowed down as the effects of incomes policy began to bite. As a result, own product real wages fell and manufacturing employment was stimulated, the latter contrary to what could have been expected on historical output and employment relationships. By the end of 1977 real profits had recovered slightly but were still well below their level five years earlier.

The author acknowledges that he is offering an interpretation of developments in the 1960s and 1970s rather than a watertight 'scientific' explanation of declining profitability. On the basis of that interpretation he emphasises that radical changes in trade union attitudes, work practices and management, bringing about an improvement in the productivity of both capital and labour, are necessary for profitability to increase.

Introduction

This paper is not the product of a substantial amount of original research and is best regarded as no more than a note for discussion. It adds little in analytical or empirical terms to (indeed in most respects offers less than) Professor J R Sargent's article 'Productivity and Profits' in the autumn 1979 issue of the *Midland Bank Review* with which I am in virtual full agreement, although this note probably ends more contentiously. It takes as its starting point Professor Hill's estimates of the share of profits and the rate of profit on capital in UK manufacturing industry over the period 1955–76[1] and attempts to

---

[1] T P Hill (1979).

indicate the macroeconomic factors that may explain why both of
these declined so drastically. In doing so, it draws on some other
relevant calculations done either by myself or by a former professional
colleague in the UK Treasury at least two years ago. These calculations
have not been revised, at least by myself, since then and may be
seriously inaccurate, but, it is hoped, not so much as to cast significant
doubt on the conclusions they support. It is probably unnecessary to
warn that all estimates of capital stock, capital productivity, capital
price, etc, which are referred to in this paper involve formidable conceptual and measurement problems. While this is so, such has been the
magnitude of the recorded changes in some of these values over the
last 20 years that measurement problems probably do not obscure the
major trends that have taken place.

It is a well recognised fact that the rate of profit on capital in UK
manufacturing industry declined substantially through the 1960s and
1970s. Table 1 and chart 1 indicate that it fell by about a third
between 1955 and 1972. In the next four years it collapsed dramati-
cally, leaving it no more than about one-third of what it was 20 years
earlier.[1]

The rate of profit on capital is related to the share of profits in
income and the capital-output ratio. Thus:

$$\frac{P}{K} = \frac{P}{Y} \div \frac{K}{Y}$$

where P is profit, K is capital, and Y is output. A rise in the ratio of
capital to output (i.e. a fall in the productivity of physical capital),
unless offset by a sufficient rise in the ratio of profit to income, results
in a fall in the rate of profit on capital.

In the 20 years we are concerned with, the capital-output ratio rose
substantially. During the same period, the share of profits in income
halved, the decline being particularly rapid in the mid-1970s (table 1,
chart 1). Thus, in formal terms, the fall in the rate of profit on capital
is easily 'explained'.[2]

---

[1] Tables B1 and B2 in the Department of Industry's background paper by W Martin
and M O'Connor broadly confirm these trends.
[2] It should be noted that the capital-output ratio is not computed independently by
Professor Hill but is implied by the other two ratios.

The capital-output ratio is related to the ratio of capital to labour and the productivity of labour. Thus:

$$\frac{K}{Y} = \frac{K}{L} \div \frac{Y}{L}$$

where L is the amount of labour 'employed with capital. A rise in the ratio of capital to labour will raise the ratio of capital to output unless the productivity of labour rises sufficiently fast to offset it.

In the 1960s, when manufacturing output was steadily rising, the capital-labour ratio rose substantially, by over 50 per cent. The productivity of labour rose by about one-third so that, again in formal terms, the rise in the capital-output ratio is also easily explained (table 1, chart 2). The capital-output ratio continued to rise in the mid-1970s, but the associated fall in output and output per unit of labour suggests that other factors were then operating. For this reason, the analysis that follows will examine the two periods 1960–1972/73 and 1972/73–1977 separately.

First period: 1960–1972/73

We have seen that in formal relationship terms the fall in the rate of profit on capital in manufacturing industry in the 1960s and early 1970s can be 'explained' by a fall in the share of profits in income and a faster rise in the ratio of capital to labour than in the ratio of output to labour. Profit share and the ratio of capital to labour are of course related to each other through the elasticity of substitution between capital and labour, but direct evidence concerning this is both scanty and unreliable. Hence we shall not make use of the concept in what follows.

A rise in the capital-labour ratio is of course to be expected in most economies as economic development proceeds, particularly in countries, like the UK, already substantially developed and whose labour force is growing relatively slowly. The rise in the ratio may be the result of the *autonomous* introduction of capital using technology (in which case it is likely to lower the price of labour relative to the price of capital) or it may be induced by an *autonomous* rise in the price of labour relative to the price of capital which encourages both the substitution of capital within existing technologies (insofar as this is possible) and the introduction of capital using ones.

It is difficult to measure the rate at which capital using technology was introduced autonomously into manufacturing industry in the 1950s and 1960s although no doubt impressionistic evidence would suggest that it was quite high. As far as the relative price of capital and labour is concerned, although difficult measurement problems are involved, it is clear that the cost of labour rose very strongly relative to the cost of capital. Table 1 and chart 2 suggest that it probably rose twice as fast, so that it is not at all surprising that capital was substituted for labour at a very fast rate. Employment in manufacturing industry at the end of this period, either in terms of numbers of workers or average hours worked, was no greater than at the beginning, and indeed as we shall show later, it fell substantially in the mid-1970s.

A number of important questions arise at this point, to which absolutely conclusive answers cannot be easily given. Why did the price of labour rise so fast relatively to the price of capital? Why did the substitution of capital for labour not pay off in terms of labour productivity, sufficiently to prevent a rise in the capital-output ratio and consequential downward pressure on profits? What prevented firms in manufacturing from raising profit share to compensate? And, perhaps most important, why did profit seeking entrepreneurs continue to invest and substitute capital for labour although the rate of profit on capital was falling so fast?

During the 1960s the real cost of labour (in terms of output prices) rose whilst the real cost of capital fell. In a perceptive article written over a decade ago[1], Professor Sargent argued that owing to a major enhancement of government tax incentives to investment at the end of the 1950s, which significantly lowered the cost of capital to industry, excess demand pressures were created in the labour market. Thus the labour force was enabled to raise its real wages in excess of productivity growth, thereby encouraging entrepreneurs to continue the process of substituting capital for labour. Professor Sargent left it unclear why labour productivity lagged behind capital substitution or why profit share fell although in the Midland Bank article quoted earlier he has since referred to the transition costs of operating equipment of various ages and efficiency at a uniform level of real wages. But other factors were probably at work.

It could be argued that the difficulty that entrepreneurs had in increasing labour and capital productivity and maintaining profits lay in the constraint imposed on the growth of output by an increasingly overvalued exchange rate in the 1960s. Relatively rising labour costs in the UK, against a background of a fixed exchange rate for sterling. made it increasingly difficult for UK manufacturers to compete over-seas and to match foreign competition in domestic markets. Inability

[1] J R Sargent (1968).

to expand output sufficiently led to capital being used uneconomically; and inability to raise prices sufficiently to cover rising costs led to shrinking profit share.

There may well be some truth in this line of explanation, at least in the first half of the 1960s. But some doubt must be attached to it since it obviously does not explain the continued and faster fall in profits and capital productivity in the late 1960s and early 1970s. On chart 1 is plotted an index of trade competitiveness produced by the Central Statistical Office[1]. It indicates the behaviour of normal unit labour costs in the UK relative to those in major competitor countries, all measured in terms of the dollar. Unfortunately it does not go back further than 1963. While it seems likely that the UK's competitive position was worsening in the years prior to 1963 as well as up to 1966[2], it is striking to note that since 1966 periodic devaluations of sterling have been sufficient to maintain a declining *trend* in UK relative labour costs expressed in a common currency at least up to the end of 1976. Yet, as indicated earlier, profit share and rate of profit on capital fell faster in these years (1966–72) than in the period before.

Apart from these empirical considerations, an explanation which puts weight on over-valuation of sterling assumes implicitly that a lower nominal exchange rate would have been associated with greater real competitiveness. In other words, that there would have been an appropriate willingness on the part of labour to accept a smaller share of the real income generated in the manufacturing sector, either through a rise in labour productivity unmatched by an equal rise in the real wage or, failing that, a fall in the real wage itself.

This consideration suggests a more political explanation of falling profit shares and falling profit rates in the 1960s, namely the existence of a strong trade union movement, with increasing political power, determined to increase the real wages of its members and to raise its income share, and able to do so in an environment in which governments sought to maintain full employment. When accompanied by an apparent unwillingness or inability, in some industries at least, of labour and management to co-operate in making best use of new

[1] *Economic Trends Annual Supplement* 1980 Edition, page 118. See also table C7 in Martin and O'Connor.

[2] Between 1961 and 1963 a loss of price but not unit labour cost competitiveness is indicated by the indices in table C7 of Martin and O'Connor. The earlier figures were not presented in the original version of the paper – *Ed.*

capital and technology being introduced, thereby retarding the productivity of both capital and labour, the inevitable result was a fall in the rate of profit on capital.

What has to be answered, however, is: why the price of capital to entrepreneurs did not rise in line with the price of labour; and why in the face of declining profit share and profit rate, profit seeking firms continued to invest and substitute capital for labour at the rate suggested earlier. The answer to both questions must surely lie in government policy itself, which, concerned with maintaining full employment and stimulating economic growth, became increasingly generous in providing tax allowance incentives to investment, whilst generally maintaining an accommodating monetary policy and low real rates of interest. By reducing or containing the cost of capital net of tax for marginal investments, these policies encouraged both a substitution of capital within existing technology and in the longer run the introduction of more capital using ones insofar as these became available. It is easy to see a vicious circle of developments emerging. Thus, owing to a rise in the cost of labour relative to the cost of capital, capital is substituted for labour without however a compensating rise in output; the consequential rise in the capital-output ratio tends to depress the rate of profit gross of tax causing a fall in the willingness of industry to invest; the government subsidises investment by fiscal measures in order to prevent investment from falling and unemployment from rising; the capital-output ratio continues to rise and the rate of profit gross of tax continues to fall. So does the profit rate net of tax but at a slower rate.

Naturally this process cannot continue for ever. At some point, apparently now reached by large sectors of UK manufacturing industry, profits fall to such a low level that investment allowances etc cannot be taken advantage of. Government is then forced to subsidise directly, often involving a take-over of equity, or even outright nationalisation, with severe fiscal and political implications. Moreover, because the method used to stimulate investment encourages at the same time the substitution of capital for labour, potential employment problems may be created. Evidence for the latter is shown in chart 3 reproduced from *Midland Bank Review* Summer issue 1979. This shows the relationship between the real product wage and employment in UK manufacturing industry, where the real product wage is derived by dividing an index of average wage and salary earnings and employers contributions for National Insurance and Superannuation, first by an index of value added prices (ie selling prices received by firms less the unit cost of fuels, materials and services bought in), and then by an index of output per employee[1]. The higher is this derived index the lower is the profitability of employing labour. One would expect therefore that employment in manufacturing industry would be inversely related to movements of the index.

In fact, we see that up to the mid-1960s an upward trend in the real product wage was accompanied by rising employment, not falling employment. The explanation provided by the author of the Midland Bank article is that in this period the marginal productivity of labour (which cannot be measured directly) was rising faster than average productivity (which is measurable). Use of the latter measure rather than the former in the compilation of the real product wage index biasses it upwards, tending to understate the profitability of employing labour. After the mid-1960s, when average productivity of labour was being pulled up less fast, the upward bias in the index was probably less; and a clear inverse relationship between the index and employment in manufacturing manifests itself. (The causes of the very steep rise in the index in 1973–74 and its impact on employment will be discussed later.) Loss of employment opportunities in manufacturing in the latter half of the 1960s was offset by an increasing number of jobs in service industries and, in particular, in the public sector (in fact, if anything, the facts appear to run opposite to the Bacon-Eltis thesis that expansion of the public sector had denuded industry of labour)[2]. However, expanding the public sector to offset decline in manufacturing creates its own problems: the consequential strain on public finances and therefore on the taxpayer reacts back on wage and salary demands, reinforcing the trend for labour costs to rise in industry, and therefore for employment to fall.

It may also be worth pointing out that balance of payments problems can also arise from policies encouraging the substitution of capital for labour at too fast a rate. Clearly, *ceteris paribus,* the higher the ratio of capital to labour, the larger must the capital stock be for a given level of labour employment, and the greater must net capital

---

[1] Readers are warned that the Midland Bank's definition of real product wages is not that used in Martin and O'Connor and differs from Professor Maynard's concept of the 'own product real wage'. The real product wage in Martin and O'Connor and the 'own product real wage' are both defined as the money wage divided by the wholesale price of output produced by the labour employed. The Midland Bank's real product wage is equivalent, in principle, to the share of employment income in value added (by manufacturing industry) – *Ed.*

[2] Bacon, R and Eltis, W A (1976). Bacon and Eltis have since modified their explanation of employment trends, so as to put more weight on the connection between high public expenditure, high taxation and consequential money wage demands. *Ibid,* 2nd Edition, 1978.

formation be to support a given growth in the labour force. Again, *ceteris paribus,* the ratio of investment to GDP must be higher. If public and private saving does not match (which is itself a function of the ratio of profits to income), then external saving must be drawn upon: thus the current balance of payments will be in deficit whatever exchange rate policy is pursued. The fact that in the late 1960s, early 1970s, the UK found it increasingly difficult to combine balance of payments equilibrium with full employment is evidence that all these factors were beginning to impact on UK economic performance.

Second period: 1973–77

In the 1960s and early 1970s although profit shares and profit rates were falling, manufacturing output continued to rise; and although employment in manufacturing expanded very little, at least it did not fall. After 1973, output and employment fell substantially; and although there was some later recovery, output in 1978 was still well below what it was in 1973, and so was employment. As indicated earlier, both profit share and profit rate showed a startling collapse.

Declines in manufacturing output and employment can be discerned in virtually every major industrial country at this time, so clearly we must look for an international cause. This seems to have been the steep rise in the commodity prices in 1973, followed by the subsequent steep rise in the price of oil at the end of the year and through 1974, although the precise manner in which this affected output and employment is open to dispute. The boom in commodity prices, excluding oil, was relatively short lived, although they never fell back to their pre-1973 level; hence oil prices must provide most of the underlying cause.

One line of argument is that the rise in oil price shifted the distribution of world income away from oil consumers to oil producers. Since, given the nature of their economies, many of the latter could spend income less readily than the former, a rise in the world propensity to save took place which exerted a demand deflationary impact on the world economy. Some governments added to this by pursuing for a time at least restrictive monetary policies aimed at containing the price inflationary effects of the rise in the cost of oil and other energy substitutes. It is however noteworthy that even after OPEC countries had raised their spending to match more closely their revenue, and even after governments in industrial countries had shifted their economic policies to a more expansionary stance through larger budget deficits and easier credit policies, unemployment in the Western world remained high, and still does.

The failure of employment in manufacturing industry to recover and for unemployment to remain high in OECD countries would seem to lie in the impact of higher real energy and raw material prices on the profitability of employing labour. In the UK, between end 1972 and end 1975, raw material and fuel input prices to manufacturing industry rose by about 115 per cent whilst manufacturing output prices rose by around 70 per cent, ie in terms of output prices, input prices rose by something like 25 per cent (table 2). Given that raw material and fuel input prices are about 40 per cent of direct costs, the implied fall in the marginal revenue product of labour at any given level of employment (assuming no change in labour physical productivity) was about 17 per cent.[1] (In the terms employed in the Midland Bank article and table referred to earlier, the real product wage – ie the cost of labour to manufacturing firms in terms of product produced – rose substantially.)

The calculation above probably overstates the implied fall in the revenue product of labour (or rise in the real product wage cost to employers), partly because of administrative time lags in adjusting prices to costs (in other words, it is probably better to relate prices in one quarter to costs two or three quarters earlier); partly because the higher level of energy prices may have stimulated the introduction of conservation measures, thereby raising 'material productivity'; and partly because the raw material input price estimate relates to raw materials and fuel only, thereby ignoring inputs of materials from domestic service industries and therefore, in all probability, overstating the increase in aggregate input prices.[2] Even so, there can be little dispute that the demand price of labour fell relatively to its supply price, so that a substantial fall in the going 'own product' real

---

[1] This can be inferred from the following equation:

$$\frac{1+w}{1+p} = \left[1 - \left(\frac{1+m}{1+p} \right) r \right] \Big/ 1 - r$$

where w, p and m are percentage changes in money wages, product price and raw material/energy input price respectively. It assumes an initial equilibrium situation in which marginal costs of production are approximately equal to direct costs which are related to price through a percentage profit mark-up reflecting the price elasticity of demand which is assumed to remain constant. Clearly, if m is greater than p, w must be less than p, ie own product wages must fall. For the period end 1972 to end 1975, m is approximately 115 and p is 71, so that $(1+m)/(1+p)$ is approximately 1.26. Hence $(1+w)/(1+p)$ is approximately 0.83.

Thus own product wages would have had to have fallen by around 17 per cent to keep them in line with the fall in the marginal revenue product of labour.

[2] See Martin and O'Connor, op. cit. pages 69/70 and Annex 1 for a discussion of the impact of rising real energy and material costs.

wage being received by the labour force was required if the existing
level of employment was to be maintained.[1] In fact, in the three years
1973−75, the own product real wage received by workers in manufacturing industry rose rather than fell, so that employment fell and
profits were squeezed.[2]

The degree to which profits in UK manufacturing industry were
squeezed in the three years 1973 − 77 is indicated in table 3. The
admittedly tentative calculations are based on a rough breakdown of
final product price in manufacturing industry into its direct cost and
gross profit components, and a further breakdown on direct costs into
raw material, fuel and labour costs, derived from summary
input/output tables for the UK.[3]

The top half of table 3 gives estimates of the percentage change in
direct costs over the years 1973−77, whilst the bottom half indicates
the *implied* percentage changes in gross operating profits, given the
percentage change in final product price that can be derived from
table 2.[4]

[1] Martin and O'Connor (ibid Annex 1) show that the method adopted above for
calculating the required fall in the own product real wage assumes that profit share in
gross output remains constant and in value added rises; in other words that the whole
burden of the adjustment to worsening terms of trade of manufacturing industry has
to be borne by labour. This assumption is not necessarily invalid in the short run. In
the longer run however owners of capital will also have to accept a lower real return
as capital is substituted for materials and labour.

[2] When assessing the welfare and policy implications of the analysis of the last two
paragraphs, it is important to distinguish between three concepts of the real wage in
manufacturing industry. First, there is the 'own product' real wage referred to above.
Second, there is the real wage itself, which is the purchasing power of money wages
over all goods and services rather than purchasing power over the product produced
by manufacturing industry (clearly the behaviour of import prices, interest, taxes etc
enter into this calculation); and finally there is the disposable real wage which allows
for the incidence of direct taxes. Clearly these three measures of real wages can move
in different directions and in different degrees. Given that real disposable incomes in
oil producing countries did not have to adjust immediately to rising oil prices (because
oil producers initially saved a large part of the increase in their real incomes), there
would have been some logic in governments reducing taxes on personal incomes so as
to maintain the disposable real wage in the hope of both restraining money wage
demands and facilitating a fall in own product wages in manufacturing industry.

[3] *Economic Trends*: Summary Input-Output Trends for 1971.

[4] The implied percentage change in nominal gross profits is approximately equal to the
percentage change in final product price minus the percentage change in direct costs
weighted by the initial ratio of direct costs to final product price, all divided by 1
minus the direct cost ratio, ie: for the 4th quarter 1972 to 4th quarter 1974, implied
change in nominal gross profits equals

$$\frac{41 - 58.7 \times 0.8}{0.2} = -29.5$$

Table 3 suggests that as a result of the direct cost and price changes which took place in the two years 1973 and 1974, not only did 'real time' operating profits[1] fall in real terms (ie nominal operating profit deflated by the rise in the price level of manufactured good output) but so did they in nominal terms. The latter fell by something like 30 per cent. In 1975 the rise in raw material prices began to slow down although fuel prices and labour costs continued to rise at a fast rate. Although manufactured good prices began to catch up the rise in direct costs, so that nominal profits recovered, they were still no higher at the end of 1975 than at the end of 1972. As indicated earlier, own product real wages received by labour were higher than their end-1972 level.

The introduction of an effective incomes policy in the autumn of 1975 slowed down the rise in money wages in the following two years, and own product real wages began to fall. Between the end of 1975 and the end of 1976 manufacturing output prices rose by about 36 per cent whilst money wages rose by about 25 per cent. As can be seen from table 2, employment in manufacturing industry began to rise in the second half of 1976 (*contrary to what could have been expected on historical output and employment relationships*) although it had not regained its end-1972 level by the end of 1977. Unfortunately policy with respect to the sterling exchange rate in 1976 produced further sharp increases in raw material and fuel prices to industry. Even so, manufacturing output prices rose relatively to direct costs, particularly in the course of 1977, and nominal and real profits showed a substantial recovery. However, although nominal profits rose strongly through 1976 and 1977, real profits were still some 10 per cent lower at the end of 1977 than at the end of 1972.

The UK was not the only country in which the rise in the real price of raw materials and energy, in the face of a failure of real wages to adjust, produced a squeezing of profits. But in all the others, apart perhaps from Italy, the rate of profit either fell less or was initially significantly higher. In the US, following an initial slight fall, profit share and profit rate rose in subsequent years as the economy pulled itself out of the 1975 recession and employment increased; and it is significant that in this country the real wage showed a greater tendency to adjust downwards than in other countries.[2]

[1] By 'real time' gross operating profits is meant the operating profits generated in a given period of time after attributing current direct costs but not overhead costs (ie: interest and depreciation charges) to current production. It also differs from the conventional profit concept by not including stock appreciation.

[2] See Hill *op. cit.* and Martin and O'Connor *op. cit.* for some international comparisons

210   Paper Six

An argument which stresses the failure of the real wage to adjust to labour's lower marginal revenue product as the cause of the rise in world unemployment and fall in profits clearly does not get universal support. Other economists put more weight on deficiency of aggregate demand and decline in capacity utilisation produced *inter alia* by tight monetary policies aimed at containing inflation. It is certainly true that some governments, particularly those of the important countries, the US and Germany, did pursue anti-inflationary policies in early 1974 if not before. Also, as indicated earlier, investment in the Western capitalist world declined at a time when the world propensity to save probably rose. However, it can be countered that even if governments had not pursued such tight monetary policies and had been prepared to allow even more inflation, employment would only have benefited if producers of raw materials and energy had been willing to see a fall in the price of their products relatively to the price of manufactured goods, and/or if the labour force in industrial countries had been willing to see a fall in their own product wages. The fact that capital utilisation fell in these years (ie the capital-output ratio rose) can hardly be put forward as an *independent* explanation of the collapse in the rate of profit. Rather, both were the result of labour being too expensive in real terms to keep either the labour force or the capital stock fully employed. Hence, it is not possible to agree with Martin and O'Connor that inflation *per se* through its impact on capacity utilisation was the main reason for depressed profitability.[1] Inflation, declining capital utilisation and falling profits were the combined effects of a common cause. Finally, as far as capital formation is concerned, we cannot overlook the fact that the severe decline in profits caused by a failure of real wages to adjust, was itself cause as well as consequence of a fall in investment.

It cannot be categorically denied that a more accommodating policy on the part of governments worldwide would temporarily have produced somewhat more employment; on the other hand, it can also be suggested that the longer term consequences of even higher inflation would have caused this to be shortlived.[2]

Conclusions

While no doubt many complicated factors were at work, it is the contention of this note that the major factor underlying the fall in the

[1] See Martin and O'Connor, *op. cit.* section C1.
[2] For a more extensive discussion of the impact of rising material prices on employment and the relevance of Keynesian demand management policies, see Maynard (1978).

rate of profit on capital in the UK manufacturing sector during the last 20 years was the determination and ability of labour to increase its share of the income created in the sector and to maintain its real wage in the face of a fall in the sector's real value added aided and abetted, albeit unconsciously, by industrial policy pursued by successive governments which kept down the price of capital relatively to the price of labour. Clearly this is a political economy explanation rather than a narrowly economic or industrial one. It embraces elements of all of the separate influences affecting profit share and profit rate listed by Martin and O'Connor (declining marginal productivity of physical capital, falling corporate tax burden, shift of market power from 'capitalists' to 'labour', crowding out by the public sector) and, in the main, separately rejected by them.[1] Obviously it offers an interpretation of events rather than a watertight 'scientific' explanation of them.

Nonetheless, it is important to emphasise that falling profit share and falling rate of profit on capital could not have continued for so long unless government itself had contributed to the process. Investment itself would have fallen off and unemployment would have risen, eventually forcing a change in the relative price of capital and labour. But governments did intervene, by giving massive tax credits to substantial parts of British industry, and by absorbing a growing labour force into public sector employment. The fiscal burden of such a policy escalated substantially, but the fact that through the 1960s unemployment was not a problem and living standards were rising moderately concealed the longer term consequences from both the government itself and the general public. It may be said that industrial policy in these years was directed solely at promoting an increase in the productivity of labour – a policy that may be good for the trade union movement, but when associated with a decline in the rate of profit on capital is not necessarily in the long term interests of the country as a whole.

The massive adverse shift in the terms of trade of manufacturing industry in the early 1970s, however, not only created its own immediate problems for industry but has also removed the veil which had blinded the public from the fundamental weakness of the manufacturing sector. The shift necessitated a substantial cut back in the 'own product' real wage in manufacturing industry if profits and employment were to be maintained. Understandably such cuts were resisted but the consequences for profits were dramatic although

---

[1] *Op. cit.* section C2.

perhaps no more than the last straw given their evolution during the previous decade. Employment could not be protected, given trade union determination to protect real wages.

At any rate, it now seems obvious that large parts of the UK manufacturing industry are at the end of this particular road. If private sector manufacturing is to survive, a radical change in management, work habits and trade union attitudes will be required that will allow a substantial rise in both labour and capital productivity to be translated into a substantial rise in profits. Fashionable remedies, such as import controls and devaluation cannot work in the absence of the changes described above and would probably be unnecessary if such changes took place. Whether or not a free profit making private enterprise manufacturing sector will remain politically feasible in the UK only time will tell. What is clear however is that the UK cannot become a viable economy, whatever political system is in being, unless there is a substantial rise in the real return on capital, even if the return on capital is, for political reasons, not called profit.

References

Bacon, R. and Eltis, W. *Britain's Economic Problem: Too Few Producers;* Macmillan, 1st Edition 1976, 2nd Edition 1978.

Hill, T. P. *Profits and Rates of Return;* OECD, 1979

Martin, W. and O'Connor, M. 'Profitability: a background paper'; this volume

Maynard, G. 'Keynes and unemployment today'; *Three Banks Review,* December 1978

Midland Bank. 'Economic outlook'; *Midland Bank Review,* Summer 1979

Sargent, J. R. 'Recent growth experience in the economy of the UK'; *Economic Journal,* March 1968

Sargent, J. R. 'Productivity and profits in UK manufacturing'; *Midland Bank Review,* Autumn 1979.

Table 1 Rate of profit on capital in UK manufacturing industry (1970 = 100)

Year	(i) Rate of Profit	(ii) Share of Profit In Income	(iii) Capital Productivity (Reciprocal Capital-Output Ratio)	(iv) Capital-Labour Ratio	(v) Output per Unit of Labour	(vi) Labour-cost/Capital-cost Ratio
1955	154.6	137.0	112.6			
1956	142.1	130.1	109.5			
1957	140.9	129.7	108.4			
1958	138.7	129.3	107.0			
1959	145.5	131.3	110.6			
1960	155.7	133.8	116.5	63.6	74.1	44.6
1961	137.5	122.4	112.3	70.8	73.4	47.2
1962	126.2	117.9	106.7	76.2	74.2	54.7
1963	131.8	124.4	105.9	75.2	78.0	62.3
1964	137.5	126.0	109.2	81.0	83.9	68.6
1965	134.1	122.4	109.5	80.8	85.3	64.8
1966	120.5	113.8	105.9	84.8	86.6	69.0
1967	118.2	115.9	101.7	86.6	90.0	75.0
1968	118.2	115.5	102.2	95.7	97.1	84.1
1969	114.8	112.2	102.0	98.6	99.5	94.1
1970	100.0	100.0	100.0	100.0	100.0	100.0
1971	97.8	101.6	96.7	103.7	103.0	102.0
1972	97.8	104.9	93.0	109.9	109.7	111.9
1973	84.1	93.1	90.2	118.0	110.6	119.4
1974	63.6	76.8	82.7	116.9	108.8	122.0
1975	51.1	65.0	79.1	115.2	101.2	104.4
1976	50.0	67.9	74.0	120.4	103.4	112.3

Source:
Columns (i), (ii) and (iii)   T. P. Hill, *Profits and Rates of Return*, OECD, Paris 1979
Columns (iv), (v) and (vi)   'In house' estimates. The capital cost estimates of column (vi) rely heavily on Flemming, Price and Ingram 'Trends in Company Profitability', *Bank of England Quarterly Bulletin*, March and June 1976.

Table 2 Employment and prices in UK manufacturing industry 1972–1977

	1972	1973				1974				1975				1976				1977			
	4	1	2	3	4	1	2	3	4	1	2	3	4	1	2	3	4	1	2	3	4
Employment in manufacturing (thousands)	7813	7814	7823	7866	7897	7802	7778	7826	7882	7715	7545	7454	7387	7275	7238	7304	7352	7324	7340	7388	7386
Unemployment (thousands)	792	699	634	581	523	578	577	618	—*	738	847	1000	1132	1220	1261	1300	—*	1329	1341	1415	1428
Prices (1970=100) Manufacturing Output	120.4	121.4	123.5	127.3	132.1	142.3	153.4	162.0	170.9	182.8	192.1	199.1	205.4	214.5	222.0	230.8	241.2	245.5	264.4	272.9	279.1
Manufacturing Input: Raw Materials	117.5	126.9	135.5	154.7	173.1	222.4	221.2	219.7	228.2	225.9	228.7	243.3	261.4	272.5	299.2	314.6	339.7	351.6	356.1	347.6	336.6
Fuel	112.4	112.4	112.4	114.3	114.6	122.4	142.7	147.9	164.2	173.3	195.8	200.5	205.2	210.1	230.6	232.0	236.3	244.8	267.8	273.0	273.3
Weekly Earnings (1970=100)	131.4	134.3	139.3	143.5	149.0	147.0	158.8	171.7	185.0	193.9	202.2	215.3	225.6	232.7	242.2	246.9	245.5	260.2	266.3	268.2	281.5
Unit Labour Cost (1970=100)	120	118	122	125	128	131	138	150	169	179	194	203	208	214	218	224	228	234	244	247	257

Source: OECD Main Economic Indicators.
*Unemployment statistics not collected owing to widespread industrial disputes.

Table 3 Changes in costs and prices in UK manufacturing industry 1972–77

	4th Quarter 1972 to 4th Quarter 1974		4th Quarter 1972 to 4th Quarter 1975		4th Quarter 1972 to 4th Quarter 1977	
	Change %	Contribution to Increase in Direct Costs (%)	Change %	Contribution to Increase in Direct Costs (%)	Change %	Contribution to Increase in Direct Costs (%)
Unit Labour Cost (Weight 60%)	+41	+24.6	+73	+43.8	+108	+64.8
Raw Materials (Weight 32%)	+95	+30.4	+123	+39.3	+187	+59.8
Fuel (Weight 8%)	+46	+3.7	+83	+6.6	+143	+14.4
Direct Costs		+58.7		+89.7		+139.0
Direct Costs (Weight 80%)	+58.7		+89.7		+139	
Final Product Price	+41.0		+71.0		+133	
Implied Change in Nominal Gross Profits	−29.5		−3.5		+110	

Chart 1 U.K. Manufacturing

Rate of profit on capital
Ratio of output to capital stock

Relative Unit labour costs
Share of profits in income
Manufacturing Output

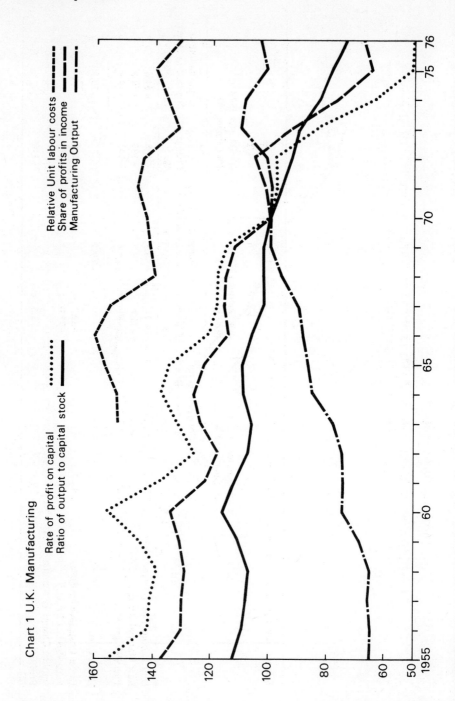

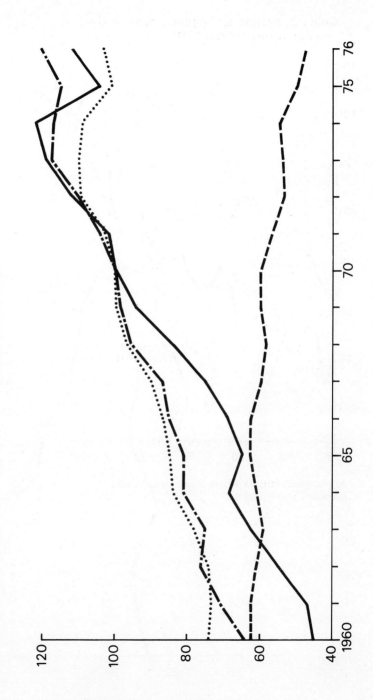

Chart 2 U.K. Manufacturing Sector

Output per unit of labour ⋯⋯⋯⋯   Ratio of cost of labour to cost of capital ⎯⎯⎯
Employment ⎯ ⎯ ⎯ ⎯   Capital per unit of labour ⎯ ⋅ ⎯ ⋅ ⎯

Chart 3 Wages and employment in U.K.
manufacturing (1970 = 100)

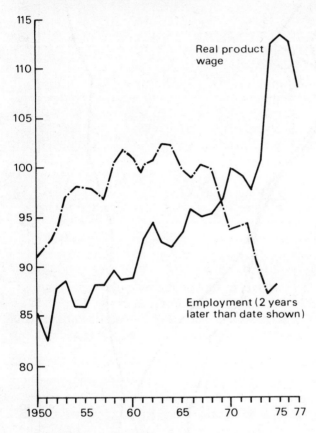

Source: Midland Bank Review, Summer Issue 1979
(see editor's note page 205)

Comment
by R. C. O. Matthews

I enjoyed Geoffrey Maynard's interesting paper and I agree with quite a lot of it. I am more agnostic than he is about his political economy explanation of why things turned out as they did although I think it is a possible explanation.

I shall begin by making one very elementary point which Geoffrey Maynard of course perfectly understands but which readers of his paper might, at one or two points, be excused for forgetting. The point is as follows. Wages share plus profit share is equal to 100 per cent. Wages share in value added is identically equal to real product wage in the sense of chart 3 of his paper.[1] Therefore, pointing to a rise in the real product wage is merely another way of restating the phenomenon of the fall in profit share and does not point to one explanation any more than to another explanation. Any fall in profit share would mean a rise in the real product wage, however it arose.

I shall follow Geoffrey Maynard's example in treating separately the periods before and after 1972–73. What do we observe in the earlier post war period? We observe, as he said, a rise in the capital-output ratio, a fall in the profit rate and a fall in profit share. This could be due to the political economy syndrome which he described but it could be explained quite easily without that. In very neo-classical terms – if one wished to use them – one could say that the capital stock has increased at a faster rate than investment opportunities. Consequently, the rate of return has fallen. The concomitant fall in profit share is consistent with an elasticity of substitution between labour and capital in the production function of less than one, which is what is normally turned out by econometric studies of the production function.

In such a model, the rate of expansion of investment opportunities is critical. The issue becomes a very general one; it is closely related to the overall growth rate of the economy and hence to our general economic problems including the foreign trade problems, problems about industrial relations and so on. Given those problems, the investment opportunities have expanded less rapidly than they might have done in more favourable circumstances.

At least an element of the declining profit rate and profit share is probably associated in this way with the very general problems of British economic growth. In this connection, I note that the fall in the

[1] ie the real product wage as defined by the Midland Bank, cf editor's note p 205 – *Ed.*

profit share and profit rate in the post war period are part of a much longer trend. I think that Mr Martin and Miss O'Connor have in this connection misread the evidence provided in the Bank of England report which they quote. The trend according to my reading of the data goes back a very much longer period than the post war period. The statistic which I find helpful to think of in this connection is that, roughly speaking, profit share in national income of the 1870s was half on a gross basis. One hundred years later on a similar measure it was a quarter. Thus the fall is not negligible and it took place in series of steps of which the fall in the post war period was only one.

Given this, the question remains; why did the investment continue in the post war period in face of these falling profit rates? There is a very long run problem here – an 1870s problem – which is interesting to me but I do not suppose it is interesting to anybody else. That problem is that the rate of capital accumulation in the 1970s was faster than in the 1870s, notwithstanding the very substantial fall in the profit rate. This clearly implies a very substantial fall in the cost of capital, the reasons for which one could explore with advantage at another time. In the post war period, I entirely agree that the tax concessions had a lot to do with it in the case of manufacturing. I do not think that they are the whole story. It is worth noting that the capital stock in the post war period grew even more rapidly in the commercial sector than in the manufacturing sector; that is, in distribution, finance and miscellaneous services, notwithstanding that that sector enjoyed very much less in the way of tax privileges than manufacturing. Further, the rate of profit in the commercial sector fell although it remained absolutely higher throughout than in manufacturing.

What I wish to imply here is that the fall in the profit rate can be seen as part of a gradual, medium term exhaustion of investment opportunities created by the great post war boom. Initially, the fall in profitability did not inhibit investment partly because of the tax reason; partly because the cost of finance fell for other reasons, for example, the direct incursion of the institutions into the purchase of equities and finance of industry. A third reason why investment was not inhibited is that, at least in some sectors, there was initially a gap between the rate of profit and the cost of finance. It does not follow that investment falls if the rate of profit falls. One has to have regard to the absolute gap between the rate of return and the cost of finance; if there is a substantial gap initially, investment may be maintained, or even rise, notwithstanding that the rate of profit is falling. I think one could regard the German case which has been quoted as a case in point. The Germans have invested a great deal, notwithstanding that the profit rate has fallen, because they had a high absolute rate of profit. So on this reckoning, I think it is possible to interpret the post war period as a long cycle from which we will, I suppose, recover in due course as new investment opportunities accrue.

I shall now turn to the period since 1973. One might well say that the further fall in profitability since then is hardly surprising in view of the under utilisation and inflation that has existed combined with elements of historic cost pricing. It is obvious that inflationary circumstances of that sort would be likely to lead to a fall in profit. Now Geoffrey Maynard will argue that the stagnation was itself due in large measure to the erosion of profitability. This is something that one can argue and something which is argued in all recessions, and it contains an element of truth. Other things being equal, a reduction in wage share in recession would remove some of the forces making for the recession. I grant though that in the recent occasion there are special points which have not been relevant on previous occasions.

The effect of the rise in raw material prices is also raised in the paper by Martin and O'Connor. It is not obvious why a rise in raw material costs should affect one way or the other the distribution of value added between profits and wages. It is not obvious to me a *priori* in which direction one would expect that effect to go. It might have no effect, it might favour wages, it might even favour profits, as it did in the old model of Kalecki. It is certainly true that if you have, for political economy reasons, a fixed real product wage, profit share must fall. I do not think anybody would suggest that fixity of the product wage was a behavioural relationship. I do not imagine that trade unions would regard it as an objective to have their wages fixed in terms of the value of the product. If anything, they would do it in terms of purchasing power; that is, they would compare it, not with the price of the product, but with the RPI. This though might have a similar effect. This brings us back therefore to the question of whether there is an innate tendency for real wages to march ahead inexorably and so eat into profits in circumstances where something has to go. This may have been the case to some extent. However I do not think one can look at the figures of trends in real wages and maintain that real wages have marched ahead inexorably. Real wages have, since 1973, gone up by less than 1 per cent per annum which does constitute a major break from what went before.

Finally, I shall make one or two remarks on the policy implications. I have been suggesting that the fall in profitability relative to the cost of finance has to be seen largely as a by-product of more general troubles; slow productivity growth in the long run, stagflation in the short and medium run. If that is correct, a direct attack on the profitability problem is unlikely to be successful. If the low rate of profit is a symptom, we are unlikely to get very far by directly attacking it. I entirely agree with Geoffrey Maynard that the problem would be transformed if we could learn how to use capital as well as labour more effectively. Experience does not suggest to me that we have policy instruments that are capable of having much influence on that and I am far from being convinced that the present Government's policy has new wisdom in this respect which we formerly lacked.

I would like to add a word about another aspect of the political economy syndrome which concerns the upward pressure on real wages. There is an element here which is important and which requires particular vigilance. This is the downward trend in hours of work. A downward trend in hours of work has a direct effect on raising real costs in a way which increases in money wage rates do not. Further reductions in present circumstances seem to me to pose a threat to profitability and to recovery.

Finally I do not see what we are going to do about the long run trend of profitability in so far as this is due to general problems of the economy. We have all discussed that hundreds of times and we have also discussed hundreds of times what to do about stagflation. There is an important question here however. It is no good saying that low profits are just due to low utilisation – that it is just a slump – if the prospect is that the low utilisation will persist for many years as it did through much of the inter-war period. Here we come back to the wage push element. Insofar as the wage push is strong, we get strong inflationary pressure. Hence, given the government's commitment to fight inflation, we get low real output; hence we get low profits. I remarked earlier that a direct attack on low profitability would be unpromising. A direct attack of course would mean an attack on real wages. That would be the only way to restore profits if we continue to have both slow productivity growth and stagflation. But in those circumstances the outlook would be dismal whatever was happening to profits and I am not sure that profitability in that context would be the worst of our problems.

General discussion[1]

Many of those who commented on this paper were, like Professor Maynard, not sanguine about the UK's present position. However, one observer did question the view that the economy was at a point of crisis; he drew considerable comfort from his interpretation of recent trends in UK export and investment performance and also from the somewhat more buoyant levels of equity, as against entity, rates of return. There was even less agreement amongst those present about the interpretation of the events which had led to this particular conjuncture; neither were people agreed upon the appropriate policy responses.

Causes

A number of doubts were raised concerning the theory that the low rate of return was due to over-investment. The connection, elaborated upon by Professor Matthews, between observed rates of return, investment behaviour and marginal rates of return, was called into question. There were many pressures on companies to invest, arising from, for example, the need to improve product quality, mechanise production processes and increase capacity, despite low rates of return on existing assets. Given that expected rates of return on new investment could differ considerably from average returns on old investment, it did not follow necessarily that the trend decline in average profitability was due to a fall in marginal profitability, reflecting the gradual exhaustion of profitable investment opportunities. Several practical examples were given in support of the view that UK companies were indeed 'resplendent with investment opportunities', but, for various reasons, had been unable to grasp them.

A further criticism of a number of the more familiar explanations of declining profitability in the UK was that they were too parochial. Declining profitability was an international phenomenon, common to a number of major industrial countries. Clearly, the special problems of UK economic growth, in particular the trade problem cited by Matthews, could not explain the experience of other economies. One observer thought it possible to explain much of the decline in UK profitability as simply a reflection of world trends and the activities of multi-national companies. The latter, through their direct investment

---

[1] Points made at the final session of the seminar, concerned with general policy, have been conflated with those made at the paper's own session – *Ed.*

policies, brought about a close, long-run inter-relationship between UK and world capital markets and, thereby, a parity of rates of return at home and abroad. The same argument was used to criticise other allegedly parochial theories of the secular decline in UK profitability. In particular, the idea that trade unions were to blame for the notable shift in income distribution towards employment income in the UK after 1969 – a phenomenon which was repeated in a number of other industrial countries – presupposed a most unlikely concatenation of militant union behaviour.

While accepting the international point, others were less convinced that the activities of trade unions did not matter. It was argued that, after 1972, the ability of unions to prevent an adjustment of real wages in line with both the lower rate of growth in labour productivity and the shift in the terms of trade against manufacturers was responsible for the profit squeeze, the fall in the demand for labour and inflation. As the calculations in table C4 of the background paper had shown, even though the growth of real wages had shifted downwards considerably after 1973 – as Matthews had noted – this was sufficient to compensate only for the lower rate of productivity growth. *Ex post,* manufacturing profits in the UK had borne the brunt of the terms of trade shock. Similar considerations had applied in many industrial countries since 1972 and were a major reason why employment in manufacturing had fallen and unemployment had risen worldwide.

This explanation was questioned on the grounds that unions had little influence over the evolution of real wages, even though they could affect money wages. One suggestion was that the profit squeeze resulted from a combination of trade unions pushing up money wages and international competition keeping down the increase in the price level. Although the evidence on unit labour cost competitiveness presented in the background paper and in Maynard's paper was not easily reconciled with this view, it was argued that the competitiveness measures were themselves unreliable. It was asserted that the trend decline in the UK's trading position could be explained by movements in competitiveness far less favourable than was indicated by the official measures. The combined influence on profitability of international competition and union bargaining behaviour was thought to have operated with particular severity from 1964 onwards. This view of the world was countered by another participant, largely on the grounds set out in the background paper; namely that during the 1960s the growth rates of labour productivity and real product wages were, on average, about equal[1]. Thus the evidence for any direct squeeze on profits

[1] See p 59 of the background paper – *Ed.*

during this period, as a result of the union-international competition nexus, was weak.

After 1972, it was argued that the unions may have affected profitability indirectly by aggravating the inflationary spiral. This, in turn, prompted deflationary action by governments leading to a squeeze on profit margins and excess capacity. The contention was that union expectations of real wage increases had been artifically raised by the increase in the marginal product of labour during the 1960s, the result of capital-labour substitution, encouraged by the fall in the relative cost of capital. The latter was partly due to the increasingly generous provision of tax allowances for investment which government had conceded, partly in response to lobbying from the unions themselves. After 1972, however, the impetus to labour productivity growth provided by capital-labour substitution came to a halt as the cost of capital rose relative to the rate of return. As a result, there was an inconsistency between the growth of real wages that the economic system could support and that which labour expected on the basis of historical experience. Unrealistic expectations, leading to higher money wage claims, and government's response to the resulting inflation, contributed towards the stagflation and profits slump of the 1970s.

Policy
This analysis of the problem led one participant to conclude that any escape from stagflation required a shift towards profits in the national income. For this disinflationary monetary policy had to be buttressed with an incomes policy. Others were sympathetic to this argument, but were concerned that a cut in real wages secured by incomes policy might prove deflationary, since real wages were an influence on demand as well as on supply. In response to this, one participant alluded to the distinction between different types of real wage referred to in Maynard's paper (page 208, second footnote): the 'own product real wage', which affected the demand for labour, the 'real wage', which affected the supply of labour, and the 'disposable real wage', which helped determine effective demand. It was quite possible for these three concepts of the real wage to move in different directions, and it need not be the case that a cut in one necessitated a cut in either of the other two. In particular, a cut in the growth of money wages secured by a reduction in income tax could, other things equal, lead to a fall in own product real wages, thereby stimulating the demand for labour and increasing the supply of output, but leave real disposable wages, and thus aggregate demand, undiminished.

A number of participants stressed the possible effects of macro-economic policy on labour and capital productivity, and thereby profitability. A strong currency was considered by one observer to be a stimulus to improved labour productivity, and the accompanying high interest rates to be a stimulus to the careful use of capital resources. This line of argument was supported by industrial experience: in conditions of excess capacity, firms were far more sanguine about rationalising their operations and improving productivity. British Leyland was cited as an example of 'monetarism in one company': not only had the imposition of tight cash limits, and thereby the fear of redundancy, encouraged considerable moderation in wage settlements, it had also enabled management to secure radical changes in working practices and rationalisation of production. Other participants thought monetarism not an unmixed blessing. While they could agree that deflation might lead to a deceleration of wage inflation and improvements in productivity in the long run, they feared that there were considerable lags in the process of adjustment. They believed that the initial effects of deflation would be to bring about a deceleration of price inflation before any reduction in wage inflation or increase in productivity. Profitability would therefore suffer, in the short run at least. This led to the belief that monetarism was not enough and that reform of the wage bargaining process was a further pre-requisite for any escape from stagflationary conditions.

A professed market economist challenged the relevance of macro-economic policy to the question of improving profitability. While there was an ephemeral relationship between the conduct of macro-economic policy and the rate of return, he believed that any sensible policy in this area would be micro-economic in nature, concentrating on the removal of distortions to the free workings of labour and capital markets. The paper by King, illustrating the enormous variation in effective marginal tax rates, was ample proof of the impediments to the market process which governments had introduced, no doubt in the belief that the investment subsidies would 'stimulate employment in some kind of misconceived Keynesian way'. Similar considerations applied to labour markets; the closed shop agreements and the various redundancy payment schemes being two notable sources of distortion. This approach to policy did not, however, go unchallanged. One observer in particular believed that macro-economic policy was of greater importance to profitability and felt that to speak of removing distortions to markets was tantamount to 'fiddling while Rome burns'. No common ground had been achieved by the end of the discussion.